THE NOVEL
ACCORDING TO CERVANTES

THE NOVEL ACCORDING TO CERVANTES

STEPHEN GILMAN

University of California Press

Berkeley · Los Angeles · London

The excerpt from Albert Camus, *La peste* (Paris: Gallimard, 1947), © Editions Gallimard, is used by permission of the publisher.

The excerpt from Jean-Paul Sartre, *La nausée* (Paris: Gallimard, 1985), © Editions Gallimard, is used by permission of the publisher.

The excerpt from Albert Camus, *The Plague*, trans. Stuart Gilbert (New York: Modern Library, 1948), © 1948 by Stuart Gilbert, is used by permission of Alfred A. Knopf, Inc., in the United States and Hamish Hamilton Ltd in the United Kingdom.

The excerpt from Jean-Paul Sartre, *Nausea*, trans. Lloyd Alexander (New York: New Directions, 1964), is used by permission of New Directions Publishing Corporation.

University of California Press
Berkeley and Los Angeles, California

University of California Press, Ltd.
London, England

© 1989 by
The Regents of the University of California

Library of Congress Cataloging-in-Publication Data
Gilman, Stephen.
    The novel according to Cervantes / Stephen Gilman.
        p. cm.
    Includes index.
    ISBN 0-520-06231-0 (alk. paper)
    1. Cervantes Saavedra, Miguel de, 1547–1616. Don
Quixote. 2. Cervantes Saavedra, Miguel de, 1547–1616—
Technique.   3. Fiction—History and criticism.   I. Title.
PQ6353.G47   1989
863'.3—dc19   88-23458
                                                          CIP

Printed in the United States of America
1   2   3   4   5   6   7   8   9

Contents

Foreword

On November 9, 1986, shortly before he died, Stephen Gilman informed Doris Kretschmer of the University of California Press that he was about to send her the manuscript of his just-completed study of the Cervantine tradition in the novel. He sent a copy of the letter to me—not only because I had been urging him to send the manuscript to the Press, but because he knew that his completing the book was as much a triumph for me as for its author.

We had met during Winter quarter 1950 at the Ohio State University, where we were both teaching. Invited to participate in a colloquium on "realism," we both made presentations at once setting forth our profound disagreement with the descriptive and impersonal formalism then regnant in literary criticism and also proclaiming the need to historicize. The modes of historicism we opted for of course differed— Gilman's deriving much from his studies with Américo Castro, mine deriving much from my studies with A. O. Lovejoy. In any case, we discovered immediately a powerful elective affinity, became fast friends, talked much about our mutual interests, exchanged manuscripts, worked at mutual criticism, taught and learned from each other.

My own mode of historicism was powerfully informed by Gilman's and that of the tradition in Hispanism in which he worked—which indeed he celebrated. Reading Gilman, then reading Castro and many others to whom Gilman directed me, I found a means, a personalistic means, of conflating Lovejovean history of ideas, New Critical formalism, cultural anthropology, and historical sociology. Gilman observed and participated in my efforts toward conflation and was primary in helping me achieve such unity in my work as it presently has. I like to think that I helped him in the same way.

Early on in our friendship I knew that Gilman had to write a book on Cervantes for non-Hispanists like me. For I realized how little aware those who study the novel were (and are) of the specifically Spanish conception of the novelistic and of its exhilarating way of celebrating the self in its history. Gilman insisted that he was "only" a Hispanist. And I insisted in response that that was precisely the point, so that he must make his Hispanism available to a larger than Hispanist readership. Over the years, as he became an heroic exegete and interpreter of writers ranging from Rojas to Galdos (with Cervantes always the nodal point), he reported that he was thinking his way toward the book I had told him in the early 1950s that he must write. He published some separate studies which would become part of that book. And on November 9, 1986, he informed me that at long last it was done.

As a man profoundly of his own time—a sine qua non for the proper historicist—Gilman felt that in the modern world the novel in the Cervantine mode was increasingly impossible of achievement, even as heroically creative adventure was increasingly impossible. The novel could no longer be written according to Cervantes. He drafted an epilogue to his study, an epilogue in which he chose to analyze long passages from Camus's and Sartre's fictions in such a way as to indicate the achievement of a specifically non-Cervantine novel. (He had no patience with recent critics who would make out the so-called self-reflexive new novel to be somehow Cervantine. How could a novel be Cervantine when there was no place in it—because no place in its historically definable culture—for an overabundant self?) He was troubled about his proposed epilogue, so he wrote me, and I am sure he would have been amenable to suggestions from readers of his manuscript that he must see his epilogue all the way to its end. A sketch, it is printed here as an appendix to the book proper.

The book is an icon of the man, whose life and work and capacity for abiding friendships manifested, in the words of a poet to whom he was very close, that "La Tierra es gran aventura."

Roy Harvey Pearce
May 18, 1988

Preface

"Pour qui écrit-on?" asks a great French humanist ("malgré lui!") of those who presume to publish what they have written. The arrogance of the question with its implicit demand for self-justification tempts "one" to retort just as arrogantly. Perhaps like Stendhal one might say: "For the 'Happy Few' gifted with sufficient understanding." In this case, however, both modesty and honesty forbid. Let me answer instead by anticipating the foreseeable disappointment of those for whom I am not writing. The four essays that follow are not intended for professional "cervantistas" who, if they take the time to read one more addition to their immense bibliography, will find many interpretations and much information with which they are quite familiar, together with other observations which may seem arbitrary or irrelevant. Nor will what I hope to communicate serve as a useful introduction or guide to the *Quijote*.[1] That is, I do not seek future readers who wish to learn what to make of its peculiar narrative behavior or how to estimate its value.

Granted, certain comments may interest—or at least provoke—my colleagues and others might be helpful to amateur addicts of fiction who find themselves disconcerted by what Francis Thompson called Cervantes's "duplicity within duplicity, a sword turning all ways."[2] Nevertheless, such readers

1. I have eschewed the English "Don Quixote" (except when citing critics who use it) because it does not permit the convenient Spanish distinction between the person, Don Quijote, and the book, "el *Quijote*," or in my text, "the *Quijote*."
2. "Was there ever so strange a book as this Don Quixote! To what class shall we assign it? Solitary, singular, it will not be pigeonholed; your literary entomologists shall ticket it, *genus* and *subgenus* at their peril. It is complex

deserve to be warned that they have not been sought for. Instead, as a Hispanist, I have tried to tell comparatists and students of literary theory what we think we know about the origin of a generic phenomenon unique in the cultural history of the West: the so-called rise of the novel. How did this special kind of fiction take its initial steps upward? What were the personal, the social, and, above all, the literary circumstances (or contexts) within which an aging would-be author, who by his own admission had failed as a lyric poet and dramatist, sat down to write: "In a village of la Mancha, the name of which I have no desire to recollect, there lived not long ago . . ."?

Faced with these questions, skeptics will reply either that the novel as narrative (a "Naturform der Dichtung") began in Eden or that there are any number of other tales and tellers—fictions and authors—with as good or better claims to priority. Among them one could mention Heliodorus (who, as we shall see, would have been Cervantes's candidate), Boccaccio (for the "elegy" of *Fiammetta*), Rabelais, Madame de Lafayette, Fielding (according to Stendhal), and Sir Walter Scott (who also favored Fielding, again for *Tom Jones*).[3] It all comes down to a question of prior definition, and definitions, when claims of this sort are at stake, are notoriously self-serving. It was just such critical hypocrisy (often reflecting professional or national zeal) that E. M. Forster challenged humorously in his first lecture, at Trinity College, Cambridge, on aspects of the novel:

---

beyond measure. It is a piece of literary duplicity without precedent or succession; nay duplicity within duplicity, a sword turning all ways" (Francis Thompson, *The Academy*, Sept. 18, 1897, p. 220). I am indebted for this reference to Louis Murillo. In the course of the essays to follow, we shall examine the apparently paradoxical combination of the generic uniqueness of the *Quijote* remarked on by Thompson and the subsequent "invention" of the novel.

3. Sir Walter Scott, *The Fortunes of Nigel*, vol. 14 of *The Waverley Novels* (Boston: Little, Brown, 1853), p. 14: "Fielding had high notions of the dignity of an art which he may be considered as having founded."

Any fictitious prose work of over 50,000 words will be a novel for the purpose of these lectures, and if this seems to you un-philosophic, will you think of an alternative definition which will include *The Pilgrim's Progress, Marius the Epicurean, The Adventures of a Younger Son, The Magic Flute, The Journal of the Plague, Zuleika Dobson, Rasselas, Ulysses,* and *Green Mansions,* or else give reasons for their exclusion?[4]

I agree. In the introductory essay, I shall forbear to trace indefensible generic frontiers and instead attempt—with the aid of two major novelists in the Cervantine tradition, Henri Beyle and Samuel Clemens—to define the way novels *need* to be read—and indeed how all the fictions on Forster's heterogenous list have on occasion been read (however unsuitably) by readers habituated to novelistic surrender and enrichment.

However, just as in Orwell's *Animal Farm* some animals are more equal than others, so too some novels are more novelistic than others, which is to say, better prepared for the kind of reading that Cervantes, as a professor of that engaging metier, was concerned to profess. Therefore, following the first essay (entitled "Definition" but in truth an antidefinition), the remaining three will examine primarily how in Part I of the *Quijote* Cervantes learned to teach naive seventeenth-century addicts of printed romances of chivalry, roguery, and sentimentality how to mend their bad habits. Lionel Trilling goes too far when he proposes that "all prose fiction is a variation on the theme of *Don Quixote.*"[5] The truth is at once more and less encouraging to those of us who care. It is not prose fiction that finds its role model in that eccentric narrative, but rather sophisticated reading of fiction. A more justifiable proposition is that of Harry Levin: "*Don Quixote* is, thus, an archetype as well as an example, the exemplary

4. E. M. Forster, *Aspects of the Novel* (New York: Harcourt Brace, 1954), p. 6.
5. Lionel Trilling, *The Liberal Imagination* (New York: Scribner's, 1976), p. 209.

novel of all time."[6] Similar testimony is abundant: Schelling, who declared Cervantes to be a modern counterpart of Homer; Sterne and Fielding, who discovered in their laughter new creative directions; Byron and Heine, whose reading generated romantically ironic tears; Georg Lukács, who in part derived his *Theorie* therefrom; and Mikhail Bakhtin, who described the fount of those opinions and emotions to be "the classic and purest model of the novel as a genre."[7] But for my purposes a comparison to be found at the end of Ortega y Gasset's *Meditaciones del "Quijote"* (1914) is the most suggestive: "What is needed is a book which would demonstrate in detail that every novel embeds the *Quijote* within itself like a secret watermark, just as every epic poem encases the *Iliad* as if it were the pit of a peach."[8]

Unfortunately (from the point of view of literary theory), the trail-breaking *Meditaciones*, which preceded the young Ortega's recognition of this necessity, does not address it. Instead, he was intent on formulating his own nascent philosophy in terms of Cervantes's novelistic portrayal of human exposure and the "perspectivism" therewith engendered. And equally unfortunately (from the same point of view), what I have to say is far too limited in scope to have satisfied Ortega. Nevertheless, to begin at the beginning, to attempt to explain how Cervantes (as unaware of his destination as Columbus) perceived his own narrative innovations and to elucidate what can be known about the literary and historical motives of those innovations is at least to clear the ground. Neither peninsular scholars nor foreign Hispanists have yet produced the definitive book requested by Ortega.[9] Like

6. Harry Levin, *Contexts of Criticism* (Cambridge, Mass.: Harvard University Press, 1957), p. 97.

7. Mikhail Bakhtin, *The Dialogic Imagination*, ed. Michael Holquist, trans. Caryl Emerson and Michael Holquist (Austin: University of Texas Press, 1983), p. 324.

8. José Ortega y Gasset, *Obras completas* (Madrid: Revista de Occidente, 1950–1961), 1: 398 (translation mine).

9. In addition to Américo Castro's illuminating introduction to the Porrúa edition published in Mexico in 1960 (translated by Edmund L. King and my-

those who cultivate other academic fields, most of us spend far too much time writing for each other. It may as a result be worthwhile for someone among us to make an effort to communicate to those outsiders who might be interested in what we profess (the verb also means "pretend") to know: just how the *Quijote* became "the exemplary novel of all time."

How do things begin? The obvious answers are triple: inventions are invented; hitherto unknown regions and unrecognized capacities or values are discovered; and living creatures (after conception and gestation) are born. And since the *Quijote* began in all three of these ways—as a result of intentional narrative invention, as a discovery of hitherto unperceived potentialities of printed fiction, and as a burgeoning of new life—each of these aspects will be considered separately. Such a procedure, admittedly, has two serious disadvantages. First, it is artificial, in that isolation of the three modes of beginning tends to disguise their organic interrelationship. Second (derived from the first), repeated examination of key episodes and passages from differing points of view is necessary. However, the only other solution I can imagine would be that of Borges's Pierre Menard: to write the *Quijote* over again and in so doing watch it in the process of becoming itself.

A word of warning to the readers I do seek, readers who contemplate "the novel" and try to explain its generic peculiarity aesthetically in any number of ways. To propose, as I have done, that the novel began in the course of composing Part I of the *Quijote* is essentially to propose that within the ocean of prose fiction there is a Cervantine Gulf Stream traceable but not rigorously surveyable that includes the very best of the good reading. This would be the content of the book that Ortega demanded and that I have not provided, except

---

self and included in *An Idea of History* [Columbus: Ohio State University Press, 1977], pp. 77–143), there is Harry Levin's thoughtful essay on the subject in *Grounds for Comparison* (Cambridge: Harvard University Press, 1972), pp. 224–44.

from time to time in lists of novels that in one way or another resemble the *Quijote* generically. I hardly need to say that it is not a question of "influence"—not even in the case of *Joseph Andrews*, "written in imitation of the manner of Cervantes." Rather, the novelists of later centuries who can be perceived as belonging to the Cervantine tradition rediscover, reinvent, and give birth anew to creatures who experience their residence on earth in a way comparable to Don Quijote and Sancho. This is the reading that matters and in terms of which we may gauge the aesthetic and ethical worth of the rest of our voluptuous immersions (both the adjective and the noun will be justified contextually within a few pages) in story books of every kind.

In conclusion, I should point out that the four essays— here substantially revised—were originally lectures delivered on different occasions.[10] Their unity is not due to a single act of composition, but rather is the reflection of a professional lifespan dedicated in large part to brooding on how the novel began and how it grew. But not lonely brooding. In the beginning there were my first teachers of the *Quijote*, Augusto Centeno and F. Courtney Tarr; then there have been colleagues, Jean-Jacques Demorest, Donald Fanger, Roy Harvey

10. The introduction was given at the English Institute and was greeted with marked hostility by the assembled scholars and later by the supervising committee, with the exception of Roy Harvey Pearce. Excluded from their 1972 volume, it was finally printed (thanks to J. Hillis Miller, who thought it had merit) in *Interpretation: Theory and Practice*, ed. Charles S. Singleton (Baltimore: Johns Hopkins University Press, 1969), pp. 153–71. The second essay, "Birth," was prepared for a symposium on Cervantes at the University of Wisconsin (Madison). A portion of it has since appeared, entitled "Don Quijote, Part I, Chapter 20: Interruption, Experience, and the Birth of the Novel," in *Homenaje a Ana María Barrenechea*, ed. Lia Schwartz Lerner and Isaías Lerner (Madrid: Castalia, 1984), pp. 241–46. The third, "Invention," stems remotely from a 1953 lecture first presented at Fordham (at the invitation of Vicente Gaos). A portion of the present text was submitted to an *homenaje* that I hope will appear before this book. Finally, the fourth, "Discovery," was the inaugural Américo Castro Lecture delivered in Princeton in 1969. In the following year it was translated, revised, and presented at the Third Congress of Hispanists in Mexico. It appears as "Los inquisidores literarios de Cervantes" in *Anales del Tercer Congreso de Hispanistas* (Mexico, 1970), pp. 3–25.

Pearce, Francisco Márquez Villanueva, and George Shipley,[11] whose generous reading and suggestions have helped immensely. I am particularly indebted to Dolores Timbas, whose editorial scrutiny has saved me from myself many times. Finally, two major "cervantistas" spent hours and days of their precious time correcting and redirecting one portion or another. I therefore dedicate what follows to my master, Américo Castro, and to my colleague, Raimundo Lida.

11. I have, of course, had far more intellectual company than I have mentioned. During the decades of their gestation these essays have been enriched by my unsystematic (after the publication of my dissertation on Avellaneda in 1950) inundation in the inexorable flood of contemporary Cervantine bibliography. As a result, those of my colleagues who may read them will surely perceive unacknowledged echoes of their contributions and ideas as well as occasional tacit disagreement. I hope they will not be offended by my decision to avoid blunting the thrust of what I have to say with a survey of their criticism. What I have done for the benefit of the readers I seek is to mention in the appropriate notes the major studies, which are our common point of departure, as well as the sources of certain still controversial interpretations that I accept as true. Here I refer most particularly to the mature work of Américo Castro.

1

Definition

*"I define the novel as the kind
of literature which produces this effect"*

Definitions constrict by definition, and definitions of the
novel asphyxiate. That is to say, to propose an answer to the
question "What is the novel?" is to predetermine a course of
meditation that should be free. If we think of that genre (as
did Cervantes, Fielding, and Gogol) as an epic in prose or,
alternatively, as a new form of fictional entertainment that
became significant when it mocked and chastised the "manners" of the eighteenth century and of major importance
when it proudly and profoundly explored the Zeitgeist of the
nineteenth, we close all other doors. These familiar definitions—the one rhetorical and the other historical—are re-
spectable and serviceable. But in the American academic
shorthand of a few years ago, they demand a choice between
Wayne Booth and Ian Watt. Let us instead ask two other
questions: "What do novels do to their readers?" and "How
do they do it?"—questions that preoccupied three of the
most sophisticated minds ever to think novelistically. I refer,
of course, to Cervantes and his most eminent nineteenth-
century disciples, Stendhal and Flaubert.

Theories of "reception" based on the notion (in the words
of Jonathan Culler) that all "propositions about poetic or novelistic discourse" should be redefined in terms of "procedures of reading" have proliferated recently.[1] However, since
I grew up in a world mostly inhabited by nineteenth-century

---

1. Jonathan Culler, *Structuralist Poetics* (Ithaca: Cornell University Press,
1975), p. 128.

people, and since the novel attained its apogee in that century, I propose that we go back six decades and listen to one of the most lucid readers the *Quijote* ever found for itself. In Ortega y Gasset's *Ideas sobre la novela* (1925) there is a preliminary answer to the first of the questions just posed:

> Let us observe ourselves at the moment we finish reading a great novel. It seems to us as if we are emerging from another existence, that we have escaped from a world out of communication with our authentic world. This lack of communication is shown by the fact that transition from one to another is imperceptible. An instant ago we found ourselves in Parma with Count Mosca, Clélia, and Fabrice; we were living with them, immersed in their air, their space, their time. Now suddenly, without any intermission, we find ourselves in our chamber, in our city, in our date; already our habitual preoccupations begin to awaken at the nerve ends. There is, of course, an interval of indecision, of uncertainty. Perhaps a brusque wing stroke of memory will suddenly submerge us again in the universe of the novel, and then with an effort, as if struggling in a liquid element, we try to swim to the shore of our own existence. If someone should observe us then, he would see the dilation of eyelids which characterizes those who have been shipwrecked.
>
> *I define the novel as the kind of literature which produces this effect.* Such is the enormous, unique, glorious, and magic power of this sovereign of modern literary forms. And the novel that lacks it is a failure whatever its other merits. Oh sublime, benign power which multiplies our existence, which frees us and pluralizes us, which enriches us with generous transmigration![2] (italics mine)

In spite of the buoyancy of Ortega's closing exclamation, his celebration of novel reading points more to the elimination of our existence than to its multiplication. As Cervantes discovered, and as Flaubert rediscovered, immersion in fiction is a peril to identity. Both the *Quijote* and *Madame Bovary* are novels about addicted readers: a desperately bored hidalgo and a desperately dissatisfied housewife who cannot

---

2. José Ortega y Gasset, *Ideas sobre la novela*, in *Obras completas*, 3: 410 (translation mine).

swim to the shore of their provincial existences. They and others like them are hooked on one of the two varieties of "volupté" that, according to Albert Thibaudet, were unknown to the ancients. The other—at that time—was tobacco, as Pierre Louys had pointed out.[3]

*"Cervantes confronted typographic
man in the figure of Don Quixote"*

Now for the second question: how do "fictitious prose works of over 50,000 words" produce these strange and interesting effects? How does the novel (a designation that at this point still includes both the *Quijote* and the *Amadís*) differ from other forms of literature? Here the late Marshall McLuhan's highly suggestive and engagingly arbitrary *Gutenberg Galaxy* will be of assistance. We have not noticeably done so, but those of us who are professionally concerned with the sudden and seemingly miraculous "publishing event" of 1605 should have welcomed enthusiastically McLuhan's observation that the novel is the characteristic literary expression of "print culture."[4] From our point of view, he redefines and refreshens what we already knew about the development of fiction in Spain prior to Cervantes.

In 1508—so our familiar lesson goes—a now lost medieval romance (a narrative in prose recounting the fantastic adventures and the exemplary love and courtesy of an ostensibly

3. See Albert Thibaudet, *Le liseur de romans* (Paris: G. Crés, 1925), pp. i–ii.

4. Marshall McLuhan, *The Gutenberg Galaxy* (Toronto: University of Toronto Press, 1962), p. 214. Both Bakhtin and Thibaudet allude in passing to this congruence of "medium" and "message." The latter merely remarks, "C'est avec l'imprimerie que la volupté nouvelle s'incorpore solidement aux habitudes humains" (Thibaudet, *Liseur*, p. 25). ("It's with printing that the new voluptuousness is solidly incorporated into human habits.") The former's realization that "the printing of books . . . served to shift discourse into a *mute* mode of perception, a shift decisive to the novel as a genre" (Bakhtin, *The Dialogic Imagination*, p. 379), is not followed up perhaps because of his search—to my mind misguided—for the origins of the modern genre in Byzantine romance.

fictional perfect knight named Amadís of Gaul[5]) was revised and published by one Garcí Rodríguez (or Ordóñez) de Montalvo, who had taken part in the Conquest of Granada in 1492. An instant best-seller, it provided welcome escape for its Spanish readers (barbers, priests, canons, young gentlemen, lawyers, and, most important of all, village hidalgos condemned by their privileged status to idleness and marginal poverty), readers who, like Montalvo, remembered vividly (or had heard about from their elders) that last flourish of chivalric prowess in the peninsula. The popularity of the *Amadís* thus resembled that of western romances shortly after the disappearance of our own frontier. The printing press was no longer a device for producing cheaply and in larger quantities hard-to-get medieval and classical texts; in addition, it had created overnight what we now call a national reading public.[6] And the result was, as Cervantes notes, that the *Amadís* was "the origin and beginning" of a flood of imitations and continuations. Exactly like best-sellers today, it engendered a subgenre: "los libros de caballería," or romances of chivalry.[7]

Reading with increasing speed and more and more silently (a kind of reading that was extremely rare in the era of the manuscript),[8] the newly constituted and insatiable public consumed ream after ream of ersatz adventures. And the more it read and was provided with reading, the better it learned how to immerse itself in the printed page and to derive therefrom unprecedented "volupté." Diego de San Pedro's sentimental and semiepistolary *Cárcel de Amor* (The

5. Bakhtin calls our attention to the fact that the *Amadís* was used as a guide to deportment, "how to converse in society, how to write letters and so on" (Bakhtin, *The Dialogic Imagination*, p. 384). Alonso Quijano can be thought of as taking this aspect to an extreme degree.

6. In widely circulated translations it performed a similar function abroad.

7. As was to be expected, the older Arthurian romances were absorbed into the genre, thanks to the printing press.

8. For further discussion, including St. Augustine's remarks on the amazement caused by St. Ambrose's miraculous ability to read silently, see McLuhan, *The Gutenberg Galaxy*.

Prison of Love, 1492), the first fictional narrative in Spanish to have been written expressly for publication, was apparently (like a manuscript) intended for reading aloud.[9] That is to say, it was intoned word for word for the enjoyment of a rapt circle of listeners.

But by 1605 an Alonso Quijano and others who shared his addiction were devouring silently (perhaps their lips still moved and their hands made gestures) all by themselves at least a volume a day: "from twilight to daybreak and from dawn to dark." Not only the regularization of type (stressed by McLuhan) but also, as just noted, the capacity of the ever more numerous presses to supply and stimulate demand resulted in the revolution in reading that made the *Quijote* possible and that is its point of departure. In addition to being silent, it was a self-accelerating process, comparable in the avidity of its absorption to the effect "of blood on a vampire" (as W. C. Fields described his first morning drink).

Surely nobody today reacts to fiction with the intoxication of such sixteenth-century Spaniards as Bernal Díaz del Castillo and his comrades, Teresa of Avila and her nuns, Ignatius of Loyola and his trainees, or Miguel de Cervantes and his creatures.[10] Only we diminishing few, fortunate enough to

9. The second edition of *La Celestina* (1500) contains instructions for reading aloud appended by the editor. Its nonnovelistic dialogue in fact demands careful oral intonation. See my "Entonación y motivación en *La Celestina*," in *Homenaje a Horst Baader*, ed. Frauke Gewecke (Barcelona: Hogar del Libro, 1984), pp. 29–36.

10. These examples are well known. Bernal Díaz in his *Historia verdadera* tells how the first sight of Tenochtitlan reminded the conquistadores of the "enchantments that are told in the book of Amadís." For further discussion, see my "Bernal Díaz del Castillo and *Amadís de Gaula*," in *Homenaje a Dámaso Alonso*, vol. 2 (Madrid: Gredos, 1961), pp. 99–114. As for Saint Teresa, she recounts in her spiritual autobiography, *El libro de su vida* (1588), the Quixotic incitement derived from such reading. And according to Pedro de Ribadeneyra's biography of Saint Ignatius (published in Latin in 1572 and in Spanish, as *Vida del padre Ignacio de Loyola*, in 1583), the sudden illumination that led to the founding of the Society of Jesus was derived from similar experiences. Miguel de Unamuno in chapter 2 of his *Life of Don Quixote and Sancho* has a vivid discussion of the matter. The mention of Saint Ignatius's "trainees" refers to the fact that the *Spiritual Exercises* were designed as if they were chapters of a divine romance. Silent reading with a visual imagination as

have lived in a world free of television (and in a house full of books), may have in our childhood been blessed with an experience of literacy remotely comparable to theirs. Eudora Welty's remarks on her early reading in *One Writer's Beginnings* indicate that she may well have come closest.[11] As for me, I was struck by the description in *To Kill a Mockingbird* of the rapt circle of children immersed collectively in a *Tom Swift* book, each attending primarily to the individual character with which he or she was identified by prior definition. Why? Because it evoked vividly a forgotten memory of similar sessions in my own childhood and of the two-dimensional personifications who so entranced us. My flesh-and-blood companions in immersion are by now dim to the point of vanishing, but Tom, Ned, Mr. Damon, and Rad still possess for me a remnant of the kind of reality that Amadís had for Alonso Quijano. In any case, at least partly because that kind of reading was, and still is, the indispensable first step for adult surrender to those special novels (the *Quijote, La Chartreuse de Parme, Huckleberry Finn, The Idiot*) on which we have traditionally depended for self-renovation, we have cause to fear that the genre may be in for trouble.

All of which amounts to saying: if not "the novel" (we must continue to evade Forster's unanswerable challenge!), then those novels we love the best and that love us the longest *need* us. Their "greatness" is not as self-evident as that of a tragedy, insofar as they depend on our capacity for what A. W. von Schlegel scornfully termed *Leserei,* meaning roughly "readingitis."[12] They depend, in short, on a disease

acute as that of Alonso Quijano was supposed to transform those who undertook the exercises.

11. Eudora Welty, *One Writer's Beginnings* (Cambridge, Mass.: Harvard University Press, 1984).

12. "Man lobt den jetzt allgemeiner verbreiteten Geschmack am Lesen, aber hilf Himmel! Welch eine Leserei ist das! Sie verdammt sich selbst schon dadurch, daß sie *so rastlos nach dem neuen greift* was doch kein wirklich neues ist. Nur die leidigste Passivität kann zu dieser Liebhaberei führen, die weder denken noch handeln mag; ja nicht einmal zu träumen müssen solche

the symptoms of which are feverish scanning, compulsion to turn pages, greediness for artificial time (as against the measured tempo of pronunciation), and mad, imaginative fervor. Just now, while correcting my text, I have read five brilliant paragraphs by Susan Sontag in which she describes the *Quijote* as "the first and greatest epic about addiction."[13]

In so saying, we have appended a qualification to McLuhan's notion of "typographic man." Although McLuhan does remark on the relation of the novel to the printing press (observing that the latter places the reader "in the hands" of the author[14]) and thereby comments perceptively on the *Quijote*, his major stress is on the linear, abstract, and rationally ordered mindset of the new readers. Here, on the contrary, we are concerned with fervid imagination shared nationwide, a mental epidemic capable of producing a literary miracle—or, as Bakhtin would say, the creation of a new and extravagant kind of generic "language" spoken in one way by the author and in other ways by the characters.

To be specific, three stages of fictional reception may be distinguished, although admittedly they can and do overlap. First, there is the invocative, oral, "truth-making," verbal magic of epics, ballads, and folktales, magic that still worked

---

Menschen verstehen, denn sonst würden sie sich weit etwas besseres imaginieren können als in ihren *Romanen* steht. Ihr eignes Leben ist unbedeutend und leer" (A. W. von Schlegel, *Vorlesungen über schöne Litteratur und Kunst* [Heilbronn: B. Behr, 1884], pp. 19–20, italics mine). ("One praises the taste for reading that is widespread now, but good Lord! What a mess and excess of reading that is! It damns itself through the very fact that it *seizes so restlessly at the new,* though it may not be new at all. Only the clumsiest of passivities can lead to this addiction, that can neither think nor act; and such people are not able to even have regular dreams, or they would otherwise be capable of imagining much better things than those that can be found in their *novels.* Their own life is insignificant and empty.") Schlegel clearly refers here to the kind of reader I term later in this essay the "adventure addict"—not realizing, as Cervantes realized, that it is through such addiction that one learns to read in the way all novels, including the greatest, should be read.

13. Of all places, in the book section of *The Boston Globe,* March 9, 1986.

14. McLuhan, *The Gutenberg Galaxy,* p. 125.

in attenuated form in manuscripts (for example, the still-believed-in Arthurian romances) written for reading aloud. In the latter, a legendary "this was so" replaced the mythical "this is so" of the former. Second, there are printed and frankly fictional narratives such as the *Amadís* and its progeny as well as the pastorals, which were (and are in their latter-day counterparts) the training pool for silent, communal immersion. And finally, in the *Quijote* Cervantes learned how to exploit fully (gave birth to, invented, discovered) the miraculous possibilities inherent in this new kind of reading—that is to say, how to enable us to augment our identity and to refresh our stale store of experience in the act of surrendering to fictional lives far more intensely and significantly alive than we are.

"The novel is like a fiddle bow . . ."

But we must not get ahead of ourselves. Ortega's definition—so convenient for evading the rhetorical trap set by Forster—may tell us something about what novels do to their readers. And Marshall McLuhan may provide elementary insight into how they do it. However, the latter's notion of the reader being "put into the hands" of the author and our own mention of Cervantes "learning how" to exploit that power indicate that our preliminary questions and answers were indeed preliminary. Even the most rudimentary story, whether oral, handwritten, or printed, has a teller, whether collective, anonymous, or a recipient of royalties. And it is equally obvious—the intentional fallacy notwithstanding—that the act of telling a story effectively presupposes a chosen beginning and ending as well as a calculated endeavor to stimulate and maintain interest between the two.

Percy Lubbock is in accord with Lukács and Thibaudet in defining novel reading as first of all a "process" or "passage of experience," but he also recognizes that the whole possesses a "size and shape."[15] He means not just a plot divided

15. Percy Lubbock, *The Craft of Fiction* (New York: Viking, 1957), p. 15.

into chapters but more significantly a predetermined "game" of communication with the author, which must be played from beginning to end, either subliminally or with critical awareness, by all readers or listeners. Even more unsatisfactory than Ortega's disregard of Stendhal as an artist and the *Chartreuse* as a work of art (for him it is only an experience) is the corollary implication that *all* works of fiction that effectively provide underwater escape are novels. Is our reading of the *Quijote* vitally more stimulating (as Ortega would have phrased it) and spiritually more illuminating than our reading of detective fiction? If so, why? Precisely because we are reluctant to relinquish Ortega's antidefinition of the novel as a special kind of reading that multiplies our existence,[16] we are faced with two far more demanding questions. How do novelists make their novels into a whole? What makes reading a novel worthwhile instead of a waste of time?

Since Ortega emphasized his gratitude for the happiness he had derived from immersion in the *Chartreuse*, it is fitting to try to amend his definition by examining two Stendhalian metaphors that take the role of the novelist into account. Furthermore, in order to prepare ourselves to comprehend what Cervantes has to say about his art, our most convenient introduction may be meditation on what his equally ironical nineteenth-century avatar has to tell us about his. Both novelists were ostensible failures, and both were at odds with iniquitous societies. Yet the Frenchman "malgré lui," because of the intensity of his historical experience (the Revolution, the Imperial campaigns, and their depressing aftermath), may serve as an intermediary for introducing the critical and

16. As a reader, Proust shares Ortega's experience of novelistic immersion. Thus he speaks with tacit regret of "la réalité qu'on retrouve en levant les yeux de dessus le livre qu'on était en train de lire et qui vous décrivait un milieu dans lequel on avait fini par se croire effectivement transporté" (Marcel Proust, *A l'ombres des jeunes filles en fleurs* [Paris: Gallimard, 1954], p. 353). (" . . . the reality which one recaptures on raising one's eyes from the book which one has been reading and which describes an environment into which one has come to believe that one has been bodily transported" [Marcel Proust, *Within a Budding Grove*, trans. Scott Moncrieff (New York: Modern Library, 1924), p. 20].)

creative preoccupations of the marginal Spaniard.[17] Although as their insatiable "lecteurs" we are the "semblables" and "frères" of both, the novels we are used to today are almost without exception far more overtly historical than the *Quijote*. The Stendhalian metaphor we know by heart is, of course, the "miroir" that the author "promène au long d'un chemin." However, the later realists and naturalists who were fond of repeating it failed to realize that the crucial word therein is not *miroir* but *chemin*. It is a miniature manifesto of open form and not of descriptive accuracy. Stendhal does not *state* that novels are better when they reflect people and places faithfully (like almost every major novelist from Cervantes to Joyce, he adored caricature); what he does *pretend* is that "size and shape" can take care of themselves. As a child—he tells us—his first memory of laughing was at the *Quijote*, and as a grown-up novelist the seemingly random road of the knight and squire (continued and perfected in the narratives of Lesage and Fielding) offered a means of communicating directly (that is, without the intrusive archaeology of Scott) the new historical consciousness of his century.

To be specific, both *Le rouge et le noir* and, in disguised form, *La Chartreuse* are composed of wayside adventures in which the wayside is Restoration France instead of the eternal and literal (read moral and brutal) wayside of Gil Blas, Tom Jones and Don Quijote. Balzac and Dickens viewed contemporary history as a temptingly delicious sociological layer cake ready to be sliced, admired, and consumed. Stendhal, however, experienced it as a rosary of ironical encounters between what John Stuart Mill called old and new kinds of human beings.[18] His novels, as a result, are "chemins" of generational incongruity along which both Julien and Fabrice in

17. The relationship of nineteenth-century historical consciousness to the evolution of the novel is most strikingly announced in the "Avant propos" of Balzac's *La comédie humaine*. Further bibliography may be found in chapter 1 of my *Galdós and the Art of the European Novel: 1867–1887* (Princeton, N.J.: Princeton University Press, 1981).

18. John Stuart Mill, *The Spirit of the Age*, ed. F. A. von Hayek (Chicago: University of Chicago Press, 1942), p. 1.

their very youthfulness and openness represent in reverse the naive obsolescence of Cervantes's fifty-year-old hidalgo. It is precisely this that Erich Auerbach failed to comprehend when he found the protagonist's age to be lacking in verisimilitude.[19] The mirror and road comparison thus expresses perfectly Stendhal's mastery of the art of apparent spontaneity, the keen joy he shared with Cervantes in arranging ostensibly haphazard encounters. But it does not tell all the truth, and he knew it. Like the *Quijote* and like any novel worth our sustained attention, Stendhal's novels possess their own unique wholeness, which he cunningly contrived and perversely denied.[20] Yet since self-revelation is the obverse of self-concealment, while writing the autobiographical striptease entitled *La vie de Henri Brûlard*, he proposed a second metaphor, at once more revealing for our purposes and more challenging to conventional criticism. The first had presented composition as a game of solitaire. The lonely writer—in the guise of the protagonist—directs his mirror with calculated irony (but apparently at random) at the passage of history within the lives of the other characters. However, the very act of publishing as well as the longed-for possibility of future editions invalidates the self-centered definition. In order to understand his own metier, Stendhal—like Ortega—would have to let the reader into the game.

Stendhal was painfully preoccupied with readers because of their extreme scarcity during his lifetime. Novelists who were blessed with a ready-made public might take them for granted or even—like Cervantes and Sterne—play tricks on them. But the semiexiled Frenchman was tormented with the fear that his irony—at least as cutting as theirs and far more self-consciously secretive—might never be understood.[21] Al-

19. Erich Auerbach, *Mimesis*, trans. W. R. Trask (Princeton, N.J.: Princeton University Press, 1953), chapter 14.
20. See my *The Tower as Emblem: Chapters VIII, IX, XIX and XX of the "Chartreuse de Parme"* (Frankfurt am Main: Klostermann, 1967).
21. Although Kierkegaard's notion that the fruit of irony is the freedom

ways intellectually preoccupied with the otherness of others, he wondered if anyone worthy would ever adopt his spiritual offspring. Could he on his own found and populate the exclusive society of the "Happy Few" with consciousnesses trained by reading to resemble his own?

More simply stated, would there come to exist by 1880 or 1935 a historically experienced public prepared—unlike Stendhal's contemporaries—to participate in the special kind of suprahistorical exaltation (or "Happyness") he was concerned to offer? Continuing worry about these—for him— really desperate questions resulted in the following marvel of wishful thinking: "Un roman est comme un archet; la caisse du violon qui rend les sons, c'est l'âme du lecteur."[22]

It goes without saying that the imaginative collaboration of the apprehender (observer, listener, or reader) is an essential factor in what used to be called the aesthetic equation. But what Stendhal and Ortega propose is that fiction (printed fiction, though neither makes that point), because it takes place in our minds, is the art form that involves us most intimately. Nor is it necessary to be as singularly susceptible as

---

derived from self-discovery (the ultimate ironist, like God, rejects understanding) would have appealed to Stendhal's radically solitary soul, it would have been unsatisfactory to him as a novelist. Rather, he felt an equal need for communication, a need to convert his possible reader into himself. In his case, as Vladimir Jankélévitch remarks, "L'ironie ne veut pas être *crue*, elle veut être *comprise*" (*L'ironie ou la bonne conscience* [Paris: Alcan, 1950], p. 51). ("Irony does not want to be *believed*, it wants to be *understood*.") Or as José Ferrater Mora puts it, "The ironical attitude is directed towards *someone*. . . . Irony may occur in solitude. But it *does occur* most often in company" (*Cuestiones disputadas* [Madrid: Revista de Occidente, 1955], p. 31).

22. *La vie de Henri Brûlard* (Paris: Le Divan, 1949), p. 227. ("The novel is like a fiddle bow; the violin that gives forth the sounds is the soul of the reader.") Without mentioning Stendhal, Harold Brodkey recently verged on the same metaphor: "Reading is an intimate act, perhaps more intimate than any other human act. I say that because of the prolonged (or intense) exposure of one mind to another that is involved in it. . . . One settles one's body to some varying degree, and then one enters on the altered tempos of reading, the subjection of *being played upon*" ("Reading, the Most Dangerous Game," *New York Times Book Review*, November 24, 1985, pp. 1 and 44–45, italics mine).

Alonso Quijano or Emma Bovary to have had the uncanny experience of having been taken over—spiritually infiltrated—by a work of fiction. Who among us has not revered rafts and tree houses without quite knowing why after having read *Huckleberry Finn* or *The Swiss Family Robinson?* And for those who no longer read, the descendants of fiction called motion pictures can have comparable (though perhaps less durable) effects.

There is, however, a crucial difference between Ortega's description of reading and Stendhal's. The former's immersion is a metaphorical extension of the commonplace "So-and-so is deep in a book," while the latter's soul melody recognizes the obvious truth that it is the book that is deep in us. And the corollary is that it is the author who "renews our life" and "takes away our gray hair" (both phrases, as we shall see, are from the *Quijote*) by calculated arrangement of the whole. Just as the violinist has his score, so too the writer, by means of symbols and emblems, allusive and elusive chapter titles and epigraphs, ironical overstatement and understatement, dreams and premonitions, and a thousand and one other forms of intervention, teaches us to remember what we have read and to anticipate what we are going to read in the very act of surrendering ourselves voluptuously to the printed page. Because prose fiction is habitually received as a process of spontaneous reading, the individual author must also take the self-conscious role of critic and teacher. At times surreptitiously (Stendhal and Mark Twain) and at times overtly (Fielding and Thomas Mann), with all deliberate speed the author trains his readers, in the words of Virginia Woolf, to "climb on his shoulders and look through his eyes" in order that they may "understand in what order he ranges the large common objects upon which novelists are fated to gaze: man and men, behind them nature, and above them that power which for convenience and brevity we may call God."[23] Meaning clearly: while absorbed

23. Virginia Woolf, *The Second Common Reader* (New York: Harcourt Brace, 1932), p. 51.

in the entrancing flow of narration, to take the configuration of the whole into account.

This, too, is the worthy task of my own profession. The author in his secondary role as teacher is necessarily limited by the historical moment in which he lives. He prepares his lesson in reading for a public to which he himself belongs. We, on the other hand, are aware that readers living in later centuries or conditioned by foreign cultures are apt to go astray. Therefore, we try to preserve as well as we can, if not a single correct meaning, at least a sense of the unique aliveness of novelistic time gone by. It is obvious that lectures and footnotes cannot by themselves teach students how to surrender themselves to forgotten and alien varieties of "happiness" or "magic power." But without them, without a responsible tradition of academic custody, how much would be lost! Even such straightforward novels as *Old Mortality* and *The Heart of Midlothian* need the annotation that Scott himself provided with admirable foresight for their resuscitation.

Unfortunately, not all teachers are to be trusted, and at this point two deplorable cases of misreading (or antireading) may be illustrative. The first is Vladimir Nabokov's notorious and almost nauseated rejection not of Cervantes (the Harvard lectures are no more than an academic spoof and have deservedly been remaindered) but of Dostoevsky. Biographically and academically, Nabokov was surely better prepared than almost anybody to lend his "soul" to the master. Nevertheless, not just in his lectures but in his conversation he was obsessively hostile. The repeated *boutade* that the author of *The Brothers Karamazov* was the Blasco Ibáñez of Russia is an odious comparison which is also unfair to the Spaniard. What Nabokov is saying in Stendhalian terms is that he is not attuned to Dostoevsky. And readers attuned to *Bend Sinister* and *Lolita* should not find it hard to comprehend his lack of response. For him and for Henry James, who reacted in much the same way, confession of their manifest failure as readers was out of the question. Rather, they justify themselves with destructive criticism: Dostoevsky's style is murky and crude;

his command of the shape of the whole, shaky; and his plots, melodramatic.[24]

At the opposite extreme there is the Spanish philosopher-philologist-poet-novelist-mystic Miguel de Unamuno, who believed himself to be so personally attuned to the *Quijote* that his commentary amounts only to an expression of passionate immersion and exaltation. Disdainful of Cervantes (like Nabokov, Unamuno was a professional poseur), unconcerned with his intricate artistry, and uninterested in his generic innovation, he preferred (or at least he so proclaimed) to read the national masterpiece in translation. The result is at best a pseudonovel, *La vida de don Quijote y Sancho* (1905), about novelistic experience. Despite its occasional insights and frequent eloquence, it is more interesting for students of Unamuno than for those who wish to bring the *Quijote* back alive.

Such estimative catastrophes are worth mentioning, if only to underline the peculiarity of the genre. If Nabokov had said about Aeschylus, Dante, or Shakespeare what he said about Dostoevsky, his opinions would not be worth a paragraph. As it is, we cannot be absolutely certain that he and Henry James are totally wrong. Like it or not, our intellects descend from Aristotle, and a novel performed as Stendhal would have it performed is manifestly non-Aristotelian. The author of the *Poetics* was able to snare tragedy in his intellectual net and then to subdivide it into five components by first defining it as an imitation of an action. However, if we accept the premise that the novel *is* an action taking place in the soul of the reader and that its primary demand is entranced violin-like submission, we must revise our modes of critical judgment. The "active" aspect of *Oedipus Rex* was relegated by the philosopher to the more or less indefinable notion of

24. Jean-Jacques Demorest, who was kind enough to read a preliminary version of this essay, informs me that Nabokov, while at Cornell, repeatedly expressed his antipathy to Stendhal. Could it have been the Cervantine tradition itself that he disliked?

mass catharsis. We, on the contrary, read the *Quijote* or *The Idiot* all by ourselves—whether in rebellion against the dictatorial violinist or submissively within the limits of our individual capacities.

"How that person feels himself existing in the happening"

Our belief that Nabokov (who stayed on shore) and Unamuno (who drowned) have indulged themselves in improper conduct—novelistically speaking—cannot be proved. But at least we can try to understand what they seem not to have understood. What is it, we asked earlier, that makes reading the *Quijote* and *The Idiot* worthwhile and not a waste of time or, even worse, an occasion for arrogant self-display? The answer is not to be found in effective style, in profound ideas, in psychological truth to life, or in Paul Bourget's demand for coherent composition, so devastatingly refuted by Albert Thibaudet.[25] A given novel may attract us because of the presence of some or all of these qualities, but none of them corresponds to what novels are really about. At this point a definition proposed by my teacher, Américo Castro, after decades of meditating on the *Quijote,* may lead us in the right direction: "The novel does not consist in telling what happens to a person, but instead in communicating how that person feels himself existing in the happening."[26] Admittedly, this definition sounds so simplistic that E. M. Forster would probably have waved it away with a condescending smile. Fortunately, though, Castro is not alone. Thornton Wilder phrases it differently, but, as a novelist, his agreement helps save the definition from Forster's skepticism: "Art does not record what the outside world is like, but what it is like to contemplate and experience the outside world."[27]

25. Albert Thibaudet, *Réflexions sur le roman* (Paris: Gallimard, 1938), chapter 1.
    26. Américo Castro, *De la edad conflictiva* (Madrid: Taurus, 1961), p. 202.
    27. *The Journals of Thornton Wilder*, ed. Donald Gallup (New Haven: Yale University Press, 1985), p. 4. After long and learned meditations on Cervan-

What makes the *Quijote* "the exemplary novel of all time," and what led Wilder later to conclude that "before Cervantes wrote this book, there was no novel,"[28] is precisely this: the birth, infancy, and maturity of experience in its pages. Not experience recollected lyrically in tranquillity; or intensified dramatically with rhetoric, self-conscious acting, and tense confrontation; or elevated epically on an exemplary heroic pedestal; or denigrated satirically from a worm's-eye view; but just the way experience was and is now—was "felt" and still "feels"—here on the page in the course of its happening. Those other kinds of fiction on Forster's list—allegories, fables, parodies, documentaries, and romances—tell us for their several purposes what happened or took place. But the novel wants its lives to accompany ours in experiencing the taking place.

Once again, how did this begin? My far-from-original argument will be that the metamorphosis gradually comes about after the initial six chapters, which comprise Don Quijote's lonely First Sally—that is to say, during the rest of Part I (the Second Sally), when the acquisition of Sancho provides his master with someone with whom to talk.[29] Thereafter each "happening" or discrete adventure becomes increasingly self-conscious. The two men, because they are together, feel themselves "existing" in what is going on and fully communicate that feeling to the reader. Admitting moments of regression to farce or of padding with sentimental artificiality,

---

tes's theory of the novel, E. C. Riley reaches this luminous conclusion: "The *Quijote* offers an extraordinary illusion of human experience, which is not a shadow or distortion of human experience, but an illumination of its nature" (*Cervantes's Theory of the Novel* [Oxford: Clarendon Press, 1962], p. 245).

28. Wilder, *Journals*, p. 95. The sentence continues: " . . . there was the 'récit' . . . which permitted by mere convention thoughts, prayers, secret motivation, but at most that was a mere rhetorical device; it was not there that the interest lay."

29. Conventionally cervantistas divide the novel into three "sallies" (the first two in Part I and the second comprising all of Part II) because of their fundamentally different varieties of narration. The difference will be clarified in the course of the essays to follow.

the rapid and schematic sequence of antiadventures often surprises us by revealing unexpectedly an underlying continuum of decelerated novelistic experience ruefully savored in the act of sharing. Thornton Wilder perhaps exaggerates Cervantes's self-consciousness in the pages of his *Journal*, written at Harvard while he gave the 1950–51 Norton Lectures,[30] but his testimony as a fellow novelist is invaluable:

> To read the first half of the First Part of *Don Quixote*, then, is to watch Cervantes discovering that the interest of fiction does not have to depend on any external importance offered by its happening—neither on surprise nor on suspense, nor novelty, nor complicated intrigue—the long consecrated structural rhetoric of narration.[31]

Wilder goes on to say that while reading, the reader can almost sense physically how Cervantes "pinched himself" in the act of writing these chapters.

The obvious objection to our rephrasing of Castro's distinction in terms of Wilder's "experience" is that in both Spanish and English the word is used in various ways. Saint Teresa writes about her mystical "experiences" in a way that seems to correspond to her childhood addiction to reading. Cervantes, on the other hand, seems to understand the word in terms of empirical testing. When Alonso Quijano finds that his makeshift visor does not withstand a swordblow, he repairs it "sin querer hacer nueva experiencia de ello" ("without caring to make another trial of it," I.1).[32] For our purposes two distinct but related temporal meanings are all that count. The first is present experience, the "now" of the happening,

30. Wilder prepared the lectures on the *Quijote* for the second semester (1951) of Humanities 2, a course devoted to the epic and the novel, which he offered, with characteristic generosity, in addition to the Norton Lectures.

31. Wilder, *Journals*, p. 96.

32. For convenience, citations from the *Quijote* are identified parenthetically by part and chapter in my text. I have borrowed shamelessly from a number of translations with such modifications as seemed necessary, mostly restoration of the indispensable "thee" and "thou" in Don Quijote's conversation with Sancho.

as in "What an experience!" The second is cumulative experience, the accretion of such "nows" in the course of living, which results in mature wisdom or disillusion, as in "a man of experience." German expresses it better with two words: *Erlebnis*, immediately lived experience (from *leben*, "to live"), and *Erfahrung*, traveled experience (from *fahren*, "to travel"). As we shall see, both constitute the very stuff of the *Quijote* as well as of every novel worth rereading.

Worth rereading? Before attempting to distinguish between kinds of reading in terms of value, let us practice with a passage that is an irrefutable example of what the novel can do at its best. It is the re-creation (not description) of the thunderstorm over Jackson's island in a narrative clearly bearing the *Quijote*'s watermark. As a lived experience in the present, it communicates the immediacy of time with singular vividness:

> We spread our blankets inside for a carpet, and eat our dinner in there. We put all the other things handy at the back of the cavern. *Pretty soon* it darkened up and begun to thunder and lighten, so the birds were right about it. *Directly* it begun to rain, and it rained like all fury, too, and I never *see* the wind blow so. It was one of these regular summer storms. It *would get* so dark that it looked all blue-black outside, and lovely; and the rain *would thrash* along by so thick that the trees off a little ways looked dim and spider-webby; and here would come a blast of wind that would bend the trees down and turn up the pale underside of the leaves; and then a perfect ripper of a gust would follow along and set the branches to tossing their arms as if they was just wild; and, *next*, when it was just about its bluest and blackest—fst! it was bright as glory, and *you'd have* a little glimpse of treetops a-plunging about, away off yonder in the storm, hundreds of yards further than you could see before; dark as sin again *in a second*, and *now you'd hear* the thunder let go with an awful crash and *then* go rumbling, grumbling, tumbling down the sky towards the underside of the world, like rolling empty barrels down stairs—where it's a long stairs and they bounce a good deal *you know*.[33] (italics mine)

33. Mark Twain, *Adventures of Huckleberry Finn*, chapter 9.

Read aloud, this splendid passage might not incorrectly be received as a prose poem that preserves a past storm in lasting beauty—meditation in tranquillity, reinforced orally by the onomatopoetic "rumbling, grumbling, tumbling." However, read silently, the way most of us have read it (the way I believe it should be read), it preys on the visual and auditory memories of the best storms of our lives. Storm-time ("pretty soon," "directly," "next," "fst!," "now," "then") is one with seen-and-heard-time—which remind us that time and weather are significantly synonymous in the Romance languages. And together they invoke life-time. Who experiences this novelistic thunderstorm, and when was (or is) its happening? Of course, it is an intense "now" for Huck and Jim, but it is also fusion of "thens," first for Samuel Clemens and afterwards for us. Even more, it will also provide a perfected version of experiences—more exactly, *Erlebnisse*—for our children, grandchildren, and great-grandchildren. Ultimately, it happens in the strange and consoling (were it not for another kind of fusion!) duration of humankind, which Huck addresses in the vast plural of the second person— "you'd hear," "you know," "you'd have."

Obviously, each of these *you*'s is also a single *you*, and as such it draws on and revivifies each reader's more or less tenuous memories of just how it did feel to exist in such a happening—camping out, comradeship, the special savor of a meal in the open, in addition to the spectacle of the storm itself. However, beneath the level of anecdotal recollection there are the primary experiences of exposure and shelter, hunger and its satisfaction, which can be shared by readers who unfortunately have never left the city or the desert. According to Lukács (who, two years after Ortega, also began by meditating on the *Quijote*), *Obdachlosigkeit*, the condition of rooflessness, at once physical and cosmic, is the primordial situation of the "heroes" of novels. And so, too, of their readers. To say the same thing in another way, each reading is unique and at the same time communal. Depending on the state of the individual soul and what is stored in the private storehouse of memory, the melody changes its tone, intensity, and quality, and yet it always remains within frontiers traced by the score and the possibilities and necessities of being human. My boyhood reading of *Huckleberry Finn* is not the same as last year's, and I suspect that new sounds await my older age. But all three readings, along with those of my grandfather, my grandchildren, and the rest of literate mankind, rather than contradict each other, reinforce each other.

Stendhal and Castro thus complement one another and, in so doing, suggest an answer to the question, What makes reading the *Quijote* and *The Idiot* worthwhile and not a waste of time? The challenge is to progress from reading books to being read by books. Those of us who greedily consume fiction in print remain content more often than we would like to admit with self-substitution—the voluptuous transferral of identity (described sensuously by Thibaudet), immersion in another *hic et nunc* (described intellectually by Ortega), the "restless" grasping of fictional suspense to the accelerated heartbeat of one's own temporal bosom (described scornfully by A. W. von Schlegel). But we need not merely aspire to the temporary solace of escape, or even to that more expansive and exhilarating happiness Proust describes in a phrase that reminds us of the metaphors of both Ortega and Stendhal: "cette multiplication possible de soi-même, qui est le bonheur."[34]

Proust said this on observing novelistically a "jeune fille en fleur" riding a bicycle, but by the time we have arrived at *Le temps retrouvé,* we are asked to esteem a happiness more profound and more lasting. The most precious blessing a text can offer is that of drawing on our experience and concentrating it into a storm far more stormy than any we can remember living through. We are then nothing less than the "lecteurs de nous-mêmes."[35] Or as Henri Bergson remarked, surely after experiencing Marcel's loss and the recapturing of

34. Proust, *A l'ombre*, p. 444. (" . . . that possible multiplication of oneself which is happiness" [*Within a Budding Grove*, p. 130].)
35. Marcel Proust, *Oeuvres complètes*, vol. 3 (Paris: Gallimard, La Pleiade, 1954), p. 1033.

time, great novels bring us back into "our own presence."[36] The essence is restored to our existence, or perhaps it is distilled from it.

The prerequisite remains, however, that before we can find ourselves (or read ourselves), we must first learn to lose ourselves. Cervantes's law is the opposite of Gresham's law in that addiction to an abundance of romances enabled the creation of what used to be called "the best of the good reading."[37] Or perhaps I should call it Saint Teresa's law, since she was the first, as far as I know, to formulate it explicitly. A novice whom she observed reading "books of chivalry and others of the same sort" remembered her saying that that habit "did not disturb her, because from them I might be brought to read good ones and that I would profit from my inclination, because the same thing had happened to her."[38]

"An adventure . . . is like an island in life"

In so relating novelistic experience to our own, we must be vigilantly aware that everything depends on such specialized vessels of experience as Huck and Jim, Parson Adams and Joseph Andrews, Frédéric Moreau and Rosanette, Ishmael and Queequeg, Mr. Pickwick and Sam Weller, or Stephen Dedalus and Leopold Bloom—to mention only some pairs in the tradition of Don Quijote and Sancho. Admittedly, they

36. Henri Bergson, *Time and Free Will* (New York: Harper, 1960), p. 134. Cited in Robert Penn Warren, *Democracy and Poetry* (Cambridge, Mass.: Harvard University Press, 1975), p. 7.

37. The phrase is the title of an extensive section of volume 8 of *Our Wonder World* (Chicago: George L. Shuman, 1914). The ten-volume set is not a juvenile encyclopedia but rather an enchanting compendium of fact and fiction. This particular section, with its enticing illustrations and selections, provoked the imagination of Eudora Welty and constituted my own introduction to silent reading on a more elevated level than that offered by "Victor Appleton." The editor-in-chief of the whole set was Howard Benjamin Grose, but the subeditor who compiled "The Best of the Good Reading" is not credited by name.

38. Cited by Francisco Márquez Villanueva, "La vocación literaria de Santa Teresa," *Nueva Revista de Filología Hispánica* 32 (1983), p. 357 n. 6.

are unequal in sensitivity, but in sharing their shared confrontation with Wilder's "outside world," we as readers learn from within ourselves just what it is like for them—according to their varieties and levels of consciousness—"to contemplate and experience" it. Story people, such as Amadís and his squire Gandalín, Pantagruel and Panurge, Cervantes's own Persiles and Segismunda, Candide and Doctor Pangloss, or Jacques and his "maître," only can communicate what happens to them and what they think about it—meaning what we should (or should not) think about it—which is a very different matter. Why? Leaving satire and allegory aside, it is time to make explicit the distinction between novel and romance that was implicit in our suspicion that a "good read" (Ortega's immersion) is as spongy a category as "good eats." In other words, some works of fiction are more novelistic than others.

What exactly is the difference between Don Quijote and Sancho exposed to the world they live in and Amadís and Gandalín encased unproblematically in theirs? Without wishing to belabor notions the meaning of which we all know intuitively, I propose an answer based on the distinction between adventure and experience suggested in an essay of the Austrian philosopher, sociologist, and source for Ortega, Georg Simmel. Entitled simply "The Adventure," it proposes that the least common denominator of happenings called adventures is not danger, excitement, or even suspense, but rather hermeticism. An adventure is a special sort of event and awareness of an event that seems cut out from (cut apart from) the ongoing flow of consciousness:

> The most general form of adventure is its dropping out of the continuity of life. . . . An adventure is certainly part of our existence, directly contiguous with other parts which precede or follow it; at the same time, however, in its deeper meaning, it occurs outside the usual continuity of this life. . . . We ascribe to an adventure a beginning and end much sharper than those to be discovered in other forms of experience. . . . The adventure lacks that reciprocal interpenetration with adjacent parts of life which constitute "life-as-a-whole." It is like an is-

land in life which determines its beginning and end according to its own formative powers.[39]

What surprises us in this definition is its replacement of our customary notion of adventures as dangerous happenings, from which we fortunately escape, with temporal delimitation. If we translate that into spatial terms, as does Simmel with his island comparison, we realize that it is not the accessories—shipwrecks, pirates, cannibals—that constitute the adventure, but the liquid frontier of the encircling shore. The very word *island* carries the connotation. And from that we may extrapolate a typology of adventurous settings: dungeons and caves, towers and tree houses, balloons and submarines, "wuthering heights" and secret passages, *loci amoeni* within impenetrable forests, green oases surrounded by impassable deserts, and many more, including the summit of Everest and the North and South poles.

Simmel surely would not deny (though he does not mention) that danger is the boon companion of adventure insofar as it carves out a discrete and more intense portion of experience. But it is not in itself adventurous any more than is

---

39. *Georg Simmel*, ed. Kurt H. Wolff (Columbus: Ohio State University Press, 1959), pp. 243–44. Again Proust and Bakhtin provide suggestive corroboration. Proust's discussion of the effects of alcohol is almost identical to Simmel's discussion of adventure: "L'alcool, en tendant exceptionellement mes nerfs, avait donné aux minutes actuelles une qualité, un charme qui n'avaient pas eu pour effet de me rendre plus apte ni même plus résolu à défendre; car en me les faisant préférer mille fois au reste de ma vie, mon exaltation les isolait, *j'étais enfermé dans le present, comme les héros* . . . ; momentanément éclipsé, mon passé ne projetait plus devant moi cette ombre de lui même que nous appelons notre avenir" (Proust, *A l'ombre*, pp. 468–69, italics mine). ("The alcohol that I had drunk, by unduly straining my nerves, gave to the minutes as they came a quality, a charm which did not have the result of leaving me more ready, or indeed more resolute to inhibit them, prevent their coming; for while it made me prefer them a thousand times to anything else in my life, my exaltation made me isolate them from everything else; I was confined to the present, as heroes are . . . ; eclipsed for the moment, my past no longer projected before me that shadow of itself which we call our future" [*Within a Budding Grove*, p. 159].) As for Bakhtin, his discussion of "adventure-time" as a distinct temporal phenomenon is equally pertinent. See *The Dialogic Imagination*, pp. 88–89.

love, despite our perception that sudden and tempestuous affairs (for example, the transitory but sharply outlined "shadow" of Proust's *jeunes filles*) perform the same operation. The Spanish poet Pedro Salinas, translator of the first two volumes of *A la recherche du temps perdu*, further illustrates the point when he compares his evanescent beloved—here today and always on the verge of disappearance—to "an island / escaped from the map, / who passed by my side / dressed as a girl / with fur of foam / on a green coat and a vast / spray of adventures."[40] Conversely, how ironical it is that Sancho's *insula* should be on dry land where he can walk away when he pleases. Once again Cervantes, who had so many genuine adventures in galleys and prisons, is engaged in teasing the fictional variety.

Although Simmel seems to be referring to actual adventures of the sort we may have had and are happy to have survived, his perception of them as essentially hermetic enables us to comprehend in a new way the episodic structure of Alonso Quijano's favorite fiction. For as Alonso Quijano read romances of chivalry, so too we read mysteries, westerns, erotic romances, and sci-fi. All of us, not without an obscure sense of guilt, from time to time join the undiscriminating public in its addiction to accelerated and compartmentalized adventures—adventures finished and already hazy as soon as consumed. Such reading resembles nothing so much as the passing of a freight train, an adventurous spectacle by its very nature. Furthermore, as the Marxist critic André Würmser points out, if we wait a few years we can escape into them again almost without remembering the first time or even the second.[41] It is easy to criticize this form of literacy as mind pollution; and instead of excusing it as indispensable training (as did Saint Teresa), certain exquisite

---

40. Pedro Salinas, *La voz a ti debida* (Buenos Aires: Losada, 1949), p. 17, translation mine.
41. See the prologue to André Würmser, *L'assassin est mort le 1ᵉʳ* (Paris: P. Dupont, 1960).

or self-righteous critics have used it to belabor all of prose fiction.[42] "What, you are reading a novel?" one of my older relatives used to ask, unaware that she was echoing A. W. von Schlegel. What she also did not realize was that the book she fastidiously called a novel, if it really was a novel, was not a waste of time but a salvation of time.

" . . . *he said he didn't want no more adventures*"

At this point we seem to have arrived at a conveniently neat set of antitheses: adventure versus experience, shallow skimming versus profound perusal, romance versus novel, escape versus self-discovery, "dropping out" versus "life as a whole," or even Tom's absurd make-believe versus Huck's pathetically novelistic and usually believable lies.[43] However, precisely because these contrasts are so neat, we should remember Mark Twain's prefatory warning to readers of *Huckleberry Finn:* "Persons attempting to find a motive in this narrative will be prosecuted; persons attempting to find a moral in it will be banished; persons attempting to find a plot in it will be shot." For the novelistic "Chief of Ordnance," motives, morals, and plots (who knows what penalties he might have devised for persons attempting to find themes, myths,

---

42. E. Noulet, in "Problèmes de lettres" (*Diogène* 14 [1956], pp. 127–44), includes a curious sampling of recent expressions of this disesteem.

43. As noted, the oral epic depends on the myth—the believed truth— of what is said. The word is the thing (as in popular etymologies), and therefore to pronounce is to create. It is the villains—Ganelon, Infantes de Carrión, Mordred, Paris—who lie. In the novel, on the other hand, printed words no longer possess oral certainty. Hence the prevalent concern of novelists with perspectivism, illusion, delusion, hypocrisy, rumor, and out-and-out prevarication. Mark Twain goes one step further, insofar as his narrator's superb gift of oral truth-telling makes him into such a convincing, inveterate, and appealing liar—appealing in contrast to the shoddy and unconscious lies society tells to itself in the language of commonplaces. Dickens, Stendhal, and Galdós, as well as Virginia Woolf and Joyce, all share the same interest in the contrast of the truth toward which their protagonists strive with the mendacious *Umgangssprache* (local speech) of their milieus. But Cervantes, with his madman, and Mark Twain, with his unrepentant liar, accentuate the contrast by putting it in reverse.

or structures?) are abstractions—that is to say, lies—whereas this novel, like the *Quijote* and all true novels, has as its only claim to merit the immediacy of its truth. As Huck says about *The Adventures of Tom Sawyer* (out of which he emerged autonomously in the same way the Don Quijote of Part II emerged from Part I): "That book was made by Mr. Mark Twain, and he told the truth mainly. There were things which he stretched"—thereby, as we shall see, meeting the requirements of verisimilitude—"but mainly he told the truth" (chapter 1). And his new narrative persona, Huckleberry Finn, proposes to go on doing the same.

We have been warned, so let us hasten to confess that the antithesis of fictional adventure and fictional experience (the first inferior insofar as it flattens life and the second superior insofar as it enhances life) is as much of an abstraction as the three that our "Chief" has forbidden. It may be useful for correcting Ortega's notion that any fictional narrative is a novel if its "magic power" works. That is, it may be useful for defining the qualitative difference between Alonso Quijano's reading of the *Amadís* and our reading of the *Quijote,* or for that matter between reading the boyhood romance of *Tom Sawyer* and the novel supposedly written by his friend. But if we go on to interpret it as delineating a rigid and impenetrable generic frontier, it is an arrant falsehood. When Huck, after the perilous excursion aboard the *Sir Walter Scott,* explains to Jim that "these kind of things was adventures," Jim, who has just lived through it as a hair-raising experience, replies that "he didn't want no more adventures" (chapter 14). Similarly, when Don Quijote, after hearing Sansón Carrasco's armor Homerically clatter on the ground, wakes up Sancho and informs him in a tremulous voice, "Brother Sancho, we have an adventure," the latter replies, "But how do you know that this is an adventure?" (II.12). In both cases it is a matter of prior definition, the kind of *vue de l'esprit* we have been trying to avoid.

Therefore, in order to avoid whatever punishment this overgeneralization might deserve, I hasten to confess that adventure is a variety of experience and that every experience, perceived and remembered as set apart from others, has an element of adventure. This confession, once made, allows us to ask and answer the obvious question posed by Simmel's definition: why is the storm scene in *Adventures of Huckleberry Finn* not just one more hermetic adventure? An island, a cave, and a storm taken together seem to fit all the requirements perfectly. Even more, the river chapters taken as a whole—centered on the raft and the wigwam and composed of such discrete episodes as the floating house, the wreck, the feud, the lynch party, and the swindles—seem fully to justify the word *adventures* in the title. The truth, of course, is that they are adventures, splendid adventures, but, as we have seen, they are nonetheless experienced in ongoing time, lived, remembered, and recounted temporally—not only as they happen ("now," "then," "next," "fst!") but also as coming from the past and going toward the future. The thunder that closes the passage cited from chapter 9—"like rolling empty barrels down stairs—where it's a long stairs and they bounce a good deal you know"—joins the entranced immediate experience of the narrative strangeling to the remembered mischief of his lost boyhood.[44] As for the future, the shared companionship with Jim and the nascent project of his liberation begin right here.

However, it is not just in the memory and imagination of Huck and Don Quijote that novelistic passage of time is perceptible. Both narratives carry within each of their episodes all that was told in the past and all that is to be told—or might be told—in the future. In the *Quijote* Argamasilla sends forth its emissaries (the Priest, the Barber, and Sansón Carrasco) in order to effect the capture and return of the errant hidalgo, and up ahead are the Insula, the tournament at Zaragoza, and the final homecoming. It is the same in *Huckleberry Finn*.

---

44. In spite of Huck's repeated assertion that he is "only a boy," the reader, after intimacy with his consciousness and capacity for experience, realizes that that, too, is a lie. For a more detailed discussion see my *"Adventures of Huckleberry Finn:* Experience of Samuel Clemens," in *One Hundred Years of "Huckleberry Finn,"* ed. Robert Sattelmeyer and J. Donald Crowley (Columbia, Mo.: University of Missouri Press, 1985), pp. 15–25.

The gloomy exigencies of the "sivilizers" of Saint Petersburg provide a lasting contrast with the freedom of the river and make necessary the concluding act of disappearance. But what is even worse is our perception that Pap's world (which refutes "sivilization") comes creeping along the ever more squalid banks in pace with the drifting raft. In both books the characters aspire heroically to "work themselves free," in the words of Virginia Woolf, and the novel as such aspires to work its readers free.[45] Admittedly, both endings are inevitably melancholy, and the consciousness of Huck (and, refracted through it, that of Jim longing for his family and prey to remorse for his mistreatment of his deaf child) is as forlorn as that of Don Quijote during and after his sojourn in the Duke's palace. Nevertheless, their consciousness does possess the magic power to transform romance into novel, to infuse adventure with experience. Time goes on being conquered through time, until Tom Sawyer (Huck's Amadís or paladin of adventure) reappears and subjects him once again to the slavery of comic squiredom.

Thus, adventure and experience are not mutually exclusive but rather complement each other. As Cervantes discovered and the novelists who have read us—or who have enabled us to read ourselves more profoundly—have known ever since, it is the intimate collaboration of the two that glues us to the printed page. In our best-loved romances—the endlessly revivable adventure classics of our childhood—the element of personal experience, whether that of Jim Hawkins hiding in the apple barrel or Tom and Becky lost in the cave, makes what "happens" all the more vivid and credible. Conversely, experience in novels is heightened and in-

45. Actually, Virginia Woolf is talking novelistically about herself. In *A Writer's Diary* she says that writing *Jacob's Room* "was a necessary step, for me, in working free," but the turn of the thought is peculiarly relevant to what novels in the Cervantine tradition are all about. As Américo Castro points out in his introduction to the 1960 Porrúa edition of the *Quijote* (p. xxv), the inhabitants of the book spend all their time either in "freeing their own lives" or in "prying into [i.e., "interrupting," as we shall see] those of everybody else" (translated by Gilman and King in *An Idea of History*, p. 99).

tensified when framed adventurously. The interminable on-goingness of life in time, the depiction of which makes so many recent *succès d'estime* unreadable, needs segmentation for its appreciation. Without experience, novels are not novels; without adventure, they are oppressive and stagnant. Proust, who observed himself in the process of novelizing perhaps even more attentively than Cervantes or Stendhal (if that is possible), explains the conjunction of the two as intense moments of "entry," which it would be "regrettable" to ignore: "L'existence n'a guère d'intérêt que dans les journées où la poussière des réalités est mêlée de sable magique, où quelque vulgaire incident devient un ressort romanesque."[46]

Here is the enchanting frontier zone that we, as inveterate readers, adore—whether in the *Quijote*, in *Huckleberry Finn*, in *Typhoon*, in *La Chartreuse*, in *Splendeurs et misères de courtisanes*, in *War and Peace*, in *Our Mutual Friend*, or in *A l'ombre des jeunes filles en fleurs*. Realism in such novels as these is derived from the way we experience outside reality (Lubbock's unfolding temporal "process"), and at the same time it is intensified and composed artistically within successive frames of adventure. For those who have learned how, such reading submits them to far more marvelous possibilities, coincidences, emotions, and milieus, as well as to far more dreadful encounters and melancholy disappointments than they might expect to experience "in all the days of their lives" (II.73). With these words Don Quijote takes leave of his adventures and foresees the rest of his sad journey homeward, to sanity and death. If he is never to see Dulcinea, adventures dissipate and the novel fades away.

"The novel begins when love seeks to know its own history"

Comprehension of novelistic life as a rosary of adventures strung on the unbroken thread of the hours, days, and weeks

46. Proust, *A l'ombre*, p. 527. ("Existence to us is hardly interesting save on the days on which the dust of realities is shot with magic sand, on which some trivial incident of life becomes a spring of romance" [*Within a Budding Grove*, p. 230].)

of biographical time effectively supplements immediate experience (the storm) with that other kind, which we referred to as cumulative, the gathering up of "nows" into the account of a whole life seen as a journey (hence the German *Erfahrung*). Accordingly, let us now follow the young Ortega to Marburg where (along with Boris Pasternak) he studied under the neo-Kantian aesthetician and philosopher Hermann Cohen. In his *Aesthetik des reinen Gefühls* (1912) Cohen was concerned, among other things, to disrupt Goethe's overly neat classification of *Dichtung* into its three "natural forms" (epic, lyric, and dramatic); and in his effort to distinguish the novel from other kinds of narration, he emphasizes the importance of *Erfahrung*. The special kind of compartmentalized adventures we call love affairs, says Cohen, can on occasion be so meaningful that they are transformed into lasting love. And the novel comes into being—is born, invented, discovered—"when love seeks to know its own history."[47]

Although this may sound as if Cohen intended to derive the whole of the genre from the tradition of pastoral romances (a notion not without a certain validity, as we shall see), I think his perception can be extended in the light of our tentative conclusions: novelistic reading begins and voluptuous identification comes to an end whenever a protagonist turns to the past for self-understanding. However apparently episodic a given work of fiction may be, if the characters (a Fabrice, a Huck, or Cervantes's pair) remember and are concerned with remembering—that is, if they begin to wonder where their freight train came from and to whom the freight will be delivered—the hermeticism of isolated adventures is over and the novel is in the wings. Don Quijote, as we shall see, is even concerned with the identity of the engineer. If an adventure is experienced rather than just "had," the ad-

47. Hermann Cohen, *System der Philosophie*, Dritter Teil, *Aestetik des reinen Gefühls*, Erster Band, Zweiter Teil (Berlin: Bruno Cassirier, 1912), p. 122. For Cohen the *Quijote* is the *Grundform* of the novel (p. 121) because in it love is an *Erlebnis* (adventure, experience) and not, as in the epic, a *Kampfpreis* (struggle) (p. 122).

venturer inevitably begins to delve into recollection and, in so doing, projects what he finds there into a vocation. Or to say it more simply, if love feels the need to be aware of its own history, it is because it wants to go on having a history.

Let us return for a moment to the stories of the bad boy and the outcast. In both we accompany Tom and Huck through the series of adventures that are explicit in the titles. Yet Tom is the hero of a boyhood romance, and Huck inhabits and recounts our nation's greatest novel. In the case of Tom, just as in that of Amadís, one adventure follows another— glade, graveyard, trial, haunted house, island, and finally the cave—with ever-increasing peril and excitement. Tom is a born adventurer whose life is (as Ortega wrote in an essay clearly derived from Simmel's) "punctiform," "spasmodic," and "exempt from today and tomorrow."[48] Aunt Polly more charitably describes him as "giddy" and "like a young colt."

Furthermore, in accord with Simmel's intuition that adventures tend to take on the quality of a dream and seem to have been experienced by another person, Tom, "as he lay in the early morning recalling the incidents of his great adventure [the treasure glimpsed perilously in the haunted house] . . . noticed that they seemed curiously subdued and far away— somewhat as if they had happened in another world or in a time long gone by." "It must have been a dream," Tom concludes.[49] And then afterward, at the beginning and at the ending of the sequel to his own personal romance, Tom loses our interest and acquires his author's disdain by going professional, inventing his dreams and rehearsing his alter egos. Loss of spontaneity—giddiness or coltishness—is the adventurer's spiritual death. One suspects that it was precisely this that Samuel Clemens feared had happened to him when he became Mark Twain.

In any case, the contrast between the artificial adventures

48. José Ortega y Gasset, "Aventuras del Capitán Alonso de Contreras," *Obras Completas*, 3: 505–6.

49. Mark Twain, *Adventures of Tom Sawyer*, chapter 27.

invented by Tom and those of Huck is both intentional and crucial to *Huckleberry Finn*. In reading both, we perceive vividly how Huck's adventures are infused with the time of his life, which in turn explores, enriches, and beckons to the time of our lives. Having just seen and heard the thunderstorm in its time, let us now reread the climactic paragraph when Huck steps on shore for good and his narrative reaches its true ending. Huck has just finished a letter to Miss Watson telling her where she can find Jim and fetch him back into slavery. But then: "I laid the paper down and set there . . . thinking over our trip down the river; and I see Jim before me all the time, sometimes moonlight, sometimes storms, and we a-floating along, talking and singing and laughing . . ." (chapter 31). Huck's decision, based on the mine of living he shares with us—time remembered as time passing, *Erlebnisse* that are now *Erfahrungen*—is to abandon conscience (which insists that Jim be returned) and to stick to his project of emancipation, even if he has to "go to hell." His life is his. It is neither the collected adventures of another person nor is it enslaved to society.

Finally, as far as Cohen's history of love is concerned, it is here patent, just as it is in the relationship of Don Quijote and Sancho, that novelistic love need not be sexual. Indeed, in such novels as these I dare say it is also shared by the author and the reader.

"Those who seek nourishment in the manna of an incitement"

Having unraveled definitions of the novel as ruthlessly as I can (and perhaps more than I should), it is now time to compensate by considering the score of the violinist. What kind of people, what kind of language, and what kind of lessons in reading have novelists in the Cervantine tradition been wont to employ in order to bring adventure and experience into incandescent fusion? As Percy Lubbock reminded us, each novel is not only a process; it is also shaped as a "whole." It has a style and, if not necessarily a plot, at least an implicit structure. It is there on our table waiting for us to pick it up, to read it again, to ponder its purpose, and to scrutinize the artistic means employed to achieve that purpose. Furthermore, although we have refused to draw frontiers between novels and nonnovels, it is clear to apt readers that, as we remarked at the outset, some works of fiction are more novelistic than others. The questions now are *how* and *why*.

These queries will be answered at much more length and in greater detail in the essays to follow. But for now, as far as the characters (or lives) are concerned, comparison of Huck with Robinson Crusoe, Marcel, Werther, Alyosha, or Yossarian (names chosen more or less at random) indicates not surprisingly that they all have a special openness, receptivity, and even vulnerability to experience, as well as excellent memories. The frequently advanced notion of antiheroism is negative in its implications. If lives such as these can be termed antiheroic, it is not because the characters are less than heroes but because they are more. They are immensely more sensitive and sentient than any self-conscious and bemedaled hero would permit himself to be. Goethe was hinting at this truth when he spoke of the passivity of the new protagonists, but he would have been closer to the mark had he recognized that vulnerability and spiritual impetus, as in the case of Don Quijote, are not mutually exclusive. Cervantes designed a hero who would seek adventures and, like poor Jim after the horror of boarding the *Sir Walter Scott,* experience the consequences.

As Américo Castro has insisted in a fundamental essay, many of the most appealing novelistic existences combine an extraordinary ability to register and recall with indomitable self-propulsion. As against the excitement of a chance adventure, "they seek nourishment in the manna of an incitement."[50] Sometimes this may be an obsession, sometimes it may be the noblest of vocations; but it is always a source of forward movement along the chosen *chemin*.

50. Américo Castro, "Incarnation in *Don Quijote,*" in *An Idea of History,* p. 27.

At first glance Huck Finn hardly seems to fit Castro's description. He is a drifter, not a charger, and, like Sancho, he is concerned most of the time with being comfortable. On the other hand, despite the acute mental discomfort of his aching conscience, he never abandons the quest for Jim's freedom. We shall return to the notion of incitement when we begin to explore the *Quijote* from within, but at this point we may observe how Castro's term illuminates the lives engendered by Stendhal, Balzac, Dostoevsky, Melville, Conrad, and Galdós:

> This is the significance of Cervantes' strange predilection for the unbalanced (for the "incited") of all types and his open disesteem for the Knight of Green Greatcoat, or for the Duke's private priest, insulated against any untoward draft that might ruffle their paralytic, generic existences. Contrast those limited lives with the inner richness of Don Quijote, in whom is incarnated the dual process of achieving the plenitude of his existence, incited by an illusion, and of being himself the creator of Dulcinea. Passing from illusion to illusion, his is an existence that finds justification and completeness in itself.[51]

All of this is a way of saying that Don Quijote and his descendants are far more intensely alive in both the active and the passive voices than we are—hence their magnetism for our lives.

Having admired both the radical otherness and the alluring aliveness of these strange beings who enhance our lives in the process of feeding on them, we should be all the more wary of imputing to them psychological verisimilitude. Admittedly, certain novels do resemble case histories, but that is not a prerequisite of the genre. The stages of our personal growth have nothing to do with the incited individuals who inhabit novels belonging to the Cervantine mainstream. If we stop to think about it, how incongruous it is that the Huck of *Tom Sawyer* or the Huck who confesses his resistance to education in the initial chapters of his own novel (he could read and write "a little") should so suddenly have expanded the range and depth of his awareness and so superbly have com-

51. Castro, "Incarnation," p. 27.

municated the Mississippi adventure-experience! There is intentionally no resemblance at all to calculated *Bildung* or *Entwicklung* in the change that occurs explosively when he is caught by Pap and taken away from Tom.

At the beginning Huck is still a boy who wants to belong to the gang and who, when alone, is afraid of the dark: "I felt so lonesome I most wished I was dead" (chapter 2). Only the familiar "twelve licks" of the town clock and Tom's "me-yow" bring consolation. But just six chapters later the flow of nocturnal time becomes the habitat—the music—of his soul and of ours:

> When I woke up I didn't know where I was for a minute. I set up and looked around, a little scared. Then I remembered. The river looked miles and miles across. The moon was so bright I could 'a' counted the drift logs that went a-slipping along, black and still, hundreds of yards out from shore. Everything was dead quiet, and it looked late and *smelt* late. You know what I mean—I don't know the words to put it in.
> (chapter 7)

And then at the end, when he submits meekly to Tom's play adventures at the Phelps's, we are just as nonplussed. Although other fictional lives may speak from the couch of the author-analyst, that kind of coherence is not essential to the fusion of adventure and experience. What has happened is something else. Huck has entranced us with the naive sensitivity of his wondering awareness; we have revived him once again with eye-to-eye and ear-to-ear resuscitation. We are not one—we do not identify ourselves with *his* adventures (they could never be ours!)—yet each of us exists in the other with a symbiotic intimacy that is strange both to psychology and to other kinds of novels.

Thus, although intensely alive, neither Huck and Jim nor Fabrice and Gina nor Don Quijote and Sancho should be understood as if they were real people or made to resemble real people. Rather, they are caricatures suddenly temporalized—that is to say, suddenly made conscious. Those recent critics who speak of the novel as the genre of passing time or as portraiture of life in time often attend primarily either to the days and years of chronicled waxing and waning—the time of diapers, crutches, spring evenings, and autumn days—or to the nexus of collective history with personal history.[52] But beneath this epidermis the novel at its best can offer something more magical: self-propelled, incited duration capable of invigorating our own. If adventure fiction is voluptuous and psychological fiction is interesting, the novel in full flower offers a far more intense and lasting form of happiness: that of encountering our best living, cleansed of daily compromise and impurity, nourished with new life, once again free and eager to search for meaning along the uncertain *chemin*.

"I have always trusted this voice"

Recognition that caricatures can be intensely conscious immediately confronts us with the problem of the language—or, rather, languages—of the novel. As readers, we know that the caricaturesque depiction of Don Quijote and Sancho, Parson Adams and Joseph Andrews, and Huck and Jim is not visual but rather oral. Granted, Cervantes amused himself (in chapter 9) with conversion of his hero into a grotesque woodcut, and Mark Twain was very much concerned with the accompanying illustrations. But what was even more important to them was to bring their creatures to life in speech—or, to be more precise, in the interplay between a character's speech and the writer's speech, both of them silent and both of them heard in the process of reading.

As we said earlier, realism is real in such novels as these not because of accurate Scottian or Balzacian description but because they present reality in the same way we know it in our lives, as an unfolding process. As a result, novel readers are trained to submit not to more or less solemnly intoned phrases (whether lyric, epic, or dramatic) but to clusters of

52. Further comments and bibliography are to be found in my *Galdós and the Art of the European Novel: 1867–1887* (Princeton, N.J.: Princeton University Press, 1981).

unpronounced, immediately assimilated speech, printed speech that draws on the latent vocabulary of our mind and rearranges it into new sequences. This is, as we shall see, what Cervantes's Canon from Toledo condemned (his criticism is far more profound than he intended it to be!) as a heretical "nuevo modo de vida"—a novel kind of life.

As for us, we are too busy to think such thoughts. We are reading, and, as Ortega pointed out, when we are thus engaged, the here and now of lamp and chair, as well as the page itself, all disappear. They submerge into a silent voice—really a chorus of silent voices that guide us down a river or across "the ancient and renowned plain of Montiel." These are not geographical settings, like the Bay of Naples described in a guidebook, nor are they myths. Rather, in the process of telling, they become a continuing symphony of experiential music punctuated with the rhythm of adventure. As Stendhal remarked simply in his marginalia, "Le roman doit raconter."[53]

The language of the novel, as distinguished from the styles of individual novelists, has been described from various points of view by Albert Thibaudet, Stephen Ullmann, Käthe Hamburger, David Lodge, Dorrit Cohn, and others. But the question suggested by the notion of the narrative voice as a form of caricature remains: how does printed speech communicate the indispensable otherness of novelistic experience? How does it turn our experience into somebody else's experience? For our answer we had best turn to a practitioner, Eudora Welty:

> Ever since I was first read to, then started reading to myself, there has never been a line read that I didn't *hear*. As my eyes followed the sentence, a voice was saying it silently to me. It isn't my mother's voice, or the voice of any person I can identify, certainly not my own. It is human, but inward, and it is inwardly that I listen to it. It is to me the voice of the story or the poem itself. The cadence, whatever it is that asks you to believe, the feeling that resides in the printed word, reaches

53. In the manuscript of Stendhal's *Lucien Leuwen*, cited in S. de Sacy, "Le miroir sur la grande route," *Mercure de France* (May 1949), p. 69.

me through the reader-voice. I have supposed, but never
found out, that this is the case with all readers—to read as
listeners—and with all writers, to write as listeners. It may be
part of the desire to write. The sound of what falls on the page
begins the process of testing it for truth, for me. Whether I am
right to trust so far I don't know. By now I don't know whether
I could do either one, reading or writing, without the other.

My own words, when I am at work on a story, I hear too as
they go, in the same voice that I hear when I read in books.
When I write and the sound of it comes back to my ears, then
I act to make my changes. I have always trusted this voice.[54]

The tongue is ours—English, French, or Spanish, as the
case may be—but it is spoken differently, both by the author
and by his characters. In its uniquely personal rhythms, vocabulary and intonations it conveys in immediate intimacy
what I can only term Huck's Huckness or Don Quijote's Quixotism. We know them and live them in their voices, precisely because those voices are the novelist's score. In short,
the language of the novel is a strange species of transformed
speech—accelerated and silenced, personalized and intensified, printed but retaining its ancient creative magic when
played in our souls. It was this speech that the great masters
of the nineteenth-century novel all learned from Cervantes.
Even as I write, I can hear the voice of Conrad's Marlow, although I have never listened to a single one of those novels
read aloud. On the other hand, the voices of Amadís and
Montalvo are so flat and stilted, so lacking in caricature, that
aural retention is fleeting.

This seemingly paradoxical notion of silent speech is so
essential to the present argument that it will be necessary to
call additional witnesses to the stand. To begin with, Bakhtin,
who, as every up-to-date critic knows, explains the phenomenon of the novel as a dialogue of "languages," has this
to say:

But this material of the work is not dead, it is speaking, signi-
fying (it involves signs); we not only see it and perceive it but
in it we can always hear voices (even while reading silently to

54. Welty, *One Writer's Beginnings*, p. 11.

ourselves). . . . Beginning with any text we always arrive, in
the final analysis, at the human voice, which is to say we come
up against the human being. But the text is always imprisoned
in dead material of some sort. . . . In the completely real-life
time-space where the work resonates . . . we find as well a
real person—one who originates spoken speech as well as the
inscription and the book—and real people who are hearing or
reading the text.[55]

Along with Bakhtin, two practicing novelists, Proust and
Wilder, provide corroborative testimony. Proust discusses
voice as a form of characterization: "Quand je causais avec
une de mes amies, je m'apercevais que le tableau original,
unique de son individualité, m'était ingénieusement dessiné,
tyraniquement imposé, aussi bien par les inflexions de sa
voix que par celles de son visage."[56] Wilder is even more helpful (in part because he is reflecting on reading the *Quijote* in
Spanish): "The whole experience has renewed the realization
that all books live by the voice of their author, that all books
are personality."[57]

This brings up the problem of oral reproduction, that social reading to an assembled group that began with writing
itself and lasted into the twentieth century. Obviously, novels
can be read aloud, and many of us remember our first experience of silent literacy as resulting from our impatience with
parental tempo. In any case, it is a matter of record that both
Dickens and Mark Twain enjoyed reading aloud enormously
on their grand tours. And so must Cervantes have done,
since Avellaneda (the author of the apocryphal continuation)
seems to have caught wind of certain episodes in Part II from
those who had heard portions of it read to others while it was
still a work in progress.[58] However, it is my belief that such

---

55. Bakhtin, *The Dialogic Imagination*, pp. 252–53.
56. Proust, *A l'ombre*, p. 579. ("When I talked with any one of my friends
I was conscious that the original, the unique portrait of her individuality had
been skilfully traced, tyrannically imposed on my mind as much by the inflec-
tions of her voice as by those of her face" [*Within a Budding Grove*, pp. 289–
90].)
57. Wilder, *Journals*, p. 110.
58. I see no other reasonable way to account for such similarities as the

performances, because of their accentuation of suspense and their search for immediate laughter, have a tendency to convert novels written for silent reading into comic romances.[59] When I recently read to my grandchildren the story told by Huck, it was received by them as a sequel to the story of Tom. Furthermore, if we listen closely and silently, say, to the voice of Jim, we realize that the comic fortune-telling in chapter 4, where everything depends on real or imaginary pronunciation of a typical dialect, by chapter 15 is replaced with personal rhythm and command of intonation. It is then that the oral experience of Jim's reproach of Huck for having played a sorry practical joke causes the latter to humble himself. Jim's voice has become his own.

To sum up, although Mark Twain comments at the beginning on the number and the accuracy of the dialects he reproduces, *Huckleberry Finn* is not a dialect novel. As a narrative it is characterized by its careful control of spelling, syntax, and punctuation, as is apparent in the passages here cited. Not the narrator (who wouldn't have known how, or how far, to go) but the author needs these forms of conventional assistance in order to direct the novel not to our vocal chords, palate, tongue, and lips but directly into our souls. There is probably no one left alive capable of reading Huck's prose correctly, but it works novelistically, all the same.

"That grave irony which 'Cervantes' only has inviolably preserv'd"

Audition of the interplay of the author's (or of his persona's) narrative voice with the characters' dialogic voices allows us

---

interruption of Maese Pedro's puppet show and the interruption of a comedia in Avellaneda, the conversion of Don Quijote into a fool at the Duke's palace and his treatment at the hands of Don Alvaro and his friends, and others.

59. One of the objections raised by several scholars who listened to the lecture on which this chapter is based at the English Institute had to do with Mark Twain's oral performances of his book. However, others pointed out that the passages he preferred to read were taken from the final chapters, when the novel (under the implacable direction of Tom) reverts to comic romance.

to comprehend Alberto Moravia's explanation of how the *Quijote* was possible: "la capacitá di Cervantes di essere al tempo stesso dentro e fuori del suo mondo."[60] In other words, the author from within the work (a fellow reader, as we shall see) communicates ironically with his public over the characters' heads. One can only surmise, more or less intelligently, how (or whether) in the seventeenth century the general public, attuned as it was to fictions lacking in irony— the chivalric and pastoral romances—heard Cervantes's voice.[61] Admittedly, there was a minority of dissident readers (disbelievers and persons of questionable lineage) who received with perverse pleasure the secreted and secretive gall that exudes from every line of *La Celestina, Lazarillo de Tormes,* and *Guzmán de Alfarache.*[62] But these, too, might have ignored

60. " . . . the capacity of Cervantes to be at the same time inside and outside his own world." *Corriere della Sera,* Sept. 29, 1963.

61. Obviously they did hear Cervantes when he regaled them with pastiches of their favorite reading, but that is not the same as listening to his own personal voice.

62. The social background of the *Quijote* obviously requires book-length, rather than footnote, discussion. But it cannot be entirely ignored even in a treatment of the aesthetic genesis of the *Quijote.* Ever since the expulsion of the Jews and the founding of the Inquisition, there had existed in Spain a marginalized caste composed of the descendants of those who in 1492 preferred baptism to exile. These people were subjected to constant observation and systematic discrimination. Various organizations (resident colleges, guilds, Knights of Saint James, cathedral chapters) required more or less exhaustive genealogical investigations for admittance to membership. It is significant that Cervantes, who was undoubtedly a good Catholic (and like other so-called New Christians was influenced by the ideas of Erasmus), never subjected himself to such an investigation. However, far more annoying than exclusion was the atmosphere of suspicion, malicious gossip, and dangerous slander prevalent in the day-to-day existence of an honor-crazed society where tongues could be more fatal than swords. Within this situation reactions ranged from fervent adhesion to bitter alienation. As an example of both extremes, Queen Isabella's confessor, the saintly Fray Hernando de Talavera, specifically warned his fellow New Christians against their prevalent "sin of irony." In any case, Cervantes, instead of expressing the resentment characteristic of his literary predecessors, treated the whole matter with a humor more reminiscent of Fielding's reference to the equally self-righteous (but less pious) horrors of eighteenth-century England. That humor was blessedly his human triumph over the society that rejected him in spite of his heroism at Lepanto and his suffering in Algerian captivity. Américo Cas-

an irony intentionally muted by the *Quijote*'s overtly comic narrative surface.

The author of that most painfully *méchant* of novels, *Bend Sinister*, like the author of *Candide*, professed to be shocked both by the cruelty of Cervantes's treatment of his hero and by the gales of laughter that that cruelty supposedly provoked. As evidence, Nabokov mentions a widely circulated anecdote concerning Philip III, who

> upon looking from the balcony of his palace was struck by the singular behavior of a young student who was sitting on a bench in the shade of a cork oak (quercus suber) with a book and frantically clapping his thigh and giving vent to wild shrieks of laughter. The king remarked that the fellow was either crazy or was reading *Don Quixote*. A rapid courtier ran out to find the answer. The fellow, as you have guessed, was reading *Don Quixote*.[63]

The implication, of course, is that Cervantes's public was as deaf to his narrative voice as were Nabokov and Unamuno.

The anecdote is possibly apocryphal and surely exaggerated, but the fact that the reader was a "young student" may be significant. When Sansón Carrasco informs Don Quijote and Sancho that "those who are most given to reading [Part I]" are "pages" and that "there are no lordly antechambers where one can't find a copy of *Don Quijote*" (II.4), he implies

---

tro has discussed the *Quijote* in these terms in *Cervantes y los casticismos* (Madrid: Alfaguara, 1966) and *De la edad conflictiva* (Madrid: Taurus, 1961), neither of which has yet been translated. Further discussion in English and a general bibliography may be found in my *The Spain of Fernando de Rojas* (Princeton, N.J.: Princeton University Press, 1972). What then *is* humor ("grave," as opposed to embittered, irony) and from what self-destructive follies does it preserve us? The answer is to be found in the *Quijote*, in *Joseph Andrews*, and in *Huckleberry Finn*, as well as in certain classic motion pictures. I certainly cannot define it verbally, but when Woody Allen is saved from despair by the Marx Brothers in *Hannah and Her Sisters*, this occurs with visual cogency. As much as *La Celestina* has meant to me, I nevertheless understand perfectly Cervantes's stricture of it: "a book in my opinion divine, if it only had veiled human depravity somewhat more."

63. Vladimir Nabokov, *Lectures on "Don Quixote"* (New York: Harcourt Brace Jovanovich, 1983), p. 53.

that these mischievous inferiors understood very well Cervantes's muted criticism of the pseudogreatness of the *caballeros* (knights of the court) and grandees of the time. The student, in other words, may have also been laughing at his neighbors, Philip III and his band of obsequious courtiers (pseudogiants all!), and not just at the beatings and the rueful dialogue they occasion. He could have heard the voice of Cervantes and could have understood how the actions and reactions of his two supremely naive protagonists are used in order to illuminate ironically a society, swollen with self-importance, that refused to make a place for him despite his past heroism.[64]

This is at best a reasonable supposition, but what is certain is that in the more or less irrepressibly satirical climate of eighteenth-century England (so different from the vicious, but blessedly stupid, vigilance of seventeenth-century Spain) the "grave irony" of Cervantes's voice was amplified and became clearly audible to a host of witty readers: Peter Anthony Motteux (1693), Alexander Pope (1728), Walter Harte (1730), Charles Jarvis (1742), William Dodd (1751), Richard Owen Cambridge (from whom the epigraph to this part of the essay is taken) (1752), and Joseph Warton (1806), among others.[65] It was precisely within such a relatively open, orally attentive, and, in certain milieus, self-consciously irreverent society that it was possible for Henry Fielding to write *Joseph Andrews* "in the manner of Cervantes." After listening with amused adoration to his master's voice, Fielding experimented in projecting his own more emphatically. He would engage his readers with facetious and worldly-wise comments, which would be validated by the often painful adventure-experiences and the naive reactions to them of Parson Adams and Joseph. And since silent reception could now be taken for granted, his intention was to capture minds one by one

64. Rabelais, Bakhtin reminds us, was even harder on those hierarchies. See *The Dialogic Imagination*, p. 240.

65. See Norman Knox, *The Word "Irony" and Its Contexts, 1500–1755* (Durham, N.C.: Duke University Press, 1961), pp. 167–71.

and so to free them from social foreshortening: from inhibitions, prejudices, "affectations," hypocrisy, and, worst of all, habitually condoned cruelty and injustice; or, as he says it himself, "to hold the glass to thousands *in their closets*, that they may contemplate their deformity and endeavor to reduce it" (italics mine).[66] They might, thanks to him, just possibly work themselves at least partially free!

It was in this programmatic formulation of the basic scheme of Cervantine irony that Fielding might be said to have invented the novel. In his reading of the *Quijote* and his writing of *Joseph Andrews* he transformed what for Cervantes (as we shall see) was not only an ageneric but an antigeneric fictional experiment into a genre, which is what Stendhal recognized when he perceptively anticipated Ortega: "Ce roman [he was referring not to *Joseph Andrews* but to *Tom Jones*] est aux autres ce que *L'Iliade* est aux poèmes épiques."[67] There are other important things to be said, particularly the compounding of Quixotesque and Sanchesque traits in the characterization of Parson Adams around a core of absentmindedness and within the carapace of an invulnerable and unquestioned religious incitement. But it was Fielding's conscious adaptation of Cervantine irony that opened the way to the future of the novel.

There is, however, another function of novelistic irony, perceived clearly by a fellow inventor, Lawrence Sterne, that

66. Introduction to *Joseph Andrews*. Perhaps I am taking Fielding's perspicacity too much for granted. Marcel Proust, in *Du côté de chez Swann*, is still amazed at the solitary intimacy within which novels operate: "Qu'importe des lors que les actions, les émotions de ces êtres d'un nouveau genre nous apparaissent comme vraies, puisque nous les avons faites nôtres, puisque c'est en nous qu'elles se produisent . . . tandis que nous tournons fiévreusement les pages du livre, la rapidité de nôtre respiration, et l'intensité de notre régard?" ([Paris: Gallimard, 1954], p. 105). ("After which it matters not that the actions, the feelings of this new order of creatures appear to us in the guise of truth, since we have made them our own, since it is in ourselves that they are happening . . . while we turn over, feverishly, the pages of the book, our quickened breath and staring eyes" [Marcel Proust, *Swann's Way*, trans. Scott Moncrieff (New York: Modern Library, 1928), p. 106].)

67. Stendhal, *Memoires d'un touriste*, vol. 1 (Paris: Le Divan, 1929), p. 52. ("This novel is to the other novels what *The Iliad* is to epic poems.")

is even more crucial. When we read in *Tristram Shandy* that that novel in reverse was intended "to rebuke a vicious taste which has crept into thousands . . . reading straightforward in quest of adventures . . . ,"[68] we realize that it is precisely the ironical intervention of the author's voice that prevents us from reading the *Quijote* in the fashion that Alonso Quijano read the *Amadís*. The rhythmic beat of adventure, at once comic and fearful, that is so audible in the *Quijote* and its offspring (and not entirely absent in any novel) entices the youthful or the unprepared seventeenth-century reader to receive it as a parody of romance. J. B. Cohen inexcusably mistranslates the title as *The Adventures of Don Quixote*, thus ignoring Cervantes's ironical equation of the name with the book itself. That is, Cervantes presents us not with a story but with a living person.

As we know and as we shall presently observe in greater detail, Cervantes was so intent on preventing this kind of elementary immersion that he added the oratorical voice of Cide Hamete and the skeptically amused voice of the anonymous Morisco translator to his own. Moreover, the oral caricature of which we have spoken and the cruel absurdity of individual episodes also prevent identification with the protagonists. We are not Don Quijote; we are not allowed to be Don Quijote; and we gradually learn that not being him allows him to identify with us, to revive in his dialogue all that we have experienced. Don Quijote comes alive with poignant intensity because he assimilates and gives new and sharply caricaturesque form both to the ongoing present of our lives and to all that we have lived through. And the more that we have lived through, the more abundant will be the cornucopia.

When Thackeray shocks us by referring ironically to his characters as puppets at their moments of most intense liv-

<hr />

68. Volume 1, chapter 20. Ten chapters earlier, he names directly the origin of the notion—"the peerless knight of La Mancha, whom, by the by, I love more and would have gone farther to have paid a visit to, than the greatest hero of antiquity."

ing, it is not only because he wants us to wonder whether we, too, may have attached strings. In addition, he wants us to be aware of the strange vital duplication, the observation of ourselves in somebody else, that novels can provide at their best. Before rejecting this paradox—the paradox of at once being ourselves and recognizing a purified, intensified, and sanctified incarnation of our personal experiences in another life—let my reader reread Huck's reflection on the brightness of the thunderstorm over Jackson's Island or Cervantes's creation of darkness in chapters 19 and 20 of Part I, which will be the subject of the essay to follow. He will then, I trust, realize how much those novels have taken from him and have done to him, as well as how important it is that it should have been taken and done.

Before concluding, I should like to meditate on a question that is implicit in these remarks. What about *Adventures of Huckleberry Finn*? How is irony conveyed in first-person narratives from which the intrusive, authorial voice is rigorously excluded? My answer is tentative but not complicated. The voice of Huck, like the voice of Lazarillo de Tormes, is also the voice of the author listening to himself, as he writes. We hear them both, and what we hear is the "history" of the author's love for his character in the very act of submitting him to the challenges of the adventures. Huck is not beaten, except by Pap at the beginning, but in his naiveté he is exposed just as cruelly as Don Quijote, Lazarillo, and Parson Adams to the most sordid, corrupt, inane, and violent experiences Middle America had to offer. It is this combination of deep affection and ruthless *Obdachlosigkeit* that fuses adventure with experience and that constitutes the pervasive irony of the novel.

As we know, there are not a few estimable novelists who, instead of listening to their characters as they "work themselves" free (and in so doing free us from the "and then . . . and then" of Forster's "naked worm" of time), bind them to evil or trap them in naturalistic determinism. We admire, experience, and teach such novels (they are not romances), although in so doing, we relinquish our own freedom and magnify our miseries. Yet definition aside, we must not ignore the miraculous potentiality of the novel to give birth to Don Quijote, Prince Myshkin, Huck Finn, Fabrice del Dongo, Parson Adams, and others—the eccentric latter-day saviors of an age, the values of which, as Lukács announced and Cervantes first discovered, are in a state of abject devaluation.

2

Birth

It is now time to reread the *Quijote* and to examine what recent critics might term its peculiar narrativity. In so doing, we may be privileged to observe clinically the future novel in the process of its delivery from the womb of comic romance. That is to say, we shall try to comprehend and describe exactly how the hermetic frontiers of adventure were first perforated by what we now call experience. As we proceed, we must keep in mind the tentative distinction just made between the novelistic irony of Mark Twain and that of Cervantes and Fielding. The former's voice—we said—was paradoxically audible and yet disguised by those of Huck, Jim, and all the other inhabitants of the river to whom we listen. In contrast to the *Quijote* and *Joseph Andrews* (and in accord with what Erich Kahler termed the gradual *Verinnerung*, or inwardness, of the genre[1]), the ironies of *Huckleberry Finn* flow beneath the surface of the story. The novelist does communicate with us; we are fully aware that we share the same secret understanding that we share with Flaubert, Proust, Virginia Woolf, and others who lead us even more deeply into the "transparent minds" of their creatures.[2] But that awareness is unobtrusive.

Cervantine irony, on the contrary, as his eighteenth-century readers perceived, is outspoken and can be heard

1. Erich Kahler, "Die Verinnerung des Erzählungs," *Die Neue Rundschau* 68 (1957), pp. 501–46, and 70 (1959), pp. 1–54 and 177–220. Translated by Richard and Clara Wilson in *The Inward Turn of Narrative* (Princeton, N.J.: Princeton University Press, 1973).
2. *Transparent Minds* is the title of Dorrit Cohn's perceptive exploration of the various ways novelists have exploited that *Verinnerung* in the late nineteenth and the twentieth centuries (Princeton, N.J.: Princeton University Press, 1978).

directly in the text. As a result, the *Quijote*'s narrativity (as well as that of some of the exemplary novellas, such as *The Colloquy of the Dogs*) can best be described as a complex play of incessant interruption. In the final essay we shall discuss what Cervantes learned from Ariosto, his mentor in the art of tale spinning and thread cutting. However, Ariosto's intention was to expose for our amusement the guiding strings of his marionette-like knights, while Cervantes not only severed the narrative thread whenever it suited him but also, as we shall see, those threads that controlled his creatures. Orlando and his colleagues ended up in the Sicilian puppet theater, but Don Quijote and Sancho in the autonomy of their personal experience have been reincarnated in one major novel after another.

Actually, as readers soon realize, Part I of the *Quijote* is composed of two antithetical modes of narration, each designed to make us aware of the peculiarity of the other. I refer, in the first place, to such interpolations as "El curioso impertinente" ("The Novella of the Curious Impertinent") and the life stories of Cardenio and Dorotea. The second, of course, is that of Cervantes himself telling us about the doings and recording the sayings of his knight and squire. As in the distinction often made by critics between the two kinds of exemplary novellas (*The Spanish English Lady* as opposed to *Rinconete and Cortadillo*), it has been customary to explain the difference in modes of narration in terms of style and decorum. Cervantes's narration is ironical and comic, mixing all levels of expression—from the rural sayings of Sancho and the picaresque language of the innkeeper and the galley slaves to chivalric pastiches and pastoral refinement. The interpolated stories, on the other hand, are confined to a single level of decorum, and because of their somewhat cloying rhetoric, they are difficult to justify to our students. As we shall see, even certain seventeenth-century readers seem to have regretted their distracting presence.

Although this distinction of Cervantes's voice from that of his surrogates (who seem to be listening complacently to themselves as they speak) is not without validity, it does not address our concerns. From the point of view of narrativity, the most significant thing about these interpolations is that they are ostensibly oral, presented as tales either told directly or read aloud. As a result, they are premised on a built-in antipathy to interruption; and if they are interrupted, violence is either a cause or an effect. Cardenio's fight with Don Quijote and the slaughter of the wineskins in the middle of the novella of Lotario and Anselmo are examples of each. The latter tale is, in fact, so densely composed that it seems to be aware of its own cohesion: when Anselmo explains his "impertinent" scheme, Lotario "did not open his lips until he had finished." Then Lotario in his turn demands equal time: "Listen, Anselmo my friend, and be patient enough not to interrupt me until I finish telling you what I think about what your desire impels you to propose" (I.33). As a veteran auditor of *La Celestina*, I am reminded of the least convincing passage of the entire *tragicomedia*—that in which Pleberio obeys his daughter's command not to interrupt her until she finishes explaining why she intends to commit suicide.

Different but comparable is Cardenio's warning to his curious audience that he will not finish his tale of woe if he is interrupted: "You must promise me that you will not cut the thread [*interrumpir el hilo*] of my sad story with questions or anything else, because at that very moment whatever I shall be telling you will come to an immediate end" (I.24). This is, of course, exactly what occurs when he happens to mention the *Amadís* and he and Don Quijote begin to argue—the one nobly and the other with characteristic lack of faith—about the chastity of the fictional Queen Madásima, just as if she and it were real. It should also be noted that later, when the Priest and the Barber encounter Cardenio "free of his furious alienation [*furioso accidente*]" and prevail on him to repeat his story, he does so with "almost the same words" and goes on to "tie up the thread broken" by the earlier interruption (I.27). His yarn is what it is (and, as we shall see, what he is), and there is no other way he can spin it. When Anselmo and

Lotario speak to each other, their narrative threads are steel wires, while Cardenio's is gossamer. But in both cases sheer continuity is what matters.

In this connection we may also note that Dorotea's complementary account of her betrayal by the same villainous grandee who had betrayed Cardenio is as uninterruptible as her character is strong. Cardenio not only is afraid of being interrupted (or of interrupting on his own, as when he fails to stop the enforced wedding of his beloved Luscinda) but also seems to be interruption-prone. He even halts his own story to apologize for his digressions. Dorotea has no such problems. When she first mentions the name of Cardenio's abducted fiancée, he goes into a spasm—making faces, biting his lips, shedding tears—"but not for that reason did Dorotea desist from going on with her story" (I.28).

The contrast of these interpolations with the printed prose of that master contriver of interruptions called Cervantes is, as we said, patent and intentional. Long before he transported *Orlando Furioso* into Sierra Morena, he had displayed his aptitude for strategic intervention. The apprentice novelist who years earlier had published *La Galatea* (1585) found in the device an indispensable form of leavening. The long and glutinous songs and narratives of amorous desperation, which are generically obligatory for pastoral characters, are made bearable in *La Galatea* by such abrupt butting-in as the following: "Teolinda had arrived at this point in the story of her love, when the shepherdesses heard a loud clamor [*grandísimo estruendo*] of shouting shepherds and barking dogs"; and: "The shepherds listened with great attention to what Silerio was telling them, when the thread of his story was interrupted by the voice of a mournful shepherd singing inside the grove."[3]

---

3. *La Galatea* is divided into "books," which do not serve for easy reference. The original Spanish of these quotations is to be found in Miguel de Cervantes, *Obras completas*, ed. Angel Valbuena Prat (Madrid: Aguilar, 1946), pp. 674 and 711.

These and the many other instances that resemble them have their counterparts in the *Quijote*, where they are used for the same reason. Again two examples will suffice. At the inn, when Don Quijote and Don Fernando are trying to outdo each other in lengthy courtesy ("comedimiento y muchos ofrecimientos"), "the arrival of a traveller dressed as a Christian who had recently arrived from the land of Moors imposed silence" (I.37). Similarly, Cervantes interrupts his own overlong explanatory narrations: "The Canon remained dumbfounded at the well-reasoned nonsense which Don Quijote had uttered. . . . And while they were eating they suddenly heard a loud noise [*recio estruendo*] and a sound of a little bell in the bramble bushes, and at the same moment there ran out a beautiful goat" (I.50). For a moment it seems as if we have reentered *La Galatea*, but when the owner of the errant animal compares its behavior to that of Leandra and the strutting soldier, Vicente de la Roca, we are relieved to find ourselves back in La Mancha with all its enchanting ambivalence—that delta world where literature is silted with history, where history is eroded by literature, and where adventure and experience flow side by side like salt water and fresh water.

Aside from its frequency, there is nothing specifically Cervantine about this sort of lateral interruption. Narratives "of over 50,000 words" intended for reading, whether silently or aloud (as opposed to brief oral tales), must perforce be broken into from time to time, if only by chapter headings. However, in Part I of the *Quijote* there is introduced a new possibility of interruption, which I shall term vertical—that of authorial voices, which intervene from above with all kinds of ironical messages. In chapter 8 we become aware of the first pangs of nascent experience, and curiously enough, it is not so much an experience of Don Quijote's as that of our own engagement in reading. It is then that Cervantes, having introduced Sancho, first seems to realize that he is involved in something quite different from the parodical exemplary novella that at the beginning he probably had intended to write. He is about to make an abrupt change in narrative course, and to prepare us for it, he contrives a stupendous practical joke.

Don Quijote and the bellicose Basque hidalgo are about to have at each other (apparently one more comic adventure, like that of the windmills at the beginning of the same chapter), when their narrator begins deliberately to decelerate the tempo of his narration. He interjects comments of his own; he emphasizes unnecessary details, thereby increasing our "mock suspense"[4] and leaving the onlookers, as if they too were readers, hanging on breathlessly ("temerosos y colgados") to the narrative thread. And then at the climax, when the swords of the two paladins are held high and they are about to chop each other in half, Cervantes suddenly chops the thread in half and goes on to comment ironically about the coincidence: "At that critical moment the tasty history stopped and was amputated [*quedó destroncada*]" (I.8).

This interruption is both unprecedented in prose fiction and crucial to the rest of the Second Sally—but not because of its surprise or because the conversion of the combatants into a woodcut is comic by Bergsonian definition.[5] Rather, its significance for the narrativity of the text is that it converts the author into a reader. "Cervantes" (who must now be named within quotation marks) is one of us; he is just as anxious as we are to find out what will happen next; and by pretending to share our annoyance, he provokes our awareness of being readers. That is to say, he is engaged in the inane pastime of believing something he made up to be real.

Chapters 8 and 9 have been discussed endlessly—and de-

4. I so described the narration at this point before reading Wilder's *Journals* and discovering that he used the identical wording (p. 98).

5. Similar interruptions are, of course, frequent in *Orlando Furioso*, but as Raimundo Lida pointed out to me, the direct source was Alonso de Ercilla's "epic" on the conquest of Chile, *La Araucana*, written "in imitation of the manner" of Ariosto. At the transition from canto XXIX to canto XXX the two furious Indian chiefs, Rengo and Tucapel, remain during nine stanzas with a blow suspended in the air, while the poet discourses on the legitimacy of single combat. He then apologizes—exactly like Cervantes—for leaving the history *destroncada* (amputated).

servedly so—but nevertheless I should like to comment briefly on the structural complexity they introduce into the hitherto more or less straightforward narrative. To begin with, we discover that the First Sally, which we have just finished reading, had two authors: the original chronicler, who claims that he cannot find any more documents concerning Don Quijote (and who is therefore responsible for the interruption) and the so-called second author, who, speaking in the first person, tells us how he found the rest of the text written in Arabic by the "historian" Cide Hamete Benengeli and how he had it translated, and from then on he reads with us. In fact, it is almost as if he were reading it to us.

The result is a triple possibility of intervention from above: first, by Cide Hamete, who, because he is a Moor, is suspected of lying; second, by the translator, who, as a Morisco (a Moorish native of Spain who knows both Spanish and Arabic), is naturally suspicious of his own kind; and third, by the Cervantine persona, who, as an equally avid bookworm, becomes our "fellow traveler." Thus, in addition to lateral interruptions as in *La Galatea*, there have been added multiple possibilities of vertical interruption. To say the same thing in another way, from the fractured adventure of the Basque there radiates through the rest of the text a network of narrative fissures waiting to be exploited ironically.

Coinciding with these intrusive voices are the impertinent chapter divisions and titles. As Raymond S. Willis has pointed out, unlike the chapters of previous fiction, they are not conceived of as genuine segments or separate episodes. Rather, the manifestly arbitrary nature of the fragmentation (attributable to Cervantes?) and the ironical rhetoric of such titles as "Donde se ponen los versos desesperados del difunto pastor, con otros no esperados sucesos" (I.14)[6] (attrib-

---

6. The translators have generally been unable to render the echo of *desesperados* (despairing) in *no esperados* (unexpected). The former (which is the origin of the English *desperado*) is a participle that refers specifically to Grisóstomo's suicidal "self-interruption," an event communicated obliquely in the poem in the words *torcida soga* and *duro lazo*, meaning "rope" and "noose." The

utable to Cide Hamete?) achieves a double effect. On the one hand, we are drawn up short, propelled out of the story. Just as in the case of the amputated duel with the Basque and the other interruptions that follow the same pattern, we are reminded that we are readers, reminded by the author (as we observed in the case of Sterne) that we should not read his book in the same way that Alonso Quijano read the *Amadís*. That is to say, we have been warned that when we laugh at Don Quijote and Sancho as if they were real, we are also laughing at ourselves for believing them to be real.

On the other hand, as Willis demonstrates, both the vertical interruptions and the maliciously segmented and titled "phantom chapters" reveal by contrast the seamless continuity of the lives we relive in our reading. The rest of the Second Sally may indeed appear to be "spasmodic," "punctiform," and "exempt from today and tomorrow," as Ortega said. But that is only an appearance. The truth is that as adventures remembered afterward, each episode grows out of those preceding it and thereby corresponds to the uninterrupted processes of our reading and of Alonso Quijano's cumulative awareness, his "self-reading" as Don Quijote. The chapter segmentation and the incessant interruptions of Cide Hamete and of our fellow readers, the translator and the "second author," push us out of the book by forcing us to maintain an ironical distance. And in so doing, they make possible, not yet the game of autonomy and self-determination that is the point of departure of Part II (the Third Sally), but something simpler and more essential. They make it possible for Don Quijote and Sancho to experience their successive adventures as their own and thereby to draw on our experience.

Chapters 8 and 9 thus are more than just a narrative joke designed to initiate an ostensible abdication of authoritative responsibility on the part of the flesh-and-blood author, who,

---

celebration that attended the pagan funeral demanded cautious treatment of the cause of his death in mortal sin.

as we shall see, later will claim to be only the "stepfather" of Don Quijote. They are also a point of departure for a fundamental narrative revolution. The writer who "hears" the stories of Cardenio and Dorotea presents them as either fearing interruptions or resolutely ignoring them. But the ironist who at the climax of the single combat with the Basque created the self-conscious novel by, in the words of Bakhtin, "separating the event that is narrated in the work [from] the event of narration itself"[7] revels in unprecedented interruptions of all sorts. Certain previous narratives (for example, Diego de San Pedro's *Cárcel de Amor,* mentioned earlier) admitted the author into the action as if he were a character—"authoritative" because present on the scene. But here, on the contrary, he withdraws in order to be able to intervene vocally whenever he pleases and in whatever guise he pleases and thereby to allow fictional experience to validate itself. The author is now the enchanter, who forces his characters to cope with the painful aftermath of each successive adventure.[8]

To the question *why,* at this point I should have to answer that unlike nineteenth-century novelists, who worshiped experience (and who wrote novels with such revealing titles as *The Personal History and Experience of David Copperfield the Younger*), Cervantes comprehended that attribute of consciousness as the unexpected by-product of abandonment and exposure—or, in Lukács's term, of *Obdachlosigkeit.* Experience was for him a dimension of existence that was at once virtually unexplored and pathetically vulnerable. Appealing, comic, and forlorn, it was the conscious precipitate of violent

7. Bakhtin, *The Dialogic Imagination,* p. 255.
8. In II.3 the identification is explicit: " 'I assure thee, Sancho—said Don Quijote—that the author of our history must be some learned enchanter.' " However, earlier he posits the existence of a benevolent "necromancer who is aware of my affairs and is my friend, because there's got to be one, or I wouldn't be a good knight errant" (I.31). At that point he is referring to the apparently supernatural speed of Sancho's trip to El Toboso, but the very proposition of a protective enchanter (as against those who transformed the giants into windmills or made his library vanish) is the seed of his future autonomy. He is beginning to be aware of his author.

interruption, the rueful result of trying to live meaningfully and not conventionally in a century and a society that revered conventionality and were prone to cut short deviant behavior with a rock, a club, or a torch. The *Quijote* itself is nothing less than an ironical two-volume interruption of the heroic version of national history that Spaniards were persistently engaged in telling themselves.

Thus, we are confronted with a form of narrativity based, on the one hand, on the endless spinning out of the *hilo*, or thread, of two intertwined, utterly unique lives and, on the other, on constant intrusion from without. So understood, it reflects not only what Ortega would call Cervantes's "posture toward life" (meaning the theme) but also the two major interruptions that are common to both his biography and his book. The first is the coincidence of the hiatus of his captivity in Algiers (and perhaps also in the prison mentioned in the Prologue as the place where the book was "engendered"[9]) and that of Don Quijote in the oxcart at the end of Part I. The second is, of course, the ultimate authorial intervention, known as death: the death of both comedy and the clown at the end of the Third Sally, an event which clearly foreshadows Cervantes's own. A year later, when writing his last words (in the Prologue to the *Persiles*), the echo of Alonso Quijano's final resignation is audible in appropriately narrative terms. In taking leave of his readers, Cervantes says: "Perhaps a time will come when, tying up this broken thread, I can continue what is missing now. . . . Farewell, humor, farewell, *donaires*,[10] farewell, my well-entertained companions."

9. Although we know Cervantes was imprisoned in Seville in 1597 (after his earlier captivity in Algiers from 1575 to 1580), scholars wonder whether this version of the book's "engendering" is a factual assertion of an age-old topos. In either case, however, the reference is to biographical interruption.

10. The word *donaire* (with which both Cervantes and Lope de Vega were enchanted) is untranslatable. Literally "gift" plus "air," its merged connotations of gracefulness, wit, timing, ease, and sparkle can only be learned by direct experience. In this case, for the overburdened old man who took such a splendid farewell to life, it refers to the expressions of long-practiced spiritual and verbal dexterity.

So far, so good. We have contemplated the narrativity of the *Quijote* in terms of the duality—interruptive and anti-interruptive—of its structure. Yet in spite of this up-to-date, or almost up-to-date, terminology, we have accomplished little more than to observe from a new angle aspects of Cervantes's art that have been amply discussed by earlier critics. However, our next step may be more pioneering. If we take into account the observation of Jonathan Culler cited earlier—"the crucial reorientation [of these new approaches] is to restate propositions about poetic or novelistic discourse as procedures of reading"—it follows that we should not distinguish the configuration of the story (the structure of happening) from the techniques of narration (the structure of words). This means simply that insofar as they both are "received" in the process of reading, the ironical interruptions of the "authors" (so frequently discussed in the past) are not in any way different (except in intention) from the naive, mad, or slyly self-interested interruptions of the characters. If we relinquish for the moment our time-honored efforts to comprehend what Cervantes had in mind and how he went about achieving it and contemplate instead our own reading, the two kinds of interruptions merge.

Let us turn, therefore, to the lives inside the work, all of which have a penchant for what we may call headlong interruptions as opposed to the vertical or lateral variety just described. For example, when Marcela halts Grisóstomo's funeral, Don Quijote in his turn stops the shepherds who would have pursued her with "loud and intelligible" threats. As the hero, he is appropriately as much a champion of interruption as his author. He halts the rotation of the vanes of the windmill, prevents the beating of Andrés, stops Maritornes in search of her Morisco lover (by "grasping her wrist strongly"), challenges all processions and passersby, implacably corrects the oral malapropisms of Sancho in midsentence (as well as those of the irritated goatherd in midstory), frees the galley slaves, silences Cardenio, and breaks up the puppet show. The fact is that the would-be knight interrupts everything that can possibly be interrupted, except, of course, the blanket tossing. The inevitable result is a rudimentary variety of experience communicated afterward in rueful dialogue usually accompanied by physical injury and attributed to hostile enchanters. This is what Max Scheler terms "the primary experience of *resistance* which is the root of experiencing what is called 'reality.'"[11] Amadís de Gaula has been treated as if he were Lazarillo de Tormes!

However, in chapter 20 during the unprecedented ("jamás vista ni oída") adventure of the fulling mills, Don Quijote's headlong incitement is itself interrupted when Sancho, who is afraid of being left alone (without his master's protection or conversation), slyly tethers Rocinante's forelegs. The result is the first exploration of how "a person feels himself existing in the happening" in fiction. Actually, nothing "happens," as both Thornton Wilder and the author of the chapter title point out,[12] but the darkness of the episode is as comic and pitch-black as Huck's thunderstorm is nostalgic and explosively bright. In this crucial adventure-experience the novel was "born"—became forever after possible—and accordingly I must request that my reader take the time to read (or reread) this chapter and the preceding chapter of the *Quijote*. It will save both of us from tiresome résumé.

This is the fourth night that Don Quijote and Sancho have spent together on the road. The first was under a grove of trees after the attack on the windmill; the second was with the goatherds in their rustic replica of the Golden Age; and the third was spent in the picaresque confusion of the "enchanted" castle-inn. The fourth night begins when dusk interrupts them laterally ("les tomó la noche") while they are

11. Max Scheler, *Man's Place in Nature*, translated by Hans Meyerhoff (New York: Beacon Press, 1961), p. 14.

12. My free translation of the title of chapter 20 would begin: "Concerning the unheard of and unseen adventure which no other famous knight ever achieved with less danger . . ." Thornton Wilder adds cogently, in relation to his notion of experience: "It is not the external event which justifies the narration but the life within the mind of the protagonists—as is shown by the Adventure of the Fulling Mills where precisely nothing happens" (*Journals*, p. 96).

lamenting the loss of their provisions and teeth in the battle with the custodians of the armies of sheep. Darkness is first communicated (in chapter 19) by the contrast of the eerie torches of the funeral procession, which in their slow approach build suspense and (as in the case of the preliminaries to the combat with the Basque) decelerate the rhythm of narration:

> They saw coming towards them a great number of lights which looked like moving stars. Sancho was stunned by the sight, nor was Don Quijote easy in his mind. The one pulled on the halter of his ass, the other on his nag's reins, and they stayed stock still,[13] attentively looking trying to make out what was going on. They saw that the lights were all the time coming nearer, and the nearer they got, the bigger they seemed. As they watched Sancho was shaking like someone who had had a dose of mercury, and Don Quijote's hair was standing on end.[14]
>
> (I.19)

As we can sense, the night is made darker not just by the contrasting light but also by being infiltrated with fear. "Can these hooded figures be ghosts?" Sancho asks his master, and the latter, while not denying that possibility, plucks up his courage and prepares for his most successful interruption.

The victory is famous, and the edible spoils most welcome. Indeed, it may well be Don Quijote's leftover exaltation at having dared to confront such an uncanny challenge that impels him in chapter 20 to take on the even more frightening fulling mills; just as it seems to be Sancho's leftover fear of the phantom torch-bearers that impels him to do all in his power to hold his master back when they hear the grim pounding. In any case, the two adventures are subtly intertwined in that the visual horror of the first prepares for the audible horror of the second. This is not a night of rural

13. Notice how the complete stasis of the next chapter is slyly prepared for here in chapter 19.

14. As has been noticed by several critics, in book 3, chapter 2, of *Joseph Andrews* the use of lights and superstition in the "night scene" indicates Fielding's appreciation of the technique of this adventure.

peace, rustic firelight, or picaresque hurly-burly but of cow-
ardice and courage, daring and dread in the teeth of threats
that the two understandably interpret as supernatural. It is a
night of high adventure awaiting full metamorphosis into experience.

Once the lights and the hoods have fled ignominiously,
master and man find themselves again alone in a darkness
communicated not by adjectival description (as a romantic or
a realist would have done) but by the heightened perceptivity
of the remaining senses. To begin with, there is taste. When
they have consumed their stolen supper, they find they have
nothing to wash it down with—neither wine nor water—a
discomfort that seems worse than their previous hunger.
Touch, however, promises a remedy. Sancho, as the reader
will learn later in the chapter, has been a shepherd boy. He
knows about pastures, and the tender freshness of the grass
underfoot leads him to suggest that they look about for a
nearby source of water. Don Quijote agrees, and because of
the total darkness, they dismount and feel their way slowly
until stopped short by their sense of hearing.

We all remember what it is they hear, but before commenting on their reactions, we should stress (as Cervantes
did in chapters 8 and 9) the extent to which a narrative structure based on continuity and interruption involves a corollary attention to gait—creeping forward (as they do now),
charging and hanging back (as they usually do), leaping
(both Don Quijote and Cardenio in Sierra Morena), plodding
(the oxen)—and to posture—riding high, knocked down,
slumped over, sitting up in bed. Among many other lessons,
it was this precise novelistic observation of movement and
stasis that Henry Fielding and Stendhal were later to learn
directly from Cervantes. When Balzac in his curious *Théorie
de la démarche* tells us that one morning he "sat down on a
chair on Boulevard de Gand with the purpose of studying the
gait of all the Parisians who, unluckily for them, would pass
by during the whole day," he implies that such observation
would reveal their secrets. And when he concludes that "fa-
cial expression, voice, respiration, and gait are identical," he

implies that the inwardness of novelistic experience is revealed most effectively when accompanied by a "physiognomy."[15]

When Don Quijote hears the rushing water, the smashing hammers, and the clanking chains of the mill combined with the gentle but no less spooky murmur of the wind in the leaves of invisible trees, he is reminded of his own oratorical rapprochement of the leafy myth of the Golden Age with the altruistic mission of heavily armored knight-errantry.[16] The rustle of pastoral darkness (capable of making even Lope de Vega's valiant Knight of Olmedo nervous) is blended with the chivalric challenge of the pounding iron—almost as if they were allegorical sound effects for the speech.

As a result, Don Quijote builds up his courage by reciting the speech again in the form of a pep talk ostensibly directed to Sancho but really to himself:

Friend Sancho, thou must know that, by the will of Heaven, I was born in this iron age of ours to revive the age of gold or,

15. Honoré de Balzac, *Oeuvres complètes*, vol. 20 (Paris: C. Levy, 1882), pp. 581–86.

16. Cervantes's profound assimilation of *Orlando Furioso* (of which more later) is evident in his amusement at the rapprochement of the same odd myth-couple (steel-clad chivalry and leaf-clad primitivism) in Merlin's prophecy to Bradamante (an Aristotelian *topikon*, or topic, used in a different way in the Cave of Montesinos) in III, 18 (*Orlando Furioso*, trans. Barbara Reynolds [New York: Penguin Classics, 1977], p. 162):

> I capitani e i cavalier robusti
> Quindi usciran, che col ferro e col senno
> Ricuperar tutti gli onor vetusti
> Dell'arme invitte alla sua Italia denno.
> Quindi terran lo scettro i signor giusti,
> Chè, come il savio Augusto e Numa fênno,
> Sotto il benigno e buon governo loro
> Ritorneran la prima etá de l'oro.

> Thence will come forth the mighty cavaliers
> And captains, by whose strategy and sword
> The pride and glory of her former years
> To valiant Italy will be restored;
> Thence princes, whose just rule the world reveres,
> As when the wise Octavius was lord,
> Or Numa reigned. Beneath the sway they'll hold
> Mankind will see renewed the age of gold.

as it is generally called, the Golden Age. It is for me that are
reserved perils, mighty feats, and valorous exploits. It is I, I
say once more, who must revive the order of the Table
Round. . . . Note well, loyal and faithful squire, the shadow
of the night, its uncanny silence, the muted and mingled sighing of the trees, the fearful sound of the water we came here
to seek—which seems to be hurtling itself down from the
highest mountains of the moon—and the endless thumping
which wounds and afflicts our ears; which things, taken all
together and each by itself, would be enough to infuse fear,
terror, and dread into the breast of Mars himself. . . . Yet all
this that I am describing so vividly for thee constitutes an in-
centive and clarion call to my courage and has the effect of
making my heart swell with desire to attempt this adventure—however arduous it may prove to be. Therefore, tighten
Rocinante's girths a little, and God be with thee.

(I.20)

Sancho's reaction to the sonorous challenge resembles that
of his master in that he, too, retreats into the past. The difference is that the former, being illiterate, has no access to the
apocryphal printed memories that fortify the latter. He has
never identified himself with Amadís (nor even with Amadís's valiant squire, Gandalín), and as a result he lacks a fictional conviction of invincibility to fall back on. Instead, losing his habitual impertinence, he reverts to childhood and
begs Don Quijote not to spur forward and abandon him:
"And if what I have said should not move or soften [your
Grace's] hard heart, let it be moved by thinking and believing
that scarcely will your Grace be gone from this spot when
from sheer fright I shall surrender my soul to anyone willing
to carry it off" (I.20). It is almost as if he were the young
Marcel being put to bed without a kiss or a night-light. The
more Don Quijote rehearses his well-memorized role as invulnerable knight-errant, the more Sancho confesses shamelessly to infantile vulnerability. The one shows off and the
other whimpers in the interaction of their dialogue. The
novel has just been born. Or perhaps it would be better to
say that the fledgling is pecking its way out of the hermetic
egg of adventure into the vast time-space of personal experience. Just as we became aware of ourselves as interrupted

readers in chapter 9, so, too, Don Quijote and Sancho, interrupted in their search for water by the sound of the fulling mill, become aware of their lives and roles as emergent from a past peculiar to each of them.

Sancho's next appeal to his master is to wait at least until dawn, which he says cannot be more than three hours away. How does he know? Because he remembers the "science" he had learned during long nights long ago when he was a shepherd boy out with his flock looking up at the constellations: "The muzzle of the Little Bear is now at the top of his head, whereas at midnight it is in line with the left paw" (I.20). Not only has he reverted to childhood, but memories therefrom return "en foule," as Stendhal phrased it. But they are only memories, for, as Don Quijote points out, the night is so dark that there is not a single star to be seen. In a marvelous ironical reversal, Sancho's fear of the noise-haunted darkness operates in exactly the same way as his master's chivalresque incitement. Sancho sees what is not there ("terror has many eyes") and now it is Don Quijote's turn to set him straight. The pattern of dialogue to which we have become accustomed has been turned inside out. With consummate narrative skill Cervantes has communicated exactly how it felt to exist in the adventurous obscurity of a night that sets the all-time record for dark nights in novels.

Having for once demonstrated that he can be a better judge of situations than his squire, Don Quijote once again prepares to go forward and undertake "esta tan no vista y tan temerosa aventura." Jarvis and others translate *no vista* as "unprecedented," while Smollett reveals the other edge of Cervantes's intentional ambiguity with the adjective "unseen." In any case, it is then that Sancho, taking advantage of his invisibility, contrives the second and definitive interruption. While tightening Rocinante's saddle girth as he had been ordered, he also slyly ties together the nag's forelegs with the halter of his donkey. The result is that all four, riders and beasts, are brought to a collective standstill lasting till daybreak. Mounted they remain—like equestrian statues or like the comic woodcut in chapter 9—with Sancho, again like a frightened child, clinging to his master's thigh. As just observed, interruption by its very nature calls attention to posture and gait.

What follows is unforgettable. Two more senses further accentuate the experience of blind helplessness and at the same time lead us to laugh as much at ourselves (insofar as we provide memories of having been afraid of the dark or of having been embarrassed by the exigencies of our bodies in inconvenient circumstances) as at the comic apprehension and misapprehension of the immobile pair. The first of these senses is not one of the familiar five: the sense of time, a sense naturally forgotten during the contained excitement of adventure but by definition present when one feels oneself "existing within the happening." And all the more so if that "happening" involves nothing more than waiting in the dark, during which past experience merges with the seemingly endless passage of one elastic minute after another. Along with Sancho's fear of what the dawn may reveal, Don Quijote's impatience (his "presurosa dilación," or zealous dilation, as Jorge Guillén phrases it in a poem dedicated to this episode, "La noche del caballero") creates acute temporal awareness. And here, too, those of us who have been pulled out of the action by a mother or a coach have experience to contribute.

The classic antidote for waiting is storytelling. The primitive raconteur clothes what E. M. Forster calls distastefully "the naked worm of time" in adventures. Hence Sancho's absurdly paratactical account of the pursuit of Lope Ruiz by the shepherdess Torralba (the dreaded *alba*, or dawn, in her name is implacably on its way but is kept from arriving by the strategy of the teller), with its endless thread of repetition:

> I say, then, that in a village in Extremadura, there lived a certain goat shepherd—I mean one who tended goats—and this shepherd or goatherd as I say in my story was called Lope Ruiz; and this Lope Ruiz was in love with a shepherdess who was called Torralba, which shepherdess called Torralba was the daughter of a wealthy cattle raiser, and this wealthy cattle raiser . . .

(I.20)

Sancho, to the irritation of Don Quijote, who interrupts at this point, dresses his story-time in a minimum of syntactical clothing, and he continues it appropriately with the embarkation of Lope's goats one by one—just as if each were a minute ticking by.

To the question, What kind of a clock is supposed to measure this post-Edenic form of scantily clad time? the answer is self-evident. The impatient chronometer is Don Quijote himself, who, when he fails to keep track of the minutes (meaning the exact number of goats who have made it to the other side of the river), cuts Sancho's thread and, to our immense regret, interrupts the story forever. It is as if the mainspring of his temporal endurance has suddenly snapped. As a folk parable of sheer narrative continuity, Sancho's tale, like that of Cardenio later on,[17] brings out by contrast the nature and structure of a novel premised on interruption. And, at the same time, it makes the interminable night seem all the longer and darker.

Cervantes, however, still has his own story to tell. Unlike Sancho, he provides a comic climax at the end: the dialogue occasioned by Sancho's cunning solution to his pressing need to empty his bowels and by Don Quijote's acute sense of smell. Who can forget Sancho's lame pretense of ignorance, "I would be willing to bet that your Grace thinks I have done something I ought not to have done with my person," and Don Quijote's untranslatably comic reply, "Peor es meneallo, amigo Sancho"?[18] It should also be noticed that all the while time has been running on (Torralba has been catching up with Lope Ruiz!) and that the chill of darkness just before dawn may have been partially responsible for Sancho's loss of self-control. Shortly thereafter they begin to discern the dim shapes of the trees, "the muted mingling and sighing" of which has been so unnerving.

---

17. When Cardenio threatens to stop if interrupted, it brings "to Don Quijote's *memory* the story his squire had told him, when he wasn't able to *remember* the number of goats that had crossed the river, and the account was left unfinished" (I.24, italics mine).

18. The phrase means figuratively, "The less said, the better," but literally, "Don't stir it around."

Full daylight brings discovery of the prosaic truth and full humanity to the clowns when for the first time they laugh at themselves. It is not now we who are amused by them, but rather it is they—when they can at last look into each other's eyes—who break into mutually infectious laughter. It is as if our previous mockery of their marvelous foolishness had been absorbed into their book and their lives, if only momentarily.[19] Immediately afterward we laugh at both again when Sancho goes too far and mimics with the uncanny accuracy of oral memory the Golden Age speech and is chastised physically for his impertinence.

Yet despite the by now familiar burlesque conclusion, this episode stands out as something entirely unprecedented both in Part I of the *Quijote* and in the previous history of prose fiction. As an adventure infiltrated by experience, what happens and what does not happen in chapter 20 prepare us for such profound episodes in Part II as the pacific encounter with the lions and with Don Diego de Miranda, the Knight of the Green Overcoat, or the frustrated pilgrimage to Toboso when "media noche era por filo, poco más o menos" ("it was on the cutting edge of midnight, more or less," II.9). The situation, the postures, and the five senses plus one interact and bring together the lives of the author, the reader, and the two participants in such a way that all four breathe in unison. We deceive and are deceived together. The adventure of the fulling mills is the very first of what Ortega calls the countless multiplications of our existence, which the strange new genre has offered us with unstinting generosity during almost four centuries.

In conclusion, the intimate relationship of interruption and experience in this chapter and in the rest of the *Quijote*— the professional interruptor interrupted and so forced to contemplate himself in his immediate situation—confirms our

19. After the lecture this essay is based on was given at the University of Washington, Professor George Shipley (to whom I am indebted for much, much more) suggested this reversal so crucial for the nascent autonomy of the pair.

earlier suspicion that Goethe's description (in *Wilhelm Meister's Apprenticeship*) of the protagonists of novels as opposed to those of drama is incomplete. In other words, they are, or at least should be, "retarding personages" highly sensitive and passively prey to "chance."[20] Cervantes's stress on Don Quijote's acute olfactory and auditory sensibility as he waits passively for morning is undeniable. But that is not the same thing as a sensitive and perceptive soul dedicated to a novel-long apprenticeship (or *Bildung*) in the craft of living. Rather, the kind of intensified experience the novel demands is better provided by lives in that state of usually frustrated exaltation that Castro terms incitement.

If we review our previous sampler of Don Quijote's innumerable avatars—Julien Sorel, Vautrin, Dmitri Karamazov, Captain Ahab, and Fortunata—we may observe that all of them, each in his own way, are prevented by their own cleverly tied ropes from moving forward to the fulfillment of their heart's desire. Adventures vary, and times change. The rope will be transformed into imprisonment, shipwreck, failure in business, membership in a lost generation, a catastrophic marriage, sexual constraints, an invasion from Mars, or simply bad weather on sea or land. The list of misfortunes could be endless, but worst of all and most frequent of all is questionable social identity and consequent exclusion from the massive yet intangible fortress of nineteenth-century society.

In so saying, we must affirm again: for these incited and impeded lives, it is their aspiration emergent from their private past and bound for their inviting future (as Guillén said of chapter 20, "tanto invita el peligro"—"it so invites danger") that produces what Dickens called personal experience. We may, and indeed should, share in the "history of the love" of Don Quijote and Sancho and of many of their fellows. But we should not identify ourselves with them and so fail to recognize their uniqueness. What we call all too facilely the

20. Book V, chapter 7; the translation is by Thomas Carlyle (1824).

rhetoric of the novel really amounts to this: the fascinating history of all the ways novelists have found to prevent their readers from reading in the way Alonso Quijano read. Only by relishing otherness can we discover our own uniqueness and thereby allow strange fictional lives to feed on our "souls"—meaning both all we can remember and all we can imagine. Only then will the blanket of the dark achieve its full obscurity and the thunderstorm attain the plenitude of its time-fraught, yet timeless, beauty.

Each novelist has his own score, but Cervantes's primordial rhetoric—his way of saving the souls of all the Alonso Quijanos who might open his book—was double in nature. Two kinds of drastic interruption were designed for his utterly untrained and adventure-avid public. By interrupting their reading from above with various voices, he hoped to make them keep their distance so that they might read with a smile of comprehension and self-recognition instead of hard breathing. And by creating the caricature of a professional interruptor who is himself interrupted within the story—first by darkness and then by guile—he opened the hermeticism of successive adventures to experience in time. It took just ten chapters of profoundly "happy" gestation, and then all of a sudden the newborn, as yet unnamed, and seemingly miraculous infant uttered its first tentative cry.

3

Invention

"Pass through, oh rare inventor . . ."

Having contemplated the birth of what was later to be called
the novel as a process taking place in Cervantes during the
composition of Part I of the *Quijote*, let us now look back
through the centuries and try to comprehend "historically"
how the parent understood his own parentage. To begin
with, although Stendhal's "fiddle bow" comparison is profoundly Cervantine, Cervantes, as an intellectual disciple of
neo-Aristotelian theorists of poetics, probably would have rejected it. The noxious way Montalvo, Lope de Vega, and their
followers were playing on the "souls" of his countrymen was
precisely what he hoped to put an end to when he set out to
write a short and exemplary comic romance.

It all comes down to what is meant by "playing" and what
is meant by "soul." And to determine those meanings in the
context of the *Quijote*, we must try to reconstruct what Cervantes thought about himself as a writer and what he
thought about his writing. He tells us repeatedly that his only
intention is to "destroy the ill-founded *máquina* [apparatus?]"
of the romances of chivalry, but the reader soon realizes that,
as a satire, his book has a far wider firing range. It even aims
intermittently at itself. From this point of view the ahistorical
notion of narrativity is no longer serviceable. What we need
to do now is to scrutinize not Don Quijote's library but Cervantes's criticism of himself as a writer both in the course of
his fictional creation and in his reflective prose and poetry—
for example, in the Prologues and, most important of all, in
the long versified meditation on his own place in the literary
panorama of his old age entitled *El viaje del Parnaso* (The voyage to Parnassus, 1614).

Cervantes, who confesses that he is as avid a reader as Alonso Quijano ("even of scraps of paper in the streets," I.9), was also an ardent reader of himself. The pose of fellow bookworm (which, as we saw, is the humorous external manifestation of the *Quijote*'s profound narrative revolution) corresponds to the way he watched himself—listened to his own silent voice—while at work. As his own best critic, he enjoyed to the full all the provocation, indirection, mockery, posturing, and ambiguity enabled by that role. Yet in the midst of the repeated challenge to the reader to play hide-and-seek with him, there is one emphatic and proud assertion, which we hear in many contexts. If not as a musician playing on his reader's soul, Cervantes does present himself as a literary Edison, an inventor who has devised an admirably clever trap for his reader's imagination. At least at the beginning the notion of exploring personal experience was still rudimentary and undefined, but if he could find a way to bring his Spaniards' wildly adventurous imagination to heel, he might be able to tame it.

Let us begin by considering Cervantes's portrait of the artist as an old man in *El viaje del Parnaso*. Ostensibly, this essay in criticism, divided into eight chapters with a prose epilogue, was a contribution to an adulatory subgenre typical of Cervantes's time: a catalogue in verse of favorite authors praised with suitable epithets. In this case, however, the writer was first of all interested in himself, in his lack of natural poetic endowment ("the gift that heaven chose not to give him," chapter 50) and in the capacity for invention that was his compensation. A poorly dressed and crippled veteran, he is accosted by Mercury while on a pilgrimage to Parnassus, and he humbly prostrates himself. However, the messenger god, bidding him rise, greets him:

> "I know that father Apollo did not
> endow in vain your breast
> with the instinct of a rare inventor.

> "Your works have reached the corners of the earth
> carried on the crupper of Rocinante
> and have incited envy to declare war on you.

"Pass through, oh rare inventor, press ahead
With your subtle designs, and help
Apollo, for your assistance matters much to him."[1]
(chapter 1)

Cervantes, of course, obeys and later presents his credentials
for admission to Parnassus to Apollo himself—mentioning
first his pastoral novel, *La Galatea*, then his plays, and finally
the *Quijote* and the *Exemplary Novellas*. These last prove that
he is "one who in invention / is superior to most, and those
inferior therein / must perforce be bereft of fame" (chapter 4).

In the similar but more wry self-portrait contained in the
Prologue to the *Exemplary Novellas*, we hear again the same
self-satisfied litany: "Some of my readers would like to see
the face and figure of a man who dares to present himself in
the marketplace *of the world* with so many inventions" (italics
mine; we shall see why later). More ironical and indirect but
at the same time more telling is the judgment attributed to
the Priest in Part I, chapter 6, of the *Quijote* (the Scrutiny of
the Books) concerning *La Galatea*:

> I've been a good friend of that Cervantes fellow for many
> years now, and I know that he is better versed in misfortune
> than in versification. His book has some claim to merit as far
> as invention goes; it proposes interesting things but concludes
> none. We must wait, therefore, for the second part which the
> author has promised; and perhaps with that repentance, he
> may be granted the pardon which we now deny him.

The writer of these lines is already on his way to becoming
the author of the *Quijote*; and having suddenly discovered
how marvelously inventive he can be, he looks back with affectionate irony at an earlier self-experimenting for the first
time with narrative fiction.[2] The meaning of these lines is not

---

1. In my translation I have rendered in English the double meaning of
the verb *pasar* as used here: "Pasa, raro inventor, pasa adelante / con tu sutil
designio."
2. A discussion of this crucial aspect of novelistic consciousness may be
found in my essay on Galdós: "The Fifth Series of *Episodios nacionales*: Memories of Remembering," *Bulletin of Hispanic Studies* 63 (1986), pp. 47–52.

arcane. It is simply this: as an inventor, how much he has improved with age!

"The posterity of the Quijote"

What did Cervantes mean when he called himself an inventor? Let us begin by avoiding the fatal, fascinating, and almost irresistible temptation offered perhaps most eloquently in 1930 by Manuel Azaña (who in the following year was to become prime minister of the second Spanish republic) in a lecture entitled "Cervantes y la invención del *Quijote*."[3] Therein the intellectual statesman was primarily concerned with the relation of biography to creation. The novelist was a dreamer (in a sense comparable to Azaña himself!) who "invented" his novel by projecting his fantasies into the exaltation of his characters. However, that process, as Stendhal observed, was not a solitary operation, not a lonely mirror perambulating erratically along a haphazard road back and forth from Argamasilla[4] to Sierra Morena and Barcelona. As a true novel, it is performed in its readers with the result that it changes them permanently: "As the posterity of the *Quijote*, we are debtors to it for a part of our spiritual life: we are Cervantes's children [or creations—*somos criaturas cervantinas*]."[5]

In so saying, Azaña refers to something far more lasting than the immediate comic prophylaxis ("pastime for the melancholy and moody breast"[6]), which, if we possess suitable

3. Manuel Azaña, *Obras completas*, ed. Juan Marichal (Mexico City: Ediciones Oasis, 1966), 1: 1097–1114.

4. Although Cervantes begins by saying he has "no desire to recollect" the name of Alonso Quijano's Manchegan abode, he cunningly attributes the satirical verses appended at the end of Part I to imaginary members of the grotesque "academy" of a one-horse village called Argamasilla, "lugar de la Mancha." The epithet is a direct echo of the first sentence of the *Quijote*. The suffix *-illa* is a diminutive, and *argamasa* literally means "mortar." The name, which could loosely be translated as "Mudville," clearly had amused him during his perambulation as a tax collector.

5. Azaña, *Obras Completas*, 1: 1100.

6. Cervantes, *El viaje del Parnaso*, chapter 4.

"souls," we may experience as freshly as did those who purchased or borrowed the *Quijote* in 1605. To be specific, Azaña, like many other readers on this side of the watershed of sensibility known as the French Revolution, was deeply impressed by the modernity of the book. After the publication in 1814 of the first nineteenth-century best-seller, Sir Walter Scott's *Waverley* (a serious historical novel with a rueful Cervantine beginning), readers increasingly began to observe their own lives, as well as life in general, novelistically. Indeed, our immediate forebears often behaved as if they were novelists looking at themselves as characters or, conversely, as if they were characters searching for a novelist to look at them—and into them.

Hence the conclusion of Ortega's *Meditations*, in which, as we saw, Cervantes is presented as two centuries ahead of his time—in contrast with Stendhal, who predicted rescue from oblivion as soon as 1880. The protonovelist's vision of life as a process of day-to-day exposure to careless circumstance might not have taught all members of his seventeenth-century public all that he had hoped to teach them: first how to read, and then how to live; or, as he might have said, how, through receptive reading and therapeutic laughter, to exchange social irrationality (for which Don Quijote's delusions provided a recognizable caricature) for personal sanity. But Cervantes's strange book undeniably has provided undreamt-of generations of future novelist-writers and novelist-readers with patterned comprehension of their alienated lives in societies submitted to unceasing mutation.

Such is also the thesis of one of the most influential twentieth-century theorists of the novel, Georg Lukács. In his *Theorie des Romans* (which he began to write in the same year Ortega published his *Meditations*) Lukács defines the genre as the literary portrait of a world bereft of value—as Don Quijote discovered for himself in the course of the Third Sally. Cervantes thus is supposed to have invented the novel in the sense that his ruefully humorous narrative experiment was the precursor of a ruefully serious genre that emerged two centuries later when historical consciousness itself was in the process of becoming obsessive. As Lukács tells us, it was the disaster of World War I that impelled him to write his *Theorie*. However, let us give the last word to the greatest nineteenth-century novelist. Ostensibly judging *sub specie aeternitatis*, in these lines from his *Diary of a Writer* Dostoevsky speaks profoundly from within his times:

> In the whole world there is no deeper, no mightier literary work. This is, so far, the last and greatest expression of human thought; this is the bitterest irony which man was capable of conceiving. And if the world were to come to an end, and people were asked there somewhere: "Did you understand your life on earth, and what conclusions have you drawn from it?"—man could silently hand over *Don Quijote.*"[7]

The proposition that the invention of the *Quijote* brought with it the invention of the novel (insofar as Cervantes anticipated a crucial variety of future consciousness) is at once tempting and patently anachronistic. Since by definition an invention (whether one of Cicero's or one of Edison's) must be consciously contrived, neither Azaña nor Lukács can help us to understand exactly what Cervantes meant when he called himself a *raro inventor*. Posterity might be said to have invented itself (in the etymological sense of *invenire*, "to come upon") in reading the *Quijote;* or, conversely and more sensibly, the *Quijote* itself might be said to have invented the novel in the readings of Fielding, Sterne, Stendhal, Flaubert, Dickens, Clemens, Gogol, Dostoevsky, Melville, and even Scott and Balzac.[8] We must, therefore, return to the past and

---

7. Fyodor Dostoevsky, *The Diary of a Writer*, trans. Boris Brasol (New York: George Braziller, 1954), p. 260.

8. Although one does not normally think of Scott and Balzac as novelists in the Cervantine tradition (the others clearly are), it is noteworthy that both *Waverley* (the first of the series bearing this name) and *La maison du Chat-qui-pelote* (the first work of fiction to be included in *La comédie humaine*) are concerned with misguidedly avid readers. Young Waverley "drove through a sea of books like a pilot without a rudder" and suffered the adventurous consequences thereof, while young Augustine Guillaume's undesirable marriage resulted from reading such romances as *Hyppolyte, comte de Douglas*. In spite of their reverence for archaeological history and social realism (both of which Cervantes scorned) the *Quijote* was a shared point of novelistic departure for

to the systematic prevalence of rhetoric in the century during which Cervantes lived most of his life in order to comprehend his self-assertion as an inventor.

"De inventione poetica"

Originally, in Cicero's *De inventione poetica* and in the long tradition it relied on, the term *inventio* was forensic: the art of finding convincing arguments for orators or of pleading a case and winning. It is, Cicero maintains, the most important *(princeps in omnium partem)* of the five traditional divisions of the discipline (the others being *dispositio, elocutio, memoria,* and *pronuntiatio*). Thus, in "Renaissance" Spain,[9] Luis de Lucena, author of the burlesque academic lecture *Repetición de amores* (1497), is praised for being a "very prudent and subtle inventor,"[10] and the Marqués de Villena in 1422 castigates bad orators who do not know how "to help themselves through invention."[11] So, too, Alonso de Proaza, professor, editor (of *La Celestina,* among other texts), and humanist, was admired

Scott and Balzac. Nor was it completely forgotten afterward, as such novels as *The Fortunes of Nigel* and *La recherche de l'absolu* indicate.

9. The word *Renaissance* is enclosed in quotation marks because of its problematical application to a nation and a culture (represented by Alonso Quijano and his fellows, devoted not only to chivalry but also to anachronistic history plays and ballads celebrating the national past) that refused even to conceive of a "Middle Ages." The long centuries of Christian reconquest were sacred not only to the mass of the people but also to such self-proclaimed humanists as Nebrija and Pulgar. Américo Castro, long before he became aware of this aspect of Spanish peculiarity, did present Cervantes as a Renaissance author, in his *El pensamiento de Cervantes* (Madrid: Hernando, 1925). And even now he might conceivably have presented him as a Renaissance mind comically and intensely concerned with the resistance of his compatriots to historical truth. For further summary and bibliography, see my "The Problem of the Spanish Renaissance," *Folio* 10 (1977), "Studies in the Literature of Spain," ed. Michael J. Ruggerio, pp. 37–54.

10. In the "bachiller Villoslada's" prefatory encomium to Luis de Lucena, *Repetición de amores,* ed. J. Ornstein (Berkeley and Los Angeles: University of California Press, 1954).

11. Marqués de Villena, *Tratado de la consolación,* ed. R. Foulché Delbosc, in *Revue Hispanique* 41 (1917), p. 123.

as an inventor or master of discourse.[12] All of them excelled in the exploitation of the Aristotelian *topika*, or topics, where arguments are "located": analogy, enumeration, differentiation, etc.[13]

Cervantes, of course, was neither an advocate nor a prosecutor; unlike Don Quijote, he much preferred ironical insinuation to oratorical display and dispute. The case of the Barber's basin in chapters 44 and 45 is a mockery of such procedures, just as the discourse on the Golden Age in the presence of the open-mouthed goatherds is a beloved travesty that nonetheless "might well have been dispensed with" (I.11). However, as we shall see, the restricted Ciceronian definition of invention—the seeking and finding of effective oral arguments—was adapted easily for poetic use during the sixteenth century. That is to say, it was transformed into literary terms that Cervantes could apply to himself as an author and to his printed narrative rhetoric. As a matter of fact, his self-praise as an inventor is an echo of the doctrine of his mentor in poetics, Alonso López Pinciano: "And so I am of the opinion that the poet should be new and rare in invention."[14]

What exactly did Cervantes do as a poetic inventor that is comparable to what forensic inventors do? As we shall see later, Cervantes, using the conventions of other fictional genres as his *topika*, set out methodically to compose not an

12. See Hernando de Castillo, *Cancionero general* (1511), ed. J. A. de Balenchana (Madrid: Sociedad de Bibliófilos Españoles, 1882), 1: 662. Cited in D. W. McPheeters, *El humanista español, Alonso de Proaza,* (Madrid: Castalia, 1961), p. 112.

13. The point is that the term *invention* was derived from a complex neo-Ciceronian tradition that antedated *El viaje del Parnaso* by at least two centuries. Marcelino Menéndez Pelayo, the father of Hispanism (against whom we frequently rebel in spite of—or because of—our indebtedness to him), studies the matter at length in chapters 9 and 10 of his *Historia de las ideas estéticas en España*, ed. E. Sánchez Reyes, vol. 2 (Madrid: Consejo Superior de Investigaciones Científicas, 1962).

14. Alonso López Pinciano, *Filosofía antigua poética* (Madrid, 1596), p. 193 (my translation). It is curious to note that a few pages later López Pinciano contradicts Cervantes's Priest (who would have burned his own father if he had encountered him in that romance) by praising the *Amadís de Grecia* as written by an author who does not "imitate" but rather "invents."

oration or a brief but his own new kind of narrative—a narrative destined to be recognized as the father (or mother) of the novel. Furthermore, because afterward he knew he had done it so well, because he knew he was such a superb inventor of prose, he even dared to demand entry into Parnassus as a major "poet." As Juan de la Cueva (a dramatist and critic who was roughly Cervantes's contemporary) enunciates in a manifesto comparable in its self-serving intention to the *Viaje del Parnaso:* "Those who in their poetry strayed from inventiveness are historians, and genuine poets those who knew how to invent."[15] This distinction between the inventor (who exploits the past for new creation) and the chronicler (who merely compiles what happened when) necessarily locates prose fiction within the larger realm of poetry. An author who can invent in prose (instead of merely copy as did those who continued the *Amadís*), in spite of all shortcomings, has every right to demand from Apollo recognition that he, too, is what in German is called a *Dichter.*

In any case, Cervantes, in the critical excursus that concludes Part I of the *Quijote,* has no hesitation in claiming for a skilled inventor's prose all of the virtues and perquisites of the classical genres of poetry. If a fictional narrator knows how to compose with

> agreeable style, ingenious invention, and as truthfully as possible, he will weave a cloth out of various beautiful skeins. . . . Because the free composition of such works allows the writer to show himself as a master of the epic, the lyric, the tragic, and the comic, with all the rhetorical qualities which are contained in the sweet and agreeable sciences of poetry and oratory; for the epic can as easily and properly be written in prose as well as verse.
>
> (I.47)

With this assertion Cervantes initiated a critical tradition. Although he could not know that his falsely modest "dry legend" was the world's first novel, those who began to follow

15. Juan de la Cueva, *Ejemplar poético,* ed. F. de Icaza (Madrid: Clásicos Castellanos, 1941), p. 124.

in his footsteps were to justify their still suspect metier in
identical terms. Specifically, both Fielding and Gogol defended the originality and the respectability of their narrative
innovations by clothing them in the mantle of the epic. This,
then, is the primordial meaning of Cervantes's eulogy of himself as a *raro inventor.* "Despite my admitted failings in verse,"
he says loudly and clearly in *El viaje del Parnaso,* "in my prose
I seek and find and weave at least as cleverly as Ariosto."[16]
As a narrator, therefore, he should not be confused with
those fictioneers and adventuremongers who confine themselves to repeating the *Amadís* over and over again. So, too,
Fielding denied all responsibility for a derivative romance entitled *The Adventures of David Simple.*[17] Genuine inventors are
poets, and they should be treated with the admiration they
deserve.

16. As was pointed out to me by a singularly alert graduate student, Beth
Tremallo, Ariosto frequently uses the comparison. For example, in II, 30, we
find the following (*Orlando Furioso,* trans. Barbara Reynolds [New York: Penguin Classics, 1977], p. 145):

> Or a poppa, or all'orza hann'il crudele,
> che mai no cessa, e vien più ognor crescendo:
> essi di qua di là con umil vele
> vansi aggirando, e l'alto mar scorrendo.
> Ma perchè varie fila a varie tele
> uopo mi son, che tutte ordire intendo,
> lascio Rinaldo e l'agitata prua,
> a torno a dir di Bradamante sua.

> Veering from stem to stern, the cruel gale
> Grows ever stronger, granting no release.
> Now here, now there, they whirl with shortened sail,
> At the storm's mercy tossed on angry seas.
> But many threads are needed for my tale
> And so, to weave my canvas as I please,
> I leave Rinaldo and the plunging prow,
> And turn to talk of Bradamante now.

See also VII, 2; XIII, 81; and XXXIV, 90. However, from my colleague Jules
Brody's book on Montaigne, *Lectures de Montaigne* (Lexington, Ky.: French
Forum, 1982), I learned the extent to which the metaphor was topical. It has
also penetrated idiomatic English, as in the phrase "spinning a yarn."
17. Introduction to Sarah Fielding, *The Adventures of David Simple* (London, 1774), p. iv.

"If in the mechanical arts it is licit to invent . . ."

In order to understand the context of Cervantes's emphasis on his own inventiveness and on the importance of invention, we must once again pause for a moment to glance at the historical and literary circumstances of the century in which he was born. From our late twentieth-century vantage point, the contribution of pedantic Renaissance poetics to the making of a strange new narrative, which, in its turn, was to invent a major genre of modern literature, constitutes a mystery that needs abundant clarification. Let us begin by turning our minds back some fifty years before Cervantes's birth in 1547, and let us try to comprehend the almost incomprehensible ebullition of Spain's crucial decades, those that ended the fifteenth century and began the sixteenth. Starting with the union of Castile and Aragon under Ferdinand and Isabella and the establishment of the Inquisition, this period was a time of change in every aspect of personal and collective life. Even the public baths were closed for good. In the year 1492 alone (an *annus mirabilis,* if there ever was one), in addition to what was discovered on October 12, Granada was taken, ending the remnant of Moorish sovereignty in the peninsula, the Jews were expelled, the first play in Castilian was performed, the first grammar of a modern language appeared, and a book of fiction for the first time was written expressly for the printing press. Everything seemed to be beginning all at once.

Although the tidal wave of political and social change that accompanied the reigns of the Catholic Monarchs and Charles V was what held most people's attention, the sudden doubling and tripling in size of the known world was a more lasting and profound challenge to consciousness. And one of the most curious symptoms of this was the return of the notion of invention to its preforensic etymological origins. Thus, for example, in 1512 a chronicler speaks of the "invention and conquest of those Indies which we now call Portuguese."[18] Cervantes, in other words, was born into a time

18. Martín Fernández de Figueroa, *Conquista de las Indias de Persia e Arabia*

when invention and inventiveness were laden with new prestige, when men who knew how to "come upon" or "come into" what they were looking for (or even marvels they were not looking for) were deservedly famous.

More familiar to our ears than the "invention of the Indies" (since we normally think that one cannot invent what was already there) was the comparable redefinition of the word in the context of literary discovery and innovation. In the year that Columbus "came into" San Salvador, Juan del Encina performed the same feat for the theater and Diego de San Pedro for an intended fictional best-seller.[19] Quite possibly in the same year, the anonymous author of Act I of *La Celestina* discovered how to use rhetorical conventions and Stoic commonplaces as *topika* in order to explore the temporality of consciousness in dialogue, an invention perfected in 1497 by Fernando de Rojas. And that was only the beginning. The literature of the century to follow (like the industry of the English industrial revolution) was a case history of sheer mutability: chivalresque, pastoral, and picaresque romances; the naturalization of eleven-syllable Italian versification; unprecedented stanzas; a unique national drama; and, by the end of the Golden Age, a variety of personal genres such as Quevedo's *Dreams*, Góngora's *Solitudes*, and the one-of-a-kind prose narratives of Cervantes and Gracián. A new geographic world and a new poetic world, each in its own fashion, returned to the etymology of the word *invent*, and de-

(Salamanca, 1512), in *A Spaniard in the Portuguese Indies*, ed. J. B. McKenna (Cambridge, Mass.: Harvard University Press, 1967), p. 20. In his commentary McKenna remarks on the fact that in a 1494 papal bull, "Inter caetera," the new lands are described as "inventas et inveniendas," p. 161. Edmundo O'Gorman in *La invención de América; el universalismo de la cultura de Occidente* (Mexico City: Fondo de Cultura Económica, 1958) uses the word in our sense of new conception, meaning that if Columbus "discovered" America, Amerigo Vespucci "invented" it; hence it was quite properly named after him. O'Gorman revised his book in English under the title *The Invention of America: An Inquiry into the Historical Nature of the New World and the Meaning of Its History* (Bloomington: Indiana University Press, 1961).

19. See my *The Spain of Fernando de Rojas*, p. 327.

rived new meaning from it. Poets devised and explorers discovered with the same verb.

Comparison of the torrent of literary change in Castilian that began in the 1490s (and continued to flow until the death of Calderón almost two centuries later) to the Industrial Revolution may appear farfetched, but it is justified literally by critics of the time. For example, Alfonso Sánchez, a professor of Hebrew at the new University of Alcalá (who was, like Juan de la Cueva, concerned with defending Lope de Vega as a "modern"), asked those who espoused what were thought to be the classical rules for drama: "If in the mechanical arts it is licit to add new things to what has already been invented—and if every day we see something new in that domain—why cannot the same thing be done in the domain of letters? Why should not Lope invent a new art of poetry?"[20] Lope himself praises Vicente Espinel, on the one hand, as "the suave inventor" of a fifth string for the *vigüela* and, on the other, as the inventor of the ten-verse stanza called *décimas*.[21]

As for Cervantes, acute awareness of the resemblance of mechanical and literary change is apparent in the Prologue to the *Ocho comedias*. These eight plays, Cervantes tells us, were never performed; indeed, they had apparently been refused in a rather humiliating fashion by professional directors after his invincible rival, Lope, had usurped "the monarchy of the drama." They remained in a drawer and were eventually published as a "book" at the end of Cervantes's career, in 1615—apparently in order to exploit the success of the *Quijote* and to provide him some much needed funds. The Prologue—it can therefore be assumed with due com-

20. In an appendix to the *Expostulatio Spongiae* (1618), a collective defense of Lope's dramatic art. Cited by Marcelino Menéndez Pelayo in his *Historia de las ideas estéticas en España*, 2: 306.

21. The *vigüela* quotation is from *El laurel de Apolo* (a poem generically similar to *El viaje del Parnaso*), in *Biblioteca de Autores Españoles*, vol. 38, ed., Cayetano Rosell (Madrid, 1898), p. 191. Lope also mentions the same invention in *La Dorotea* and elsewhere. As for the ten-verse stanza, Lope goes on to say, "and the sweet, sonorous espinelas," which should not be called "décimas."

passion—was an attempt to compensate for his past chagrin with a miniature history of the theater designed to emphasize his role as an inventor who had contributed to its evolution. One Navarro, Cervantes tells us, had initiated elaborate stage effects by "inventing clouds, thunderstorms, and battles on stage." However, he himself in earlier and more successful plays had taken the decisive step of reducing the awkward five-act classical form to three acts. He had thus invented on his own what was commonly thought to be one of Lope's major innovations.

The most significant thing about the Prologue from our present point of view is not Cervantes's self-serving thumbnail history of the theater but the fact that he does not distinguish that external "coming into" or "coming upon," which corresponds to our technological notion of what inventors do, from poetic insight. In the same sentence and without transition he goes on to claim that he "was the first to represent on stage the imagination and hidden thoughts of the soul, thereby creating moral figures." We shall return to this assertion later because of its relevance for the narrative art of the *Quijote*. Its mention now is only intended to suggest that Cervantes as a creator-critic quite properly does not distinguish form from content. The introduction of a theatrical machine, the structural reinforcement or improvement of a genre, and the exploration of a soul were all alike—conscious literary achievements of which the inventor might be equally proud.

Thus, although Cervantes might have appeared to be *caduco* ("over the hill" or "worn out") to "a certain kid whose profession is poetry" (mentioned in the *Viaje del Parnaso*, chapter 8), he was no reactionary in the sense of only wishing to preserve tradition. Already in the Prologue to *La Galatea* he attacks "those narrow-minded souls who, in order to conserve the brevity of our antique language, wish to eliminate the abundance of present Castilian,"[22] that is, those who

22. Cervantes is apparently referring to the traditionalist Cristóbal de Castillejo and his followers, who were engaged in a bitter polemic (in the concluding chapter we shall gauge its cruel extent) against innovation—

do not "understand" nor wish to exploit the marvelous literary "freedom" of that "fortunate age." Let them, Cervantes says, realize the advantages of the "open, fertile, and spacious field" that is now before us and that offers new "facility and sweetness" combined with "gravity and eloquence" as well as a "diversity of sharp, grave, subtle, and elevated conceits."

In conclusion, it is evident in these prologues as elsewhere that Cervantes as an inventor was concerned above all to assert that he knew what he was doing—that his innovations were conscious and intentional. Lope and his generation, as we shall see, had presented themselves as naturals, *ingenios* capable of producing without ratiocination all the lush variety of versification, forms, and genres of their hothouse Golden Century, but Cervantes was determined to continue the calculated creative experimentation of earlier decades. And once he got started, he proved his point: he changed the shape and function of chapters; he incorporated dramatic techniques into narration (as Fielding, Stendhal, and Gogol were to do in his wake);[23] he played ironically with his own simultaneous presence and absence as an author; and, above all, redefining the forensic definition, he wove the traditional story "skeins" at his disposal into an unprecedented tapestry. In other words, without forewarned awareness of the self-consciousness of its art, the marvel of the *Quijote* will seem merely miraculous. The terms *Renaissance* and *Baroque*,

---

meaning "Italianization"—in versification and vocabulary. However, sixty-four years after Castillejo's death, Cervantes in the *Viaje del Parnaso* expressed his own pessimism regarding new tendencies. For him Castillejo was what might now be termed a premature Jeremiah.

23. F. W. J. von Schelling in his *Philosophie der Kunst* (1802) observes: "In dieser Beziehung könnte man den Roman auch als eine Mischung des Epos und des Drama beschreiben" (*Sämmtliche Werke*, ed. K. F. A. Schelling, Part I [Stuttgart und Augsberg, 1859], 5: 674). ("In this connection one could describe the novel as a mixture of epic and drama.") Jill Syverson further develops this perception in connection with the *Quijote* in an excellent doctoral dissertation at Harvard University (1980), *Theatrical Aspects of Cervantes's Prose*, which will shortly be published. In the meantime see her "Theatrical Aspects of the Novel: *Don Quijote, Joseph Andrews*, and the Example of Cervantes," *Revista de Estudios Hispanicos* 9 (1982), pp. 241–48.

though useful in certain contexts, are misleading in this one: by transferring authorship to the Zeitgeist, they cover up what was actually going on. We are quite simply dealing with an old man's well-meditated choice of Daedalus over Orpheus. If not as a singer, as an inventor he claims mythological welcome.

"To overthrow the poorly made machine . . ."

Having launched this ex-post-facto manifesto, we are now ready to scrutinize, as Cervantes would have said, the initial versions or experimental models of the invention that we began by calling a clever trap for the reader's imagination. In the introductory essay we mentioned briefly the silent, voluptuous, and unprecedented symbiosis of author, hero, and reader initiated in 1506 when a mechanical invention (the printing press) transformed a medieval genre, the romance of chivalry. What we did not stress sufficiently and what matters now was the concomitant transformation of the reader into a member of a public.

In the oral or semioral world prior to the printing press, what we now call "literature" was transmitted directly from one person to another, although others, of course, were invited to benefit tangentially. One sang to a lady in order to win her favors or at least to show off one's skill; one wrote treatises in order to provide a friend with philosophical consolation or a future monarch with lessons in wise government; one composed satirical verses in order to insult an enemy; one confessed one's sins in writing to a priest in order to be absolved; and one addressed letters to anyone, from a fellow scholar to a dead celebrity, in order to show off one's erudition. At the most, when mimicking the voices of *La Celestina*, singing a ballad, or reading aloud from a chivalric romance or saint's vita, a group might be summoned to listen, limited in its immediate size by the range of the human voice. But now Spaniards, united in faith and nascent patriotism by Ferdinand and Isabella and in fictional adventure-escape by the printing press, came to constitute a public. Being Amadís together, and at the same time belonging together fervently to a paradoxically "medieval" nation-state, provided a collective identity—with all the consolation for daily misery or boredom therewith made possible.

That primordial collectivity of readers—despite the prevalence of illiteracy—constituted a national market larger and more homogeneous than markets of other European nations, far more fragmented into classes and dialectal regions. As such, it literally demanded and was supplied with the stories of Amadís's children and grandchildren as well as those of new rivals and such ancient predecessors as the fellowship of the Round Table. The book created a public, and the public, avid for more of the same, converted the book into a genre or subgenre. Then some fifty years later, readers who were beginning to be surfeited with chivalric deeds (particularly the increasing number of shut-in women readers) welcomed another subgenre, the pastoral romance initiated by Jorge de Montemayor in *La Diana*. Alongside tapeworm or express-train narratives of ever more incredible deeds of arms, there appeared on the market lyrically decelerated fiction combining idealized "green worlds" with printed love songs and stilted dialogues and monologues. Violence did not disappear completely (insofar as the two varieties of literate pleasure existed in a state of voluptuous osmosis), but at the center of the glade the inaction was primarily in the past. Instead of swordblows the performers each in turn exchanged amorous tales of woe designed for the sentimental participation of both the auditors and the readers.

Then after another five decades (although the anonymous novella called *Lazarillo de Tormes*, published in 1554, had been a precursor) there appeared the genre of the picaresque antiromance, that is to say, strings of antiadventures designed to provoke the laughter of Schadenfreude from ignorantly cruel readers and awareness of social hypocrisy from those whose marginal lives attuned them to bitter irony.[24] The date was 1599, and the book, Mateo Alemán's *Guzmán de Alfarache*, was

24. See chapter 1, n. 61.

to have a crucial role in the history of the novel, insofar as its enormous success and its perverse portrayal of all that was (and still is) shameful in human existence was the "necessity" that led to Cervantes's "invention." Cervantes, having read and disliked *Guzmán de Alfarache* as much as Fielding disliked *Pamela,* set out to write a work of fiction that not only would restore humanity to our laughter but also would present life with the profundity and multiplicity admired therein by Dostoevsky. E. C. Riley explains Cervantes's innovation in terms of decorum:

> The narrow literary dogmas of decorum and style reflect a now obsolete world-view arranged on hierarchical lines. *Don Quixote* is an ironic vision in which the old world-view is compounded with one that is essentially modern, with the ideally exalted and the basely material coexisting as distinct but separate parts of human experience. In that novel Cervantes served up not a slice of life, but, more nearly than anyone had done in a work of fiction before, the whole cake.[25]

Riley's description of what we find in the *Quijote* cannot be faulted, but the implied explanation (anticipation of nineteenth-century Hugoesque and Balzacian rupture of neoclassical levels of style) seems to me to be erroneous. Riley does not take fully into account the fact that in Spain medieval mimesis (as presented by Auerbach) was never abandoned—not only in *La Celestina* (the corrosively ironic audition of which anticipates the humorously ironic reading of the *Quijote*) but even in the exquisite neo-Virgilian and neo-Petrarchan eclogues of Cervantes's favorite poet, Garcilaso de la Vega. The inevitable result of that oversight is that Riley imposes on Cervantes's inventiveness criteria that are alien to it. Decorum as such does not take into account what the present essay is intended to establish: that these three sixteenth-century genres of printed fiction—the chivalresque, the picaresque, and the pastoral—constitute the primordial poetic *topika* (later there would be many others including his own

---

25. Riley, *Cervantes' Theory of the Novel,* p. 145.

Part I) where Cervantes seeks and finds threads for his increasingly "sutil designio." Although when read in terms of prescriptive rhetorical rules these genres seem to represent different levels of style, they certainly do not correspond to an "old world-view" that Cervantes was concerned to surpass.[26] Rather, it was their very modernity (their printed condition and public appeal) that he was concerned to utilize.

However, in order to understand how these three species of romance contribute to the art of the *Quijote*, we must first examine Cervantes's criticism of them. The trouble with Mateo Alemán, for example, was not just that he presented a one-sided worm's-eye view of life that needed correction but, more important, that his initial invention satisfied him and his readers. Just as Montalvo and Montemayor and their readers had been satisfied. Cervantes, too, as he himself confesses, was fond of individual works belonging to the chivalresque and the pastoral (while feeling that the *Guzmán*, the literary success of the moment, was structureless in its autobiographical imitation of life), but he was critical precisely of their generic quality. Each is a "machine," a closed narrative pattern, sent from press to public full-grown but half-baked. They were, in other words, sudden inventions, insufficiently perfected and thoughtlessly enjoyed and admired, which ought to be "overthrown," as the imaginary friend who helps him with the Prologue advises. Yet the very fact that the *Amadís*, the *Diana*, and the *Guzmán* possess a potential assembly-line quality provided Cervantes with a chance to use and improve on his narrative inheritance. Faced with the revolutionary standardization that McLuhan attributes to Gutenberg's invention and the resultant standardization of its literary offspring, Cervantes realized—in what must have been a sun-burst of marvelous illumination—what a better and more conscientious inventor could make out of those three rudimentary narrative contraptions or, as he termed them, *máquinas*. In their case the medium had indeed gov-

---

26. Today, of course, instead of levels of style, they would be called (more revealingly) codes, or, as Bakhtin would have it, languages.

erned the message, a lamentable form of determinism he intended to put in reverse.

Leaving the Prologue and entering the text of the *Quijote*,
we find these conclusions supported explicitly in Part I, chapter 6, the "scrutiny" and immolation of Alonso Quijano's library (Don Quijote, once having invented his role, no longer
needs to read!), which we shall examine from another point
of view in the essay to follow. During that literary Inquisition,
Cervantes's Priest-critic observes to the Barber-critic that
Montalvo's "was the first romance of chivalry to be printed in
Spain and that all the others took their origin and inspiration
from it." Therefore, it deserved to be burned. Not so, replies
his friend, because it is "unique in its art it ought to be pardoned." Similarly, the Priest remarks later, "it is the honor of
La Diana to have been the first of such books." Alonso Quijano, given his literary tastes, had purchased no picaresque
fiction, but as Claudio Guillén has pointed out, Cervantes
clearly foresaw that the *Guzmán de Alfarache*, too, would become the patriarch of a future genre, or *género*—a term at
once mercantile and literary in Cervantes's ironic usage[27]—
unless he could persuade booksellers and buyers that his
own purposefully ageneric (and so radically unpredictable
and infinitely more profound) version of the comedy of life
exposed to a careless world full of both kind and hard-
hearted inhabitants was the superior product.[28]

27. The much discussed passage occurs in I.22, while Don Quijote is engaged in interrogating those condemned to the galleys. One of them, Ginés
de Pasamonte, a malicious caricature of Guzmán (who ends as a galley
slave), is engaged in writing his autobiography. When the knight asks him if
it is finished, he replies that it cannot be finished until he is finished. This,
of course, questions the verisimilitude of the pretense of *ich-Erzählung*, or
first-person narration. Ginés also predicts boastfully that his book will eclipse
the *Lazarillo de Tormes* and any others of that "género" that in the future might
presume to compete with it. See Claudio Guillén's essay entitled "Genre and
Countergenre: The Discovery of the Picaresque," in his *Literature as System*
(Princeton, N.J.: Princeton University Press, 1971), pp. 135–58.

28. "We have already said that the novel gets on poorly with other
genres. There can be no talk of a harmony deriving from mutual limitation
and complementariness. The novel parodies other genres (precisely in their
role as genres); it exposes the conventionality of their forms and their lan-

How would Cervantes accomplish that aim? Quite simply, by taking advantage of what was wrong with the chivalresque, the picaresque, and the pastoral: the fact that they had been (or would be) produced en masse for a mass public whose collective mind was habituated to—and, indeed, saturated with—the simple patterns of their fiction. By cleverly and mischievously bringing them together in a single narrative, he would "invent" not only "in" the innumerable printed romances he himself had read but, more importantly, "in" the very minds of his readers. Then as each reader came to appreciate and to laugh at Cervantes's play with generic rigidity—his delightful tangle of fictional expectations—mass identification would no longer be possible. The public would disintegrate, and the individual would once again be alone and, to the extent of his capacity, in ironical communication with the author. And the most extraordinary thing is that what might well have been a parody relevant only to its own times (like Fielding's *Shamela*) should still work for twentieth-century readers who have never opened a single one of those primitive romances! Cervantes's genius was able to communicate across the centuries not only the foolishness and conventionality of avid sixteenth-century reading but also its savor and fervor.

"A cloth woven from various and beautiful skeins"

The Scrutiny was a pause for literary assessment placed at the end of the initial five chapters of primitive invention customarily referred to as the First Sally. As readers of the time were immediately aware, that initial portion of the *Quijote* consists of a juxtaposition of chivalresque and picaresque motifs, or "skeins." To say it more directly, it portrays a head-on collision of a fantasy castle with a sordid inn, prostitutes

---

guage; it squeezes out some genres and incorporates others into its own peculiar structure, reformulating and re-accentuating them" (Bakhtin, *The Dialogic Imagination*, p. 5).

with damsels, trout with codfish, a rascally innkeeper with a noble seneschal. Like a stand-up comic "orator," Cervantes invented those first chapters by finding (or "coming into") patterns from fiction already familiar to his readers and pitting them against each other.

Recognition of this parodical technique allows us to draw two preliminary conclusions. First, although Cervantes's primary intention may well be that which he proclaimed—to wreak havoc with the romances of chivalry—the world of Mateo Alemán is also submitted to caricature. As we remarked earlier (and as critics generally agree), it was the appearance and success of the *Guzmán de Alfarache* in 1599 that was the initial catalyst of Cervantes's new narrative. Evidently, that narrative must have been undertaken shortly thereafter.

The second conclusion is more important for our present purposes: as the author soon realized, this direct clash of antitheses was self-destructive. The brutality of picaresque cynicism (which, as we shall see, is not at all the same as realism) would overwhelm chivalric folly and lead to Don Quijote's definitive defeat. Accordingly, the First Sally is brought to an abrupt ending with the hero's complete derangement. The sardonic merchants have dared to make fun of his Lady's beauty; his trusty steed has dumped him ignominiously on the ground; and he has been beaten mercilessly by the most unworthy of all possible opponents, an adolescent muleteer. The result is that by the ironclad logic of his delusion the erstwhile hidalgo can no longer sustain his assumed identity as a knight-errant. If Amadís was invincible, by definition he is to be no less so. His only recourse, therefore, is to change roles and to believe himself to be first the treacherously defeated hero of an absurd neo-Carolingian ballad.[29] And then

29. As Ramón Menéndez Pidal, Spain's greatest medievalist, has shown, the initial stimulus of the *Quijote* was an anonymous comic interlude entitled *El entremés de los romances* ("romances" in Spanish are oral ballads), in which a deluded man identifies himself with his interlocutors. See *Un aspecto en la*

(after having been rescued and taken home astride a donkey by a kindly peasant neighbor) there is the episode of Abinderráez, a young and handsome Moorish lover taken prisoner by Christians whose interpolated story is told in *La Diana*. The literary satire of the First Sally, perhaps originally conceived of as an independent novella, comes to its inevitable ending. All that remained for Cervantes to do was to arrange for the Barber and the Priest to draw the proper critical conclusions and preside over the atrocious "auto-da-fé" of the library.

The problem was now sharply delineated. If the book was to continue—if Cervantes was to show readers and writers of fiction what a conscientious inventor could make out of popular generic raw material—Don Quijote had to be better defended. Means would have to be found for him, if not to conquer (although that was to happen once in a while, too), at least to survive and retain his adopted identity. As Cervantes himself might have said, Don Quijote would have to be protected from the excesses of his mad *ingenio* by the author's gift for invention. The first step, of course, was fundamental: the creation of Sancho as a sort of human buffer state between his master and the stony implacability of what was out there in the world. The kind peasant neighbor, who shows up with his donkey and tactfully brings the brutally beaten hidalgo home at night in order to avoid scandal, is replaced in the Second Sally by Sancho Panza, who is institutionalized in chivalric terms as a squire. Both share the same social class, both ride the same beast of burden, and both speak with good sense and good humor.[30] Don Quijote's

---

elaboración del "Quijote" (Madrid: Ciudad Lineal, 1924). As is evident here and elsewhere in the *Quijote* (above all in the Cave of Montesinos episode), Cervantes, unlike Lope, perceived as comic this and other manifestations of Spain's marvelous oral tradition, such as Sancho's proverbs. That is to say, he perceived them as just as ridiculous and grotesque a falsification of history as the romances of chivalry—and without the solace offered by reading.

30. As when in I.5, Sancho mimics Don Quijote's chivalric jargon upon bringing him home.

first rustic savior, thus, is clearly a precursor of Sancho—a signpost toward an immense novelistic future.

But what about the occasions (and there are quite a few of them) when knight and squire are both laid low? In addition to providing a more prudent companion with comforting saddlebags, purse, and provisions, some way would have to be found to lessen the implacability of the novelistic world, to soften the granite hardness and careless cruelty Don Quijote inevitably encounters in his headlong assaults. Fortunately, a third skein, the pastoral romance (perhaps suggested by Don Quijote's self-transformation into the gentle captive Abinderráez and by a number of titles in his library), was at hand to be woven in for this very purpose. Increasingly during the Second Sally the novel would rest on a comforting background of shady groves, green meadows, clear streams, and quiet intervals for song and story—all ready-made for the rest and recuperation of warrior and squire. Admittedly, these were artificial and highly stylized *topika*, which our inventor had first "come into" in *La Diana* and which he did not hesitate to criticize in *The Colloquy of the Dogs*.[31] At the same time, it was an absolutely indispensable thread if the *Quijote* was to grow into a novel.

However, aside from both the narrative utility of the pastoral and Cervantes's occasional criticism of its lack of verisimilitude, we should also remember that of the three printing-press genres of fiction it was the one he preferred ("books dreamed but well written," as one of the dogs remarks) and to which he himself had contributed in *La Galatea*. In fact, one whole episode of the *Quijote*—that of Marcela and Grisóstomo—seems to represent the "enmienda" (the aesthetic penitence or self-correction) that was promised for that romance in the Scrutiny. There the knight and squire, after the speech on the Golden Age, fade into the background and

31. In *The Colloquy* Berganza recalls his service as a sheepdog, remarking that his thievish masters, unlike literary shepherds, sang with hoarse voices and, instead of devoting their time to amorous pursuits, only scratched at their fleas and mended their wooden sandals.

become observers—allowing Cervantes to show us, as if he were Louis Armstrong playing a waltz, what he can do with the pastoral climax of his earlier romance within the new context of the *Quijote*. The contradictory pastoral exigencies of passion and freedom are now explored with sympathy, irony, twenty-twenty binocular vision (a personal perspective that is absent from the stylized and conventional stories and poems of *La Diana* and its successors), and the characteristically imperceptible blending of literature and life Cervantes shared with Lope and Velázquez.[32]

Nevertheless, in addition to the calculated charm and the noncommittal profundity of this miniature masterpiece, the importance of the episode of Marcela and Grisóstomo to the novel as a whole is to have introduced the pastoral skein. And it was that that kept the mirror moving along the road. After Don Quijote's picaresque lapidation by the ungrateful galley slaves he neither loses his identity entirely nor does he have to go home. Instead, prudently advised by Sancho, he retreats from the forces of law and order to a pastoral *locus amoenus* in the protective fastnesses of the Sierra Morena.

But the pastoral had much more to offer than an asylum for the mad knight or a chance for him to explain rhetorically and experience "personally" the Golden Age. It also imported into the previously slim text what novels have to have in order to fulfill their destiny: a narrative world. As Cervantes soon discovered, what had begun as an experimental variation—at once playful and functional—provided him with an unsuspected treasure: three-dimensional space replete not just with soft grass and restful glades and groves but also with mountain ranges, rivers, lagoons, caves, and seashores; in short, what we described earlier as a typology of adventurous settings. This sudden spaciousness is in di-

32. For Lope see Leo Spitzer's classic essay on *La Dorotea, Die Literarisierung des Lebens in Lopes' "Dorotea"* (Bonn and Cologne: Kölner Romanische Arbeiten, 1932). As for Velázquez, one only has to remember visually such paintings as that in which the transition from mythology (Bacchus) to contemporary rusticity (the grizzled peasant topers) resembles the reception of the Golden Age speech by its audience of goatherds.

rect contrast to the empty scenes of the First Sally, where a two-dimensional series of comic cartoons take place on the "ancient and celebrated" but featureless plain of Montiel. It is curious to note the difference in the enchanting but romantically anachronistic illustrations of Gustave Doré. At the beginning Doré confines himself to interiors, postures, pratfalls, and folkloric sketches, whereas later Don Quijote and Sancho (so immense in their dialogue) are made to resemble Saint Jerome in Manneristic paintings. They are almost swallowed up by the lavishness of the strange landscape. However, within our text the pastoral scene is no longer conventional: it is an environment which enables myriad possibilities for narrative maneuver and creative play.

Equally important is the immense amplification of the cast of characters, many of whom are incited by erotic compulsions and reluctances. Just prior to the First Sally, Alonso Quijano only glances occasionally at Aldonza Lorenzo from a distance, and later, when in his still unrehearsed role as Don Quijote he takes the "draggled and loose" prostitutes at the inn for "illustrious ladies" of the castle, he feels neither attracted nor threatened. As Caroll Johnson has pointed out convincingly, although we may disagree with his psychoanalytical approach on the grounds that literature is not life, sexual consciousness and amorous dilemmas of many kinds do pervade the Second and Third Sallies.[33] As in both *La Diana* and *La Galatea*, the web of intrigue that surrounds the doings and dialogue of the two protagonists is mostly made up of a series of *casos de amor* (case histories of love). The first symptom of the change occurs when Don Quijote and Sancho enjoy the rude hospitality of the goatherds. As we recite mentally the knight's oration on the Golden Age, we can almost hear his titillation when he contemplates in his mind's eye the scanty vegetable attire of the innocent and unmolested *zagalejas* (rustic maidens).

The scene, the speech, and the chaste maidens all lead

<hr/>

33. Caroll Johnson, *Madness and Lust* (Berkeley and Los Angeles: University of California Press, 1984).

necessarily to the Marcela and Grisóstomo episode,[34] centered on a romantic suicide amidst a horde of artificial shepherds driven mad by Eros. Then, by way of comic contrast, even Rocinante catches the "plague of love" when with disastrous results he smells the Galician mares. And so it goes throughout the rest of the book, from Maritornes through the tangle of love affairs in Sierra Morena to the elaborate goings-on at the Duke's palace, where the climax is the immensely comic and somehow touching bedroom encounter of Don Quijote and Doña Rodríguez. This alternately comic and serious (sometimes both at once) aspect of the *Quijote* Henry Fielding perceived—"received"—and recreated with remarkable sensitivity and Mark Twain found scandalous and uninteresting.[35] And though profoundly Cervantine in its elaboration, it was made possible by the weaving in of the pastoral romance.

Finally and crucially, the introduction of the pastoral, with its limitless fictional space and its complex variety of erotic relationships, enabled Cervantes to explore what Leo Spitzer in a fundamental essay was to christen "perspectivism." In the First Sally, as Aristotle would have it, things either are or are not: the castle *is not* a castle; the inn *is* an inn. However,

34. Johnson reveals the hidden cunning of Cervantes's play with nomenclature in this episode. Grisóstomo is an Hispanicized version of Chrysostom, and the fourth-century saint who bore that name was well known for a treatise entitled *De virginitate,* translated from Greek into Latin by Erasmus. As for his friend Ambrosio, his namesake is Saint Ambrose, who composed a treatise recommending virginity directed to his sister Marcellina, *De virginibus, ad Marcellinam sororem libri tres.* See Johnson, *Madness and Lust,* pp. 97–99.

35. Mark Twain's attitude is evident in the sexlessness of his utilization of the *Quijote* in *Huckleberry Finn.* In a well-known passage from a letter to Livy dated March 1, 1869, he "seriously advised [her] not to finish the book until he could censor it for her: 'Don Quixote is one of the most exquisite books that was ever written and to lose it from the world's literature would be as the wresting of a constellation from the symmetry and perfection of the firmament,' but 'neither it nor Shakespeare are proper books for virgins to read until some hand culled them of their grossness'" (Alan Gribben, *Mark Twain's Library: A Reconstruction* [Boston: G. K. Hall and Co., 1980], p. 76; the interior quotation is from *The Love Letters of Mark Twain,* ed. Dixon Wecter [New York: Harper and Brothers, 1949] p. 76).

after chapter 9 the soothing intervention of the pastoral provides a literary world in which all sorts of unexpected combinations, ambivalences, and syntheses are possible, depending on the point of view. Or perhaps I should say depending on the point of *desire*. One looks from near or far and, as we shall see, judges and interprets in terms of who one is and what one seeks—that is to say, in terms of one's private (and often amorous) incitement. For the disinterested goatherd, Marcela is modest and virtuous; for the suffering Grisóstomo, she is cruel; for Ambrosio, who hates her for making his friend suffer, she is a "fiery basilisk"; and for Don Quijote, who is always alert to incitement in others and who is characteristically extreme in his enthusiasm, "she should be honored and esteemed by all good men in the world, for she has proved that she is the only woman living with such pure intentions" (I.14).

The variety of ways in which these conflicting views are expressed is also significant. As we listen to the speakers, we hear first a story, then a poem read aloud, then two antithetical harangues (Vivaldo's "j'accuse" and Marcela's "I was born free"), and finally Don Quijote's challenge and the poetic epitaph. From now on events, objects, and people will not be what they are (or are not) but as they seem to somebody who tells them and shapes them verbally in the act of telling. In *La Celestina* perspectivism was based on prejudiced preconception (for Calisto, Melibea is a goddess, while for Elicia, she is physically repulsive), but in the *Quijote*, as Spitzer points out, it is also linguistic.[36] Thus, Sancho's comic fusion of basin (*bacía*) and helmet (*yelmo*) into "baciyelmo." It may look like a basin, but he learned from experience its utility as a helmet when the stones thrown by the galley slaves were flying thick and fast. Without it, Sancho says, his master "would have had a hard time." We shall return to this hybrid noun later. At this point I only wish to present the death of Grisóstomo and its aftermath as evidence that the perspectiv-

36. Leo Spitzer, "Linguistic Perspectivism in *Don Quijote*," in his *Linguistic and Literary History* (Princeton, N.J.: Princeton University Press, 1948), pp. 41–73.

ism that differentiates the Second and Third Sallies from the
First Sally was initiated by the introduction of pastoral *topika*.
Along with comfortable seating and pleasant scenery, the incessant interchange of experiences and points of view in
story and song was a decisive contribution of the pastoral.

A major critic has proposed that Cervantes really wrote
two very different novels: the *Quijote* of 1605 and the *Quijote*
of 1615.[37] This is, as I see it, a foreshortened description of
the process of invention that takes place before our very eyes
as we read from chapter to chapter. The truth is that each of
the three sallies has its own peculiar anatomy, which despite
previous gestation is a spectacular innovation. We are talking
about nothing less than an almost incredible process of literary growth. After the initial clash of the picaresque and the
chivalresque, the pastoral skein functioned as a shock ab-
sorber and prepared the way (as we shall see in the final essay) for the introduction of recognizable patterns taken from
the theater, from Ariosto, from comic interludes (Cervantes's
most successful and appealing plays), and, at the end of the
Second Sally, from the Byzantine tale.[38] Then, at the beginning of the Third Sally, we are treated to the most unexpected
and "daring" (as Cervantes remarks wryly and proudly in
the Prologue to the *Exemplary Novellas*) invention of them all:
utilization of the previous two sallies themselves as a source
of *topika*, thereby freeing Don Quijote and Sancho from ser-
vitude to their creator-enchanter. But it was when the pastoral was added in chapter 9 that the tapestry began to ac-
quire the narrative richness we adore.

"You have an untutored ingenio*"*

Both the Cervantine metaphor of the narrator as a weaver-
inventor unwinding and recombining skeins drawn from the

---

37. Joaquín Casalduero, *Sentido y forma del "Quijote" (1605–1615)* (Madrid:
Insula, 1949).

38. In the so-called Captive's Tale, which comprises chapters 39–45, the
Byzantine pattern of Mediterranean wanderings, escapes, adventures, and
eventual reunion in perfect love is subtly combined in Cervantes's own memories of combat and captivity.

generic expectations of the reading public and the Stendhalian metaphor of the novelist as a musician drawing a melody from the soul of the individual reader challenge the familiar Romantic interpretation of the *Quijote* as a conflict of the real with the ideal. Indeed, since this view is based on a facile and mistaken identification of the chivalresque with the ideal and the picaresque with the real during the First Sally (and in such individual adventures in the Second Sally as that of the windmills), it is clearly misleading. As we shall see, if Cervantes himself had been asked to explain what the *Quijote* was about thematically, he would have replied (along with Mark Twain and every novelist in the tradition about their own works): the immediacy of its truth amidst falsehood. And now on our own initiative (leaving truth enclosed within parentheses) we may subdivide novelistic falsehood into illusion, delusion, outright prevarication, and the hypocritical commonplace beliefs and assertions of society.

Even these varieties of falsehood, however, are still abstract and ahistorical. In order to grasp the way Cervantes himself, as a man of arms and letters personally and patriotically concerned with the nexus of literature and life, understood the literary errors of his time, we must submit ourselves to a brief lesson in seventeenth-century critical theory. Specifically, we must venture to make a perhaps too rigid distinction between the two closely related (and often confused) notions of *inventiva* and *ingenio*, as Cervantes understood them. We must ask, What is the difference between the *Quijote*, as a cunning product of Cervantes's inventive skill, and the imitation romance of chivalry, which flows automatically and without impediment from the fervid fantasy of the "ingenious hidalgo"? What does the adjective *ingenioso* mean? On becoming acquainted with Don Quijote, we soon realize that the usual English translation of the title, "ingenious gentleman," is incorrect.[39] Rather, according to the Dictionary

39. Otis H. Green, in his "El *ingenioso* hidalgo" (*Hispanic Review* 25 [1957], pp. 175–93), having examined past English translations of the word, concludes that Robinson Smith's "the imaginative gentleman" (1910) is the most

of the Spanish Royal Academy, it refers to "the faculty in man for prompt and effortless discourse and invention." The "gentleman," in other words, is *ingenioso* because he has a natural and spontaneous gift for making things up—and, by extension, for falsehood.

In the sixteenth and seventeenth centuries, *el ingenio* and *la invención* were often used to signify two phases of the creative process. *Ingenio* engenders or generates *(engendra)*, while *invención*, governed by the understanding *(entendimiento)*, slowly and conscientiously gives artistic form and coherence to whatever was engendered.[40] Thus, Cervantes's

---

accurate. I, of course, agree. He then proceeds to explain Don Quijote's madness in terms of the theory of humors as presented by Dr. Juan Huarte de San Juan in his *Examen de ingenios* (Baeza, 1575). The matter has been discussed at length by scholars and seems to me more interesting and fruitful than the many anachronistic psychological and psychiatric treatments of the subject. However, it, too, is ultimately extraliterary and ignores the development of the living imagination and experience, which emerges from reading and which is our reading.

40. As those who have read *Examen de ingenios* know, Huarte de San Juan uses the term *ingenio* to refer to human mental ability and capacity in general and then subdivides it (causal humors aside) into categories corresponding to imagination, memory, and understanding (chapter 8), all of which are indispensable for "invention," understood in the postrhetorical sense. As a result, he does not confirm the above distinction between the two terms. However, if for our purposes we may confine *ingenio* (as it was used by the poets of the time) to the imaginative variety, the *Examen* is helpful. The initial problem posed is not unlike that of Cervantes: why do men "make so many different and particular judgements?" Why are there "so many different kinds of madnesses and follies?" If the world really seems to be an enormous "madhouse," what is the cause? The answer offered is, of course, the book itself, with its theory of humors affected by human ages, regions, climates, and (since the author was a traditional male chauvinist) gender. However, as we suggested in the previous note, the proffered explanation is less important than the notion of imaginative imbalance, which recurs time and again during the discussion. For example: "When a man of very vivid imagination comes to exercise his understanding, he appears to be ready for the straitjacket [*loco de atar*]" (chapter 1). Or again: "From heat imagination is born [and thus] everything that is said by delirious patients belongs to the imagination and not to understanding or memory" (chapter 8). And finally, in relation to poetry: "Aristotle tells us that [a certain poet] was better when he was out of his mind. And that is because the imagination peculiar to poetry needs so much intense heat that it vitiates understanding" (chapter 11). Is

fellow pioneer as a pre-Lope dramatist, Juan de la Cueva, in 1588 defines *ingenio* as "the soul and source of invention."[41] As for Cervantes himself, we have already heard him praise indirectly (via the Canon of Toledo, I.47), his talent for *ingeniosa invención.* And in the Prologue to the *Exemplary Novellas* he boasts in the first person that his *ingenio* engendered them, after which "his pen gave birth to them." In other words, it is indispensable to possess the gift of *ingenio,* but it must be guided and shaped by invention. Only in tandem can they produce the "subtle design" Mercury had praised when Cervantes approached Parnassus.

However, when, as in Don Quijote's mad romance of himself, *ingenio* is divorced from invention and allowed to run wild, only bizarre and arbitrary apparitions can be expected. Windmills will become giants, and herds of sheep, strange armies. In this sense the *Quijote* as a whole might validly have been understood by its contemporary readers as an immense and hilarious dialogue between the knight's unbridled *ingenio* (which, it goes without saying, was also that of Cervantes as an equally avid reader of romances of chivalry) and his author's inventive meditation.

As we detected from his remarks on *La Galatea* twenty

Don Quijote, then, ready for the straitjacket? Not at all, because he is one of those exceedingly rare *ingenios* who combine "much memory and much imagination" (chapter 8). As for Cervantes, he is one of those equally rare *ingenios* who "up to the age of sixty" should be "writers of books" (chapter 3) because they use their "memory to retain images for the moment when the understanding wishes to contemplate them"; that is to say, they use it "to infer, distinguish, and elect" (chapter 8).

41. Juan de la Cueva, *Ejemplar poético,* p. 127. Elsewhere he admits that "although it is true we know some / who only with their ingenio have merited fame . . . , excellent judgement" is also indispensable for lasting "grandeur," pp. 120–21. Here he seems more in accord with Juan de Valdés, Spain's first self-made Renaissance literary critic, who contrasts *ingenio* and invention, which "discover what to say," to judgment and composition, which choose the best of what is discovered and put it into its proper place (*Diálogo de la lengua,* ed. J. F. Montesinos [Madrid: Clásicos castellanos, 1928], p. 165). In any case, if the terminology is not consistent, the duality is— which is what matters for understanding the dialogue between Cervantes as "inventor" and Don Quijote as "*ingenioso.*"

years afterward, Cervantes, like other novelists (Fielding, Stendhal, Galdós, and Virginia Woolf at once come to mind), was engaged in a lifelong dialogue with himself and with his creations. Thus, when in 1605 he looked back over Part I of the *Quijote*, he realized that its humorous critique of the special category of *ingenio* classified by Dr. Juan Huarte de San Juan in his *Examen de ingenios* (1575) as imaginative could also be used to castigate the overprolific younger generations of poets and playwrights. The very fact that they referred to themselves as *ingenios* (not writers, but human incarnations of *ingenio*) resembled Alonso Quijano's mad self-reincarnation as Don Quijote. The result was *El viaje del Parnaso* (not only an at once rueful and complacent self-portrait but also a scathing continuation of the Scrutiny and the dialogue of the Canon of Toledo with the Priest), much of which consists of an attack on the literary inflation of those who followed in the footsteps of Lope de Vega, the so-called Phoenix of *ingenios*. Proud of their naturalness and facile spontaneity, these poetic upstarts irritated the deliberate inventor-weaver, who had finished Part I of his self-conscious and ironical tapestry.

Not only were these young pseudocelebrities brash and self-assured; they were also transient. They recited and published with "ligera consideración,"[42] that is to say, with careless *ingenio* and without inventive meditation. They prated of lasting fame, but in their impatience they were really more concerned with showing off to each other and with impressing their contemporary fans. The *Quijote*, on the contrary, was written with *entendimiento* (brains, or understanding), as Cervantes proudly informed the anonymous author of the apocryphal continuation in the Prologue to Part II. As a result, its future would be endless and limitless: "There would be no nation nor language in which it would not be translated" (II.3). This and similar predictions are, as usual, ironical and not to be taken seriously. As we shall see, Cervantes ruefully and hesitantly seems to have staked his immortality

42. Cervantes, Prologue to *La Galatea*.

as a poet on a very different sort of "epic in prose," the serious neo-Byzantine allegory (often funny in spite of itself) *Persiles y Sigismunda*. But even in the case of the *Quijote*, composed with such ingratiating pleasure, he would have objected strongly to Sir Philip Sidney's definition of invention as "Nature's childe, . . . fleeing stepdame Studie's blowes."[43] For him the only conceivable path through time was the meeting of minds.

The point is that in the Spain of Cervantes's late middle age the notion of the poet as a "natural" was carried to extremes unheard of in Sir Philip Sidney's England. Beginning roughly in the 1580s, Castilian society underwent—or produced—what can best be described as a volcanic eruption. Poets wrote copiously, recited implacably, and begat incessantly more and more of their kind (Cervantes describes them as swarming like bees[44]), and all taken together, they trace a steeply ascending curve of composition, recitation, and—though less vertiginous than in our own century because of the limitations of the handpress—publication. When compared to the exquisitely parsimonious poets who preceded them (Fernando de Rojas, Juan del Encina, Saint John of the Cross, Garcilaso de la Vega, Fernando de Herrera, and their fellows), these later generations of *ingenios* seemed literally to have become poetic machines dedicated to mass production. Just as in the case of the continuations of the *Amadís*, the initial patterns of rhetoric had been endlessly reproduced, and to a certain extent the same thing is true of the comedia and other Golden Age genres. But a far deeper preoccupation for Cervantes was the substitution of deceptively enchanting virtuosity for the search for genuine insight into the human condition that had characterized Spanish letters earlier in the century. It was to that quest that he was still deeply committed.

43. Sir Philip Sidney, *Astrophel and Stella*, ed. Mona Wilson (London: Nonesuch Press, 1931), p. 1.

44. The phrase from *El viaje* contains a hybrid term: "¡Cuerpo de mí con tanta *poetambre!*" (chapter 2), from *poeta* and *enjambre*, meaning "swarm."

Accordingly, when in the *Viaje del Parnaso* Cervantes stops talking about himself and turns his attention to his younger colleagues, he describes them as "absorbed" in their mad verbal "dreams" (chapter 1). Conversely, as Quevedo pointed out bitterly, at a time when Imperial preeminence was becoming more and more phantasmagoric, a world of empty words gradually was replacing the world of things.[45] The new poets thought of themselves as unique and marvelous fountains of *ingenio*, but for Cervantes, who had survived his wound and his captivity, who had failed as a writer and a bureaucrat, who foresaw the bleak literary and political future (for him they were not distinct) of his nation, and who was burdened with an accumulation of years, debts, and infirmities, they were a pack of born liars. Their substitution of irresponsible *ingenio* for conscientious invention was so spiritually poisonous that (like the prevarications of the foolish hero of *La verdad sospechosa*, a play by Cervantes's friend Juan Ruiz de Alarcón, adapted by Corneille in *Le menteur*) it "left truths themselves without credibility" (chapter 8).

This summary review of the well-known historical, biographical, and literary circumstances that contributed to what we would now call Cervantes's alienation is intended to suggest not only how he initially conceived of the "ingenioso hidalgo" (as a satirical representation of a special kind of national aptness for delusion) but also why as a playful "author" he alternately praises and pretends to denigrate himself. For example, when in the *Viaje* Cervantes calls himself an "ingenio lego" (chapter 6), the intention is not to confess lack of awareness of what he was up to or ignorance of rhetoric (as certain past critics believed) but rather to separate himself from the rest of the pack. In the Prologue to Part I of the *Quijote* we find the same false modesty: "What could my sterile and uncultivated *ingenio* engender but the history of a

45. See one of Quevedo's last letters, dated August 21, 1645, and addressed to Don Francisco de Oviedo, in *Epistolario completo de d. Francisco de Quevedo-Villegas*, ed. L. Astrana Marín (Madrid: Instituto Editorial Reus, 1946), p. 503.

parched, wrinkled, and capricious child?" And in the following paragraph: "After having spent so many years sleeping,
forgotten by all, in the silence of oblivion, I now emerge to
tell a story as dry as straw and foreign to invention."

At first, we are puzzled: why does our inventor, so proud
of himself elsewhere, pretend at this point in the Prologue to
be so humble? Evidently, irony is intended since, as we have
seen, he was not at all dissatisfied either with his *ingenio* or
with the capacity for invention that transformed it into art.
The tip-off is the sly attack on the canned erudition of Lope
de Vega, which was perceived by the first readers. But more
important than literary in-fighting was the combination of
facile pomposity (rather than genuine learning) with effortless effusion (rather than careful craftsmanship) that was
blighting not only the lyric poetry but also the drama and
prose of the period. Cervantes did admire Lope as a "monster of nature,"[46] but he scorned "the more than twenty thousand prematurely hatched" songbirds who followed in his
wake.[47] His own poetry, as we have heard him admit, may
have been lacking in certain respects, but these were "vain
and hollow apparitions" only comparable in the vegetable
kingdom to "gourds" (chapter 5). As for the *Quijote,* he knew
how good it was but not how it would be received. Later he
would proclaim its success and remark complacently that it
had "incited envy to declare war on him." But now when an
utterly unprecedented book was on the verge of meeting the
public, he sought to protect it with an ironical preemptive
strike. You may not like my stuff, the message reads, but let
me tell you, I am not a fake like so many others; nor am I in
a feverish delirium, like the person remarked on by Huarte
de San Juan, all of whose ravings emerged in rhyme (chapter 7).

There is a complementary passage within the text of Part I

46. In the Prologue to *Ocho comedias.* In the *Viaje del Parnaso,* however,
because of Lope's manifest jealousy of the *Quijote's* success, he reverses the
compliment ironically by terming envy a monster of nature (chapter 8).

47. The term used is "veinte mil sietemesinos" (chapter 1), or "born in
the seventh month."

of the *Quijote*, which reverses the irony of the Prologue and thereby reveals clearly how proud its ostensible modesty really is. As is not infrequent in that gallery of mirrors, a character refers to the author hypothetically—in this case as an *ingenio* so superbly gifted that his real existence taxes belief even more than the fictional variety of Don Quijote. We are in chapter 30, and the Curate is asking Cardenio (in one of his sane intervals) what he thinks of Don Quijote's madness:

> "Isn't it a strange thing to see with what ease this unfortunate hidalgo believes [Dorotea's] inventions [her unskillful lies while pretending to be the Princess Micomicona] only because they imitate the style and manner of his books?"
>
> "It is indeed so rare and unheard of," answered Cardenio, "that I can't imagine how there could exist an *ingenio* so cunning as to be capable of *inventing* such a thing on purpose and fabricating such a lie out of whole cloth." (italics mine)

Once again *invención* and *ingenio* have joined but with an added twist. Taken together in context, they question the supposedly absurd (but true!) proposition that there could possibly exist a flesh-and-blood author-liar so accomplished that he could make us believe in a believer sufficiently mad and naive as to swallow Dorotea's clumsy impersonation of an African princess in distress. And since in fact as readers we are used to believing in heroes far more unlikely than Don Quijote (indeed, we would believe in him all the more if such passages as this did not interrupt the process of identification), the sly suggestion is that the book might well be interpreted as a prodigious product of irresponsible and mendacious seventeenth-century *ingenio*. The reader who ignores the inventive skill of the "epic in prose" is the butt—not Cardenio or the Priest. The writer here knows and wants us to realize that if we read the text as a prevarication so enchanting that it cannot be disbelieved, we are as gullible as Alonso Quijano. Cervantes does not deny (as he has done in the Prologue) his undeniable gift for the kind of spontaneity that derives from *ingenio*. But, at the same time, he suggests that his inventive exploitation of it is far better than Dorotea's (not to mention the poetic "gourds") and that, therefore, we should not be as eager to believe as his hero. To fabricate a lie out of whole cloth and to fool candid dupes may take a lot of gall and a certain amount of rudimentary imagination, but it is not the same thing as genuine artistry. The nimbus of irony, which in the title surrounds the notion of *ingenio*, is here once again quite apparent.

"He who flees from verisimilitude cannot achieve these things"

So much for the curious literary variety of seventeenth-century falsehood that Cervantes intended primarily to confound. It is now time, if not yet to free truth from its parentheses, at least to try to comprehend Cervantes's carefully devised literary remedy. If the Scrutiny had been the only critical excursus in the text of Part I of the *Quijote*, we would only know from its fragmentary observations that in addition to parody and satire of the romances of chivalry, Cervantes proposed to "reform" the assembly-line fiction of the last hundred years and, at the same time, to salvage and reuse whatever was meritorious therein. Thus, for example, he praises *Tirante el Blanco* because, like Don Quijote, its hero eats and sleeps, but he also implies that inventively it is naive.[48] And although he thinks *La Diana* may be spared because it is written with "understanding" (*entendimiento* again!), he recommends amputation of its magical conclusion. Fiction as such may be a lie—that is the implication—

48. The reference is to what has been called the most obscure phrase of the *Quijote*: "Con todo eso, os digo que merecía el que lo compuso, pues no hizo tantas necedades de industria, que le echaran a galeras por todos los días de su vida" (I.6). Translated more or less literally, it means: "In conclusion, I declare to you that he who composed it, since he did not perpetrate so many follies cunningly, deserved to be sent to the galleys for all the days of his life." The wordplay with *galeras* (galley slave, galley proofs) is obvious in the forensic context of the Scrutiny; the real puzzle is presented by *necedades* and *de industria*. If *necedades* means "smut" and not "foolishness," as Riley proposes, Cervantes's comment may be interpreted as excusing with benevolent superiority the author's candor and lack of the ironical malice with which such matters are treated in the *Quijote*.

but it works better when it is a convincing, artistic lie, which is precisely what he intended to tell.

The Scrutiny, however, is not our only textual window into Cervantes's self-contemplation and self-congratulation as an inventor. At the end of the Second Sally the pattern of the First is repeated with a concluding section of meditation (chapters 47 through 50) on the nature of narration and the *grandeurs et misères* of literature as an institution. And this time—as becomes a writer, not on the verge of writing what would later be recognized as the world's first novel, but who has just accomplished that feat—Cervantes is far more explicit and confident. He now abandons all feigned self-deprecation and semijocular allusions to rivals and predecessors. Instead, in a dialogue between our old friend the Priest and a learned Canon (who meet on the road while the Priest is bringing the caged Don Quijote back to Argamasilla for the second time), he gives, among other literary judgments, an explicit (although incomplete, as we shall see) statement of his views on the poetics of prose fiction. Even though he could not foresee the immense influence his way of telling a story would have in the far future, the doctrine emergent from his recent creative experience has much to communicate to modern readers and students of the novel.

What does Cervantes conclude about what he had accomplished in Part I perhaps a week or so before he finished writing it? To begin with, he reaffirms that it is intended as an antidote to the narcotic habits for those addicted to daily doses of romances of chivalry. "I have read the beginnings of almost all that have been printed," says the discriminating Canon, "but I have never managed to read one right through. For they all seem to me more or less the same, and there is no more in one than in the other" (I.47). It is a confession that at this point tacitly amounts to advertisement of the *Quijote's* uniqueness. But what is even worse—according to this canonical rhetorician—is pseudochivalric violation of the rule of resemblance to truth, or verisimilitude, which was fundamental to Renaissance theories of composition: "And even though the principal aim of these books is to delight and not to teach, I do not know how they can succeed in doing so, seeing the monstrous absurdities with which they are filled." He then goes on to exemplify and elaborate:

> When they want to describe a battle, first they tell us that there are a million fighting men on the enemy's side. But, if the hero of the book is against them, inevitably, whether we like it or not, *we have to believe* that such and such a knight won the victory by the valor of his strong arm alone. . . . If you reply that the men who compose such books write them as fiction, and so are not obliged to look into fine points or truths, I should reply the more it resembles the truth, the better the lie, and yet at the same time the more provocatively doubtful or barely possible it is the better it pleases. Mendacious fables *ought to match the "entendimiento"* of their readers.[49] (italics mine)
>
> (I.47)

These remarks are not as ambiguous as they may sound today. Rather, they reinforce our previous contention that while certain episodes seem to justify the romantic opposition of the real and the ideal, Cervantes himself was primarily concerned with the effectiveness of fiction. When in the next sentence he equates verisimilitude with "imitation," he does not mean description of recognizable sensory data but rather the congruence (the "marriage," in Spanish) of the "lying fable" with the "mind" of a discriminating reader. Cunning combination of the adventurous marvel of the remotely possible with harmony and proportion was what was needed to entice a person such as the Canon "to read the book right through." Only the ignorant (the Innkeeper, his family, and the circle of open-mouthed reapers—of whom more later) and the hopelessly addicted (Alonso Quijano, Dorotea, and Cardenio) can create imaginary truth in the

---

49. A writer as concerned as we have seen Cervantes to be with his own *entendimiento* and with the lack of it in his colleagues naturally sought this quality in his unknown readers. It is the Cervantine version of Stendhal's "Happy Few." As early as the Prologue to *La Galatea* he proclaims that work was "composed" by his *entendimiento* for others, and at the end of the last chapter he promises a second part, which "will be seen and judged by the eyes and *entendimiento*" of the public.

process of identifying themselves with a hero or a lady during one totally absurd and disconnected episode after another. Entranced with the joy of naive belief, they do not demand that the narratives they adore possess borderline credibility or organic consequence.

The readers sought by Cervantes, on the contrary, were either those conceivably capable of education or those already gloomily overeducated—that is to say, those who, like himself, were or had been avid gourmands of the printed page but somehow found the diet unsatisfactory. The Canon begins by confessing to the Priest that he had "read, induced by idleness and perverted taste," the beginnings of almost all the romances of chivalry that had ever been printed. But he could not bring himself to believe that a single knight could rout an army, nor could he proceed from one adventure to another without some sense of the "shape of the whole." As a result, sooner or later he would inevitably find himself stranded on the shore of his discriminating but boring here and now. Any writer naturally embraces every possible reader, but he also must have in mind his personal answer to Sartre's "Pour qui écrit-on?" That of Cervantes is unambiguous: silent readers, at once satiated and addicted, who had been waiting, without being fully aware they were doing so, for what he was concerned to contrive.

The reading public was a century old. Among its members there had to be (as indeed there were) individuals capable of comprehending Cervantes's immensely daring and ambitious invention: a new, sophisticated form of fiction, in which skeins drawn from the three genres of their habitual reading could through a process of mutual interruption (thus the metaphor of weaving) compensate for each other's inherent unbelievability. The picaresque could bring the chivalresque and pastoral down to earth; the chivalresque could elevate the sights of the picaresque; and the pastoral, as we have seen, could allow the whole to take "harmonious" shape by providing a comforting narrative world in which the other two might at least partially coexist. The process of rhetorical invention, in other words, resulted in *an* invention: the *Qui-*

jote, itself, an exemplary literary lesson for an age of stampeding *ingenio* and farfetched falsehood.

Verisimilitude is, thus, not an end in itself. It is not a censorious or melancholy substitution of the real for the ideal, of the psychological for the typical, and, above all, of the humdrum for the outlandish. Cervantes did not propose to write *Eugénie Grandet, La princesse de Clèves,* or that pathetic novel entitled *Mr. Bailey, Grocer,* to which one of George Gissing's characters devoted his entire creative life. Verisimilitude—according to the prescription of Cervantes's surrogate and his well-known sources—has nothing to do with description of recognizable milieus, with psychological analysis, or with so-called real life. It is rather an invented sham credibility, which through malicious selection and cunning juxtaposition preserves the admiration, savor, and joy of old reading from its inherent generic foolishness and repetition.[50] Its aim is to enable mature readers to reexperience the pleasure of past surrender to their favorite romances without having to revert to second childhood. Like many of the greatest novels—*Adventures of Huckleberry Finn, Moby-Dick, La Chartreuse de Parme, Bleak House, Splendeurs et misères des courtisanes, Don Segundo Sombra, Cien años de soledad, War and Peace,* to mention but a few—the *Quijote,* with its intricate game of possibility and probability, with its engaging confluence of adventure and experience, is a juvenile classic for grown-ups—or, conversely, a grown-up classic for such exceptional children as Heinrich Heine, Gustave Flaubert, and Henri Beyle.

> *"Your grace will see how . . .*
> *these books . . . will improve your disposition . . ."*

After the Canon and the Priest finish their academic discussion, Cervantes uses a third interlocutor to pose a crucial

---

50. Don Quijote stresses admiration and suspense ("admiran" and "suspenden") in his defense of the romances of chivalry. Both constitute the rhetorical effects sought by Ariosto—as contrasted to the verisimilitude of the theorists—which he enjoyed teasing (see, for example, XXXVIII.33 and 34). For further cogent discussion, see Daniel Javitch, "*Cantus interruptus* in the *Orlando Furioso,*" *Modern Language Notes* 85 (1980), pp. 66–80.

question to which the *Quijote* as a whole constitutes the implicit answer. This new critic is the caged knight, and the question is simply: how can self-conscious, make-believe believability be used to preserve a delight that depends on unquestioning acceptance of everything that is on the page? Don Quijote's splendidly moving defense of the sheer elation and the spiritual therapy of reading had not been taken seriously by critics prior to Alban Forcione, who interprets Don Quijote's "sensuous pleasure" in the "disordered order" of his fanciful account of the adventure of the lake as a Baroque reply to the Canon's Renaissance poetics.[51] The stylistic analysis on which the interpretation is based is acute, but the conclusion fails to illuminate what seems to me to be the real subject of the debate: the relation of reading to living.

As far as the romances of chivalry are concerned, the Canon finds himself at a vital impasse. His mind and his imagination are hopelessly at odds. Although he reproaches Don Quijote (referring to him as "señor hidalgo," the status that society had conferred on him, not the status that he had conferred on himself) for succumbing to a "disgusting and idle" genre, he confesses for the second time that he, too, had read such books with pleasure. It is only when he "realizes" that their ability to infect lives with fake identities resembles heresy that he throws them against the wall or into the nearest fire. The Inquisitional solution is, of course, not a solution at all but rather an abolition of the problem, which Cervantes, as we shall see in the next essay, was far from advocating. The Canon had earlier tried to write a new romance restrained in the straitjacket of formal harmony and verisimilitude, but, he informs the Priest, it had not worked out:

> For my part I have been somewhat tempted to write a book of chivalry observing all the points I have mentioned. To tell you the truth, I have written more than a hundred pages. And to see if they corresponded to my estimation of them, I have

---

51. Alban Forcione, *Cervantes' Aristotle and the "Persiles"* (Princeton, N.J.: Princeton University Press, 1970), pp. 107–24.

shown them to those who are passionate devotees of that kind
of reading—both to those who are learned and possess good
judgement and to those whose pleasure comes from absurdities, and from all of them I received welcome approval; but,
for all that, I have not continued.

(I.48)

The Canon's explanation of his lack of perseverance is unconvincing in view of his complacency and his professorial
pleasure at the sound of his own voice. In the first place, he
says, it was a task unfitting to his profession, and in the second place, "because I found that the ignorant were more numerous than the wise, and, although it is worthwhile to be
praised by the wise, to be misunderstood by a crowd of fools
is not.[52] I do not wish to subject myself to the muddled judgement of the empty-minded populace who are generally given
to reading such books." In the context of the *Quijote*, however, a more imperative reason is apparent. As Cervantes
knew, and as any fool of an innkeeper could have told the
wise Canon, verisimilitude thoughtfully and artistically
transplanted into the organism of a romance of chivalry could
be liable to speedy rejection.[53] To insist on believability for
such tales might well result in a lack of appeal and eventual
disbelief. Indeed, as the case of Alonso Quijano demonstrates, the less lifelike the fictional event, the more one en-
joys believing it and the more one needs to believe it.

The Canon makes this very point ("we have to believe that

52. The Canon uses the past participle of the semantically equivocal verb
burlar: he does not wish to be "burlado de los muchos necios." Most translators render this as "to have given fools the pleasure of reading nonsense," or
as something similar. This translation, I think, is mistaken, first because the
Canon surely would not refer to his reformed romance as "nonsense," and
second because *burlar* usually means "to make fun" or "to fool" someone (as
does the *burlador* of Seville, Don Juan) rather than "to have fun." Thus, J. M.
Cohen has the Canon "mocked" by fools who presumably do not understand
his art. My own choice would be "misinterpreted by fools," since *burlar* also
means "to copy" or "to reproduce" more or less exactly. That is to say, the
Canon does not wish to be reproduced inadequately in their reading.
53. The author of *Tirante el Blanco* gets away with it, from Cervantes's
point of view, precisely because, unlike the Canon, he is both naive and
funny.

such and such a knight won the victory"), but without real-izing what he has really said. Indeed, the more one thinks of his discourse in its Quixotesque context, the more his literary doctrine seems incomplete. He has not given us a clue either to Cervantes's inventive (today we would say intertextual) play with printed genres or to what we shall see to be his ironical reassignment of responsibility for verisimilitude. The Canon is academic, even slightly pompous, and it is precisely his lack of irony that disqualifies him as the official spokes-man of his author. It is, in fact, his bloodless solemnity that opens the way both for Don Quijote's insanely funny disqui-sition on the historicity of chivalry and for his eloquent dis-course on the joys of believing the impossible in chapter 1. He who in reading identifies himself with a fictional knight "finds himself in flowery fields . . . where the sky is more transparent and the sun shines with new radiance. . . . Oh, sir," he concludes, "believe me; read these books and you will see how they will send into exile whatever melancholy may afflict you and how they will improve your disposition if it should perchance be in bad straits" (I.50).

The significance of Don Quijote's rebuttal can only be com-prehended in terms of the speaker—an inveterate reader de-fending what he loves best of all. The rhetorical strictures of the Canon do indeed constitute the doctrine Cervantes had learned, accepted, and applied in the *Quijote*—insofar as in it he eliminates the utterly incredible and skillfully weaves its pattern of episodes into an artistic whole. Yet at the same time Cervantes knew that he had created a strange, buoyant, life-giving book that Renaissance critical theory could not possibly account for. He had preserved and immeasurably enhanced that century-old joy called reading. As a devotee of the printed page, he had banished our melancholy and improved our disposition, and in a way far more profound than chivalresque submersion (Don Quijote's anticipation of Ortega's metaphor is no coincidence!) in the "flowering fields" beneath the "fearful lake." In the *Quijote* learned lit-erary prescription not only confronts and frowns pedanti-cally on the new practice of unregenerate silent reading but also, and in spite of itself, enables those addicted to such reading to experience a vital self-renewal that humanists could only describe. Theory and practice, neoantique ratiocination and *moderna voluptas*, in these chapters encounter each other in the same fashion as wrestlers embrace. What one meditates on critically and what the other creates imaginatively are at once independent and interdependent, and the result is nothing less than a book christened *Don Quijote de la Mancha*.

The Canon had only proposed to "match" the minds of discriminating and sophisticated readers who were "learned and possessed good judgement." Cervantes, however, knowing, from personal surrender to print, the literate vulnerability (and, from personal experience, the social predicaments[54]) of all those who might purchase or borrow his book, intended to commune ironically with each one in the course of overhearing together how Don Quijote and Sancho speak their minds in what George Bernard Shaw would have termed the endlessly entertaining continuity of dialogue that consoles their odd and homeless domesticity. The mad reader and his illiterate companion would—without know-

54. Most biographers either are not aware of or prefer to ignore the not too remote "stains" in Cervantes's lineage. The evidence is circumstantial but abundant. To begin with, the *ciervo*, or "deer," in his name is a variant on the animal nomenclature that along with place and saintly names was often used at the moment of conversion and baptism—for example, the surname Cerf in France. Then there are the five physicians (as is well known, a typical profession of Spanish Jews and *conversos*) in his family. But most important are the sardonic references in the *Quijote* and elsewhere to the national myth of cleanliness of blood. He may have loved Sancho, but he was merciless with Old Christianity as such, and those who claimed that variety of social preeminence were equally (and more dangerously) merciless with those whom they suspected of being *ex illis*. For further discussion and evidence see Castro's *Cervantes y los casticismos*, cited previously. These origins, of course, mean nothing in themselves, although they did lead Salvador de Madariaga, who was the first to discuss the matter, to propose foolishly that Cervantes was a Sephardic Jew ("Cervantes y su tiempo," *Cuadernos* 40, 1960). What is important is to comprehend the social situation of an educated man who was above all a patriotic Spaniard, who on his return from the Mediterranean wars, where soldiers were judged by their prowess, found an ingrown genealogy-crazed society, which made no worthy place for him and which he perforce contemplated from an ironical distance.

ing it, for such is the nature of irony—serve as a superconductor between the author and each one of us. Cervantes's reading, Alonso Quijano's reading, and our reading do indeed coalesce in such a way as to improve our disposition immeasurably. To say the same thing in another way, what Cervantine irony does, and was intended to do (as against the mass catharsis of Sophoclean irony or the elite pessimism of *La Celestina*), is to convert a collective public unhealthily avid for naive escape into individuals who not merely would learn good judgement in his company but, far more important, would experience the spiritual therapy both of adventure and of laughter at adventure. A brand new internalized version of Horace's antique *ridendo castigat mores!*

But what is it exactly that we commune ironically about? Countless books and articles have been written to explore the widely varying reactions to the *Quijote* of successive centuries, foreign societies, and such individual readers as Fielding, Dickens, and Mark Twain. But from the elementary standpoint of literary satire, all of us have one thing in common with Cervantes's contemporaries. In the First Sally we laugh along with the narrator at the folly of his fiction-prone, addle-pated knight-errant. In the Second, however, when, as we have seen, the addition of the pastoral skein makes us increasingly aware that the process of fictional invention involves us directly as readers, we—and Cervantes, too—begin also to laugh at ourselves.

We are led to remember all of the absurd printed fiction (whether chivalresque, picaresque, and pastoral or their latter-day descendants that swarm in drugstores and airports) we have swallowed whole without gagging. As habitual readers, we, too, have been miniature replicas of Alonso Quijano. But it is not only a question of self-criticism and literate therapy. Our very amusement at our role in the fictional process not only recaptures and excuses lost transport but also adds to it an increment of consciousness and distance that makes it all the more exquisite. Cervantine invention, with its ironical play with conventional literary patterns, has provided us with that "conscience dans le mal" that Baudelaire felt to be the essence of pleasure. Or, as Cervantes phrased it less perversely, what began as literary satire has been transformed into a marvelous "pastime for the melancholy or moody breast."

In prescribing the *Quijote* for any "melancholy or moody breast" (in the *Viaje del Parnaso*) and any romance of chivalry as a remedy for the Canon's ailing disposition (in Don Quijote's rebuttal), Cervantes sends us a disguised but simple message. In indirect confrontation with Renaissance pedantry he tells us that we really need not worry ourselves about details of verisimilitude and harmony—that, accordingly, we should relax and enjoy his gift of good reading as much as Alonso Quijano had enjoyed his flawed reading. It would be wrong to call it bad, because reading as such is good, and even better if we know what we are about. The Canon had only wanted to reach the *entendimiento* of the ex-future readers of his unfinished novel, whereas Cervantes demands not only their understanding but their "disposition."

In other words, what centuries later would still be called the rhetoric of fiction is none of our business. Cervantes has taken care of it in the act of composition. Therefore, we do not need to worry about the probability, the possibility, or the facilitated impossibility of the *Quijote*. As in the case of *Dead Souls, La Chartreuse de Parme, Moby-Dick, Misericordia, Cien años de soledad,* or *Splendeurs et misères des courtisanes,* the act of reading frees us from that irksome responsibility. Our very awareness of the fictitious quality of the narrative keeps us from having to throw it against the wall or into the fire. And to the question, Why, then, chapters 48 and 49, with all their insistence on how properly to write a romance? I should have to answer, first, that Cervantes as a critic was deeply concerned with methods he was trying out for the first time in prose fiction; and second, that verisimilitude is not only a rhetorical recipe for composition (which, of course, it is) but Cervantes's principal subject. Unlike the lives we relive in the nineteenth-century novels just mentioned (in which the "reality" of self and world is usually taken for granted), the peculiarity of Don Quijote and Sancho is their constant preoc cupation with their own novelistic condition: the probability, the possibility, and the facilitated impossibility of themselves and all that they encounter.

"Those shapes which appear over there"

The reader's unremitting and delighted awareness of the fictionality of the *Quijote* (exacerbated by Cervantes's constant tickling of that awareness) has an until then unprecedented effect on the two protagonists. They, of course, do not think of themselves as fictional but as alive and real: "'I know who I am,' replied Don Quijote, 'and I know who I can be'" (I.5), while Sancho, whose identity is resolutely singular ("Sancho I was born, and Sancho I intend to die") is equally proud of the unambiguous layers of Old Christian fat that cover his *panza*.[55] And yet, for all that confidence, the *chemin* of their lives is traced quite maliciously through one of the strangest artificial habitats ever to have been created: a basin-helmet world in which nothing is certain and all those things a realistic novelist would call *vrai* (windmills, cruel farmers, rural manor houses) serve only as the webbing for the varied literary skeins of the tapestry. If Don Quijote and Sancho had been creatures of the Canon's aborted romance, they would have known where they stood and how to handle his domesticated adventures, but in the world invented by Cervantes it is they who must "see and make out" the ceaseless kaleidoscope of questionable "shapes which appear over there" (I.7), wonder together what they portend, and cope with them as best they can. Cervantes has turned over the problem of verisimilitude to the knight and squire, as if they were their own authors.

Critics have noticed this transformation in connection with such key adventures as Don Quijote's descent into the Cave

55. *Panza*, of course, means "paunch." Cervantes maliciously converts the commonplace reverence for cleanliness of blood into cleanliness of fat when Sancho boasts about the "four fingers of Old Christian blubber" protecting his midriff (II.4).

of Montesinos or Sancho's ascent to the heavens on Clavileño (after which each doubts the verisimilitude of the other's tall story). But I would maintain that this constant and imperative need of interpretation is precisely what makes the *Quijote* a novel from the beginning of the Second Sally until the end of the book. It was this need that the future genre was to adapt in ever new ways. Don Quijote and Sancho are heroes (meaning extreme human examples) confronting the day-to-day challenge of a world of far more deceptive novelties, appearances, and ambiguities than that in which we ourselves live and which we believe to be real. As readers submitted to more or less humdrum circumstances, we nevertheless recognize in their lives an intensified (Castro would say "incited") representation of the process of our own daily encountering, wondering, concluding tentatively, and coping hopefully. Verisimilitude has been used not only to match the demand of our minds for harmony and proportion and to facilitate our belief; more importantly, doubt and interrogation are the substance of the unprecedented Quixotesque and Sanchesque dialogue that increasingly enchants us as we read from page to page and from episode to episode. All of this amounts to a tacit declaration of independence, of which the first article is a guarantee of free speech.

In chapter 1, "Definition," we described the language of the novel as resulting from the fusion of speech with print, of silent reading with the otherness that is expressed in the words, rhythm, and intonation of spoken language. It was precisely this revolutionary rapprochement that Cervantes "came upon" when he transferred the responsibility for verisimilitude from himself as the author to the two protagonists in their novel-long continuity of dialogue. Let us again look back briefly and consider the traditions available to Cervantes before he began. On the one hand, there were the *Amadís* and its successors, which had enthralled and bemused Alonso Quijano with their unadulterated adventure, with the capacity of the printed page to narrate silently the breathless "and then . . . and then . . ." of sheer marvel. As for the dialogue therein, it was sparse and as stilted and conventional as that of pastoral monologues. On the other hand, there were *El Corbacho* (1438) and *La Celestina* (1499), which had inaugurated self-conscious exploration of the creative possibilities of writing spoken Spanish in prose.[56] As we pointed out earlier, these are books designed for reading aloud, books that demand skilled oral imitation of the accents and intonation of the speakers on the page.[57] Thus, if Amadís is the printed and programmed prisoner of the impatient narrative of his sorrows, challenges, and triumphs, Celestina, Melibea, and the rest of the cast are the tragicomic victims of their own decelerated elocution. In the *Quijote*, however, where the two are synthesized and genuine speech is read silently, interpretation of the world and self-discovery (on the part of both the speakers and the readers) are expressed in kaleidoscopic dialogue. We and the two immortal clowns live and experience together in oral freedom.

Freedom of speech has as its inevitable corollary freedom of choice. The endless problem of reconciling illusion with impossibility, possibility with probability, has the gift of liberating Don Quijote and Sancho both from the narrative control of the author and, little by little, from the tyranny of their own roles. The solitary knight of the First Sally is doubly enslaved: on the one hand, by the tale in the third person and the past tense ("he did this"; "he thought that"); and on the

56. Previously, spoken Spanish (as in the case of other modern languages) had been the vehicle for a wide variety of oral poems (epics and ballads) as well as for other poems written in verse for reading aloud (for example, the thirteenth-century miracles and saints' lives of Gonzalo de Berceo), while prose was primarily a more or less syntactically developed code for imparting information (chronicles, laws, how-to texts) or dispensing moral advice (apologues, fables, epistles). There was even a fictional history of an exemplary knight, "el caballero Cifar," whose Sancho-like squire, "el Ribaldo," eventually ascends in rank and becomes an equally exemplary chivalric companion-in-arms. What is crucial to the possibility of the *Quijote*, however, is not this presumptive antecedent but rather the prior existence of a tradition of written dialogue and monologue—exclaimed from the heart or directed to an auditor—on every level of decorum from *Umgangsprache* to high-flown rhetoric. Almost a century before Rabelais, Spanish writers were preparing the way for the novel by experimenting with ironically "overheard" aural realism.

57. See chapter 1, note 9.

other hand, as we remember, by having to speak and act exactly like Amadís. But with the development of the process of invention in the course of the Second Sally, both characters increasingly live in the apparently free, spoken present of their comic arguments and rueful reconciliations. At the same time, the constant necessity of making sense or finding meaning in a half-and-half world, where peasant goatherds commingle with shepherds from pastoral romance and where more or less unfamiliar new inventions for exploiting natural energy either look like giants or convert gentle darkness into dreadful night,[58] infects them with its ambiguity. The more they are forced to interpret, the more the simpleton begins to seem unaccountably wise and the madman unaccountably reasonable. Here is the really unprecedented capability of the invention: the literary self-consciousness that the author induces in the reader gives birth to the independent and ever-changing self-consciousness of the two protagonists.

Much critical meditation has been devoted to the paradoxical freedom of fictional characters both in this novel and in others.[59] It is a commonplace of Cervantine criticism to explain how the author of the *Quijote* was the first to create—or contrive—what are called autonomous characters, in two giant steps. The first is, of course, the step taken in chapter 9 of Part I: Cervantes's abdication of his responsibility for his own inventiveness by returning that proud passport to Parnassus to its etymology. As we have seen, the text of the "first author" comes to an abrupt end because of a lack of "sources," and the "second author," adopting the role of fel-

58. Cervantes clearly enjoyed the juxtaposition of his own process of literary invention with the mechanical inventions of the time. Later the pair will encounter water mills (II.29), and Don Quijote will visit a printing establishment (II.62).

59. The classic essay for Hispanists is J. E. Gillet's "The Autonomous Character in Spanish and European Literatures," *Hispanic Review* 24 (1956), pp. 179–90. Further bibliography may be found in the revised edition of Américo Castro's *Pensamiento de Cervantes*, ed. J. Rodríguez Puertolas (Madrid: Noguer, 1972), p. 108. Castro himself has a provocative essay, "Cervantes and Pirandello," in *An Idea of History*, pp. 15–22.

low reader (which, of course, he is), literally comes upon (and then enters into) the rest of the text by chance in the street. Aside from the multiple possibilities for creative interruption thereby provided, what matters to our present discussion is the fact that the new-old author, Cide Hamete, is vehemently suspected of lying, which is in itself a means of liberation. Don Quijote and Sancho (along with the reader) from now on will have to rely on themselves for determination of the truth.

The second, and equally noteworthy, act of emancipation occurs when the two—by this time old friends—discover as they are preparing to set out on their Third Sally (Part II, published ten years later) that mysteriously a book has already been written about their past adventures. Cervantes and his readers, as we said, together convert their best beloved reading (Part I) into a new *topikon* and thereby further intensify Don Quijote's and Sancho's sense of the reality of their life together in contrast with the fictitiousness of its story. They now are more convinced than ever that they are free to determine whatever it is they wish to do: for example, to go to Barcelona instead of to the jousts at Zaragoza as they had planned and as Cervantes had intended.[60] Don Quijote had begun by freeing himself from the monotonous role of village hidalgo; then the supposed unreliability of Cide Hamete freed him in our minds from subservience to his author; and

60. At the end of Part I "the author of this history" hints at things to come in Part II by remarking that while he cannot find any "authentic facts" about the Third Sally, "fame has left a tradition in La Mancha that Don Quijote . . . went to Zaragoza and was present in a famous tournament in that city and there he met challenges worthy of his valor and excellent *entendimiento*" (I.52). However, when the knight learns in II.60 that his unworthy double (a spurious Don Quijote created by Cervantes's unidentifiable rival in an apocryphal Part II that appeared in 1614) did compete in those jousts, he avails himself of his "autonomy." In order to prove "to the world" that he is the only authentic version of himself, he decides on his own to go to Barcelona instead. Not only does Part I exist in the minds of the characters and readers of Part II but also its malicious imitation. For a brief comparison in English of the two Part IIs see my "The Apocryphal *Quijote*," in *Cervantes Across the Centuries*, ed. Angel Flores and M. J. Benardete (New York: Dryden, 1947), pp. 246–53.

now even the door to his cage of print has been unlocked. He and Sancho now can be themselves in any way they choose—and their behavior as a result often seems to come as a surprise, as when the translator judges Sancho's speech to his wife to be apocryphal, or when Cide Hamete puzzles over the truth or falsehood of Don Quijote's adventures in the Cave of Montesinos.

Such ironical play with autonomy has diverted readers over the centuries; in Spain it was imitated by two of the *Quijote*'s most fervent admirers—by Galdós in *El amigo Manso* and by Unamuno in *Niebla*. There is a difference, however. Both Galdós and Unamuno employ the device in order to meditate novelistically on free will and determinism, whereas Cervantes uses these two overt proclamations of emancipation to call our attention to the genuine freedom that is inherent in his narrative invention. Once verisimilitude is transformed from a rhetorical recipe into the central problem for the inhabitants of the fiction, they are necessarily on their own. In this sense the *Quijote* may be thought of as not only the first but also one of the most subversive novels ever written. Mickey Mouse was banned first by Hitler and then by Stalin as an impudent symbol of defiant freedom, but had they read it and understood it, both dictators would have found the *Quijote* far more menacing. To relive the lives of Don Quijote and Sancho (as did Samuel Clemens and Henri Beyle) is to accept the challenge to break our own chains, the enmeshment of our biographies with the fictions imposed on them by society: honors, promotions, medals, bank accounts, superstitions, conventions, commonplace beliefs, class distinctions, and the rest. As Virginia Woolf implied, the ultimate justification of the genre invented by Cervantes is that it may enable us "to work ourselves free."[61]

61. See chapter 1, note 45. Castro and others have stressed that one of the principal themes of the book is its celebration of freedom—not the idea of liberty, but the quest for personal liberation engaged in by those who matter: Don Quijote, Marcela, Don Diego's son, etc. See, for example, Américo Castro, "An Introduction to the *Quijote*," in *An Idea of History*, p. 96.

*"I, although I may seem to be
the father, am the stepfather of Don Quijote"*

If the benefits of this invention include the release of both the readers and the characters from temporal and social captivity, what advantage does it bring to the inventor? Is he only a great emancipator, or does he, too, participate in the *Quijote*'s heady access to freedom? The Canon, as we remember, answers these questions by pointing out that once the strait-jackets of the *Amadís,* the *Diana,* and the *Guzmán* are ripped apart at the seams, the narrator can alternate their several generic points of view, "because the free composition of such works allows the writer to show himself as a master of the epic, the lyric, the tragic, and the comic" (I.47). The Canon seems to mean that the author not only can tell his "epic" story but also, by adapting the dialogue form of the drama, can reach lyrically into what Cervantes called in the Prologue to the *Ocho comedias* "the imagination and hidden thoughts of the soul."

In pastoral romances such so-called moral figures express themselves directly in stilted monologues, but in the kind of reconstituted narratives we now call novels, they come alive in print as they speak to each other. The typical chivalresque romance was mostly a third-person narration of one stereotypical adventure after another; the picaresque was a sordid and seemingly endless *ich-Erzählung;* but now all three, cunningly compounded and leavened with paired dialogue (Don Quijote and Sancho, Cipión and Berganza, Rinconete and Cortadillo[62]), offer hitherto unsuspected creative freedom.

---

62. The last two pairs are included in order to suggest that the invention of Sancho not only provided the possibility of the Second Sally but also dialogic leavening for those *Exemplary Novellas* that were written during or after the composition of Part I. Carriazo and Avendaño, the two aristocratic picaros of "La ilustre fregona," are a third example. These two "incited" young men of high station find freedom in social descent, in contrast to the village hidalgo, who is regarded as bumptious by the local caballeros for seeking his own freedom in a fictitiously noble incarnation of their own degenerate rank. Even more than the myths of cleanliness of blood and peasant honor, the presumptuous pride and power of the so-called grandees (who had nothing

Diderot, Fielding, and Wieland[63] were to play with the same
pattern with illustrated irony, but until Samuel Clemens lost
and found himself in the dialogue of Huck and Jim, nobody
(not even Dickens in *The Pickwick Papers*) came close to Cervantes's gift for pairing and revealing lives in speech.

An additional freedom particularly stressed by the Canon
is the seemingly limitless choice of subject matter suddenly
available to the author's imitation divinity. In an earlier portion of his discourse to the Priest, it appears (as has been
noticed by the critics) as if the Canon were writing a book-
jacket blurb not for the *Quijote* but for Cervantes's last major
narrative creation, the strange and pretentious Byzantine allegory entitled *The Toils of Persiles and Sigismunda* (*Historia de
los trabajos de Persiles y Sigismunda*):

> Yet—he continued—in spite of all he had said against such
> books, he found one good thing in them: the fact they offered
> a good intellect [that *entendimiento* Cervantes found lacking in
> the author of the spurious Part II] a chance to display itself.
> For they offered a broad and spacious field through which the
> pen could run without hindrance describing shipwrecks, tem-
> pests, encounters and battles, now painting a brave captain
> with all the features necessary for the part, . . . now a beauti-
> ful lady chaste, intelligent, and modest. . . . Sometimes the
> writer might show off his knowledge of astrology or his excel-
> lence at cosmography or music, or his wisdom in affairs of
> state, and he might even have the opportunity of showing his
> skill in necromancy.
>
> (I.47)

---

to show for themselves but their clothes, their possessions, and their lineage)
was, as indicated earlier, the major target of the book's criticism of society.
As Castro points out in *Cervantes y los casticismos*, these, along with certain
sectors of the ecclesiastical establishment, were Cervantes's own "giants" (p.
177).

63. We have already mentioned the first two. Christoph Martin Wieland's
Don Sylvio von Rosaura, in which fairy tales (as in Michael Ende's *Die unend-
liche Geschichte*) substitute themselves Germanically for romances of chivalry,
is a pleasing imitation not of the "manner" of Cervantes but directly of the
Quijote.

Here, just as in the case of verisimilitude, the Canon's poetics of the novel is at once enlightening and incomplete. His
breathlessly enthusiastic paean to narrative freedom is in its
own way an anticipation of the creative scope of such novels
as *Fortunata y Jacinta, War and Peace, Nostromo, Os Maias,* and
Moby-Dick, not to mention such more recent epics in prose as
Terra nostra, U.S.A. and *The Flounder.* Albert Thibaudet in his
brilliant *Le liseur de romans* gives the impression that he has
just finished reading chapter 47: "The novel is like a drawer
into which the contents of the pocket can be emptied. . . .
Tragedy, comedy, political pamphleteering, history, . . . tears,
laughter, everything can and should be present in a novel."[64]

Yet this is only half or a quarter of the story. As against the
Persiles, in which the characters are bound to a "moral" allegory from which autonomous "hidden thoughts" are excluded, in the *Quijote,* as we have just seen, the knight and
the squire possess their own complementary—however
painful—freedom to wander across "broad and spacious
fields" trying to comprehend all they encounter. As Américo
Castro concluded almost half a century after writing the book
that initiated his serious concern with Cervantes's achievement, "Novelistic characters, up till that time entirely programmed, shed their programs and launched themselves
into the liberty of fields open to all, each one in his own way
and according to his particular incitement."[65]

Thus it was that the *Quijote,* which Cervantes feared might
be considered merely an "entertainment," and not the *Persiles*
on which he wagered his immortality,[66] became the world's

64. Thibaudet, *Le liseur de romans,* p. 25.
65. The citation is from a personal letter to me from Castro. In "Cómo
veo ahora al *Quijote,*" the marvelous preface to the "Editorial magisterio español" edition (Madrid, 1971), he remarks even more incisively: "In literary
works prior to the *Quijote* the literary personage met all sorts of obstacles and
adversities, but we know of none in which the central theme consists of the
convention of someone who has chosen his own identity and those who are
determined to deprive him of it" (p. 65).
66. In the Prologue to the *Exemplary Novellas* Cervantes announces the

first and most durable novel. And thus it is that those of us who still read novels are still "Cervantine creatures." Just as in the case of verisimilitude, in that of narrative freedom the discrepancy between the Canon's theory and Cervantes's practice is due quite clearly to the understandable limitations of literary theory at the time. The achievement of the *Quijote*—as its author knew intuitively but not with critical complacency—is the everlasting possibility it offers of reliving immensely enhanced human lives in all their simplicity and complexity. "Death," Don Quijote's enemy and virtual assassin, Sansón Carrasco, has to admit at the very end, "did not triumph over his life with his death."[67]

As far as a theory of the novel as a genre is concerned, the Canon's hybrid formulation "epic in prose" was repeated by most critics (including Schelling and Friedrich von Schlegel) until about three generations ago, when Hermann Cohen, Georg Lukács, and others began to meditate seriously on such reading. However, Cervantes, who probably would have been surprised if he had been told that what was for him a unique invention would, like the *Amadís*, propagate its kind indefinitely, seems to have sensed its insufficiency. As a result, in the Prologue to Part I he proposes a metaphor of his own, which is suggestive from our present point of view: "I, although I may seem to be the father, am the stepfather of Don Quijote."

Here is an assertion Cervantes surely would not have made about Persiles and Segismunda. In their allegorical neo-Byzantine romance (in which, as suggested, he only exploits the Canon's external freedom) all the characters, like good children, obey paternal rhetoric. Precisely because they

---

forthcoming publication of that strange narrative with his customary rueful mixture of skepticism and pride: "If my life does not abandon me, I shall present to you *The Toils of Persiles*, a book that dares to compete with Heliodorus, unless, because of its sheer daring, it be shooed out of doors with its hand on its head." Once again, the book is a person who may be rejected by the reader like a drunk being thrown out of a tavern.

67. In the epitaph in verse, II.74.

were created by the rules and for a didactic purpose, he expected a great deal more of them than do skeptical and cruel stepfathers. But what did Cervantes mean exactly in so describing his relationship with the knight who was eventually to be the indispensable visa on his passport to Parnassus? Ostensibly, he is continuing that mock-modest mockery of himself as an inventor which begins in the Prologue and culminates in chapter 9 when he tells us he "came upon" the rest of the book in an Arabic manuscript. Cide Hamete is the author-father in truth and in falsehood, and Cervantes is only the stepfather. Whatever is wrong or untrue about the book—he goes on to say in the Prologue—is not his fault, and he has no need to beg the reader's indulgence "with tears in my eyes, as others do."

In the world of the *Quijote,* however, it is safe to say that whatever is ostensible is by definition untrustworthy. Therefore, it is licit to suspect that this curious kinship metaphor also alludes to that expulsion into a shelterless and hostile world that in remote homage to the myth of Genesis constitutes the core of epic, romance, and novel—in Spanish, from the *Poema del Cid* through the *Amadís* and *Lazarillo de Tormes* to *Martín Fierro, Don Segundo Sombra,* and, most recently, Juan Goytisolo's *Juan sin tierra* and Carlos Fuentes's *El gringo viejo,* the titular hero of which carries the *Quijote* in his knapsack.

Cervantes hints at this further meaning at the end of the Second Sally in the Captive's Tale. The Captive (a wish-persona who represents Cervantes's years in Algerian captivity) recalls a statement by his father just before sharing his fortune with his children and sending them with that protection out into the world: "From now on I wish you to understand that I love you like a father and have no wish to destroy you like a stepfather" (I.39). The verb *destruir* seems significant in the case of the *Quijote.* Not only is the liberation of the knight and squire a matter of ironical abdication of authority and of ironical emergence from a previous book, but far more painfully it is the work of a hidden author who challenges his stepchild's incitation (the illusory vocation that impels him to carry his mirror along the road) with all sorts of apparently arbitrary mistreatment—practical jokes, pitfalls, barriers, beatings, and every other sort of mental and physical discomfort.

Fathers—particularly the literary fathers of the time, such as the ones remembered by the Captive, Don Diego de Miranda, and Don Beltrán in Alarcón's *La verdad sospechosa*—are supposed to attempt solicitously to direct the footsteps of their offspring into safe paths leading toward honor and fortune. But the stepfather (like Lazarillo's blind first master) contrives liberty through daily mistreatment, the kind of mistreatment that made the *Quijote* seem so pointlessly brutal to—of all possible writers!—the author of *Candide:* "One is interested in Roland, but nobody is interested in Don Quijote, who is felt to be a senseless fellow upon whom malicious tricks are continually played."[68]

What Voltaire (like Nabokov) failed to understand is that Cervantes's apparently unrelenting malice (in the long run we realize how much he secretly loved his brainchildren) enhanced Don Quijote's and Sancho's freedom to react in ever-changing ways. The ability to cope with increasing patience, to interpret with increasing wisdom, and to comment with increasingly untrammeled dialogue emerged not only from the ambiguity of the Cervantine world but also from its relentless challenge. Even the more relaxed pastoral intervals, which allow the second two sallies to reach book length, can often be the scenes of cunning deception (the Wedding of Camacho), provocative mystery (Cardenio in Sierra Morena), or stark fear (the Adventure of the Fulling Mills). In such a world one really is on one's own.

Ortega in *The Dehumanization of Art* portrays the true artist as painting "at a maximum of distance and with a minimum of sentimental intervention."[69] This may or may not be the case in the plastic arts (what's wrong with Murillo or Eakins, after all?), but it certainly does not describe the special

68. Voltaire, "Epopée," in *Dictionnaire philosophique* (1764).
69. Ortega y Gasset, *Obras completas*, 3: 362.

irony—at once implacable and affectionate—of novelists in the Cervantine tradition. Beyond the limits of the Spanish-speaking world, Stendhal in *Le rouge et le noir*, Fielding in *Joseph Andrews*, Mark Twain in *Huckleberry Finn*, Dostoevsky in *The Idiot*, Gogol in *Dead Souls*, Dickens in *The Pickwick Papers*, Flaubert in *Madame Bovary* and *L'education sentimentale*, Balzac in *Les illusions perdues* (as in the previous lists, *my* reader is invited to continue this one on his or her own) are all—each in his own new and original fashion—stepfathers.

Thus, in the *Quijote* Cervantes has, as it were, divided his *entendimiento* (meaning now not only his critical understanding but his consciousness as an inventor) into two parts. On the one hand, he constructs a threatening and uncertain world where strange appearances and brutal passers-by represent a continuity of challenge. On the other, he watches how those two detached portions of his own existence named Don Quijote and Sancho respond—attacking, fleeing, coping, interpreting, suffering, and always trying in speech to reconcile their antithetical or complementary notions of verisimilitude. The writer lived, and readers have ever since lived, this book as an intensified—at times even caricaturesque—representation of the daily tragicomedy of the human condition.

What is it that we and they have in common? The question has already been answered. Christened by Friedrich von Schlegel romantic irony (with God as *our* ironical author), by Lukács *Obdachlosigkeit*, and by Heidegger, taking even greater advantage of the German language, *Inderweltgeworfenheit* (thrust-into-the-worldness), the meaning is roughly the same. The author smiles maliciously and tenderly, and the characters sally and stumble and get up and interpret as best they can. And if we accept Lactantius's "Naturam non matrem esse humani generis sed novercam" ("Nature is not the mother of the human race but its stepmother") in terms of our innate superstitious belief in Her consciousness (acting as if She were also an enchanter), then Don Quijote and Sancho are our brothers in fiction.

"A history which derives its force from truth"

We cannot remain with the complementary interpretations of the *Quijote* suggested thus far—literary satire, heroic salvation of the joy of reading, fictional representation of, and consolation for, the enigmatic human condition—because however valid each may be on its own terms, Cervantes in his role as critic resurfaces well inside the Third Sally with a comment on his invention that is far more profound and daring: the *Quijote* is really true. This apparently paradoxical assertion (echoed by Fielding, Mark Twain and Thornton Wilder, as we have heard) is attributed with intentional irony to the Morisco translator whose voice has been silent for some time. As we remember, he, like the "author" Cide Hamete, belongs to a caste and culture that was traditionally believed to be addicted to lying, a belief that allows Cervantes to tease contemporary neo-Aristotelian concern with the opposition or collaboration of historical truth and fiction.[70] There are some questionable details (is Sancho's last name Panza or Zancas?) in the manuscript, "but they are of little importance and do not affect the true narration of the history, and no history is bad if it is true. If doubt may be cast on the truth of this one, it can only be because its author is Arabian" (I.9).

Both Cervantes and his characters (as soon as they become aware of the printed existence of Part I) express from time to time similar doubts about the exaggerations or omissions of Cide Hamete. However, by the time he had finished writing the Adventure of the Lions (an adventure so unequivocally devoid of enchantment that it causes the hero to change his chivalric designation from Knight of the Rueful Countenance to Knight of the Lions), Cervantes became aware that out of fiction and out of play with verisimilitude he had created a new form of truth. After Don Quijote, armed only with his dull sword and rusty shield, has defied the bored maneaters, he and Sancho are about to enter the restful shelter of the rural manor house belonging to Don Diego de Miranda, an

---

70. See Castro, *El pensamiento de Cervantes*, chapter 1.

individual who is himself sheltered warmly in the garment of his epithet, the Knight of the Green Overcoat. At this juncture "Cervantes," in his role as fellow reader of the translation, interrupts:

> Here the author paints in exhaustive detail the house of Don Diego, painting for us everything that the house of a rich gentleman farmer contains, but the translator of this history thought it better to pass over in silence these and other minutiae, because they did not further the principal purpose of the history—a history which derives its force from truth and not from frigid digressions.
>
> (II.18)

At first glance this may seem to be one more whimsical reminder of the fictiveness of what we are reading, or it may perhaps be interpreted as a tacit confession that the translator has grown tired of his interminable task. However, aside from echoing past ironical play, the extraordinary thing about this aside is its explicit distinguishing of the "true" from the "real." Incredibly, Cervantes has foreseen the marriage of the future genre (which he could not have known he had invented) first with local color and romantic historicism, afterward with positivistic realism, and finally with scientific naturalism. Then in the same sentence he rejects those as yet undreamt-of *isms* as alien to his own narrative art. Why this ostensible aversion to description?[71] The semiconcealed answer lies, I think, in the present participle *painting* and in the adjective *frigid* (meaning frozen)—both of which signify lethal paralysis of the enchanting movement forward of narrative time. The romances of chivalry had exploited that voluptuous progression candidly and unartistically. Nevertheless Cervantes did not propose to trade it in for the moralistic

71. As Alban Forcione points out, after this disavowal Cervantes goes on to describe Don Diego's milieu in much greater detail than he had previously employed for setting such scenes as Alonso Quijano's abode or the inn. Thus, he at once predicts and rejects future fictional emphasis on the relationship of experience to environment. See Forcione, *Cervantes' Aristotle and the "Perciles,"* p. 163.

interruptions of Mateo Alemán or the static caricatures of Quevedo. Rather, as we have seen, he intended to reform and save the art of writing for entranced reading. In the hands of an expert narrative enchanter what had customarily produced arrant falsehood could be used to conjure not just a likely story (as the Canon recommends) but the one truth that is self-evidently true, that of consciousness in time.

It is not that the lions are truly dangerous with "true" claws "seen" by Sancho (Cervantes or Cide Hamete made them up), nor even, as Unamuno maintains, that Don Quijote invents himself in authentic courage. Rather, that comic "moment of truth" (which significantly follows the doubts raised by the disconcerting discovery that the vanquished Knight of the Mirrors is an exact copy of Sansón Carrasco) raises the issue once again with an urgency that is no longer merely facetious. After facing the lions, Don Quijote's vocational self-confidence soars again: "How does this seem to thee, Sancho? Are there any enchanters who can prevail against true valor?" (II.17). This stress on the words *truth* and *true* is further emphasized in the magniloquent interruption of Cide Hamete, who is described once again as the "author of this true history," and by Don Quijote when he allows the keeper to close the cage: "My devoir is fulfilled, and away with enchantments, and may God save reason and truth!" After the mirror play invented by that archliar Sansón Carrasco, Cervantes, Cide Hamete, the translator, and the characters—each in his own way, but as if in secret collaboration—cry the same cry: Truth!

If Sancho had been the only witness and interlocutor, there the episode would have ended: one more profoundly ironical and superficially clever variation on the interchangeability of truth and lie as the two sides of the coin of humanity. But he is not. As Américo Castro was the first to observe, the inevitable result of an adventure in which truth and madness merge completely is intensification of the mutual awareness of Don Quijote and Don Diego. Each is conscious of his own variety of consciousness (madly incited or sanely prudent and humdrum) in terms of that of his interlocutor.[72] On their first meeting, the two had been struck by each other's appearance and antithetical ways of life. It is not made explicit, but the text suggests that it is Don Diego's doubts about knight-errantry ("Is it possible that there exist histories about true deeds of chivalry?"), as well as Don Quijote's jealousy of Sancho's worship of this "saint on horseback," that motivates his most perilous feat of arms.

After the adventure is over, each of the two continues to contemplate the other and himself, the one with augmented pride and the other with augmented stupefaction. Both are Spaniards of more or less the same age, both are called caballeros, but nevertheless they are alien species. Don Diego "said nothing, being absorbed in observing Don Quijote and in taking careful note of his deeds and words, which seemed to him those of a sane madman and of a madman gravitating towards sanity." Don Quijote then addresses him: "Who can doubt but that your grace should not be of the opinion that I am an eccentric madman? And no wonder, if such should be your thoughts, for my actions indicate no less. Nevertheless, I would have your grace know that I am not quite as mad or witless as I may have appeared to you" (II.17). To prove it, he goes on to compare quite reasonably (and quite maliciously on Cervantes's part!) the socially accepted and celebrated

72. See "Incarnation in *Don Quijote,*" (in *An Idea of History,* p. 34) for Castro's illuminating remarks on this encounter of exaltation with prudence. My colleague Francisco Márquez Villanueva, taking Castro as a point of departure, meditates further on Cervantes's ironical portrait of Don Diego. Ostensibly, the domestic knight is an example of Erasmus's "Christian" variety, but his choice of clothing belies this generally accepted typification. His green coat adorned with colored ribbons, his gaudy saddle and green spurs, his fancy hat, and even his token scimitar (useless for combat) all identify him as a fool, a personification of folly. Excessive and complacent prudence, Cervantes implies, can be an even more foolish way of life than that driven by incitement to explore the frontiers of impossibility. The interpretation is as daring as Cervantes thought his *Persiles* to be, but I cannot disagree with it. Cervantes, as Márquez points out, has exploited (invented) the fundamental paradoxicality of Erasmus. See Márquez, *Personajes y temas del "Quijote"* (Madrid: Taurus, 1975), pp. 219–27.

folly of bullfighting, indulged in by vain "knights of the court," with his own lonely lion-baiting.

Aside from the audible echo of Erasmus's *Moriae encomium*, however, what matters from the point of view of the final perfection of the invention is the face-to-face and mind-to-mind encounter of errant and domestic knighthood. Don Quijote's three sallies, or *chemins*, are composed, in addition to acts of violence, of a succession of intense meetings of disparate individuals. Who can forget, for example, the occasion when the cowardly lunacy of Cardenio and the exalted delusion of Don Quijote embrace and stare?[73] But among them all, this is the most self-evidently "true," the one that invites us most peremptorily to project our own humanity—the sheer experience of our being alive, of having felt ourselves exalted by exposure to danger and comforted by shelter—into the thoughts, words, and actions of the heretofore fictional participants. As we said of Huck Finn's thunderstorm, exposure and shelter, danger and security, and adventure and order constitute the polarity of experience that is central not only to the *Quijote* but to the novel as a genre. Accordingly, it is in this episode that we are most aware of the music drawn forth from our "soul" in the process of reading. And Cervantes knew this at least intuitively, which is why he pauses to remind us that it is not the lions, not the whey dripping ridiculously into the heroic beard from under the helmet, and, above all, not the artifacts of domesticity that are true; rather, it is the time-fraught and time-fragile interlocking of self-awarenesses that he has invented in our consciousness and in our accumulated experience.

In other words, what the Morisco suggests is that narratives are true "narratively" and not, as latter-day novel readers came to believe, because of faithful description. We re-

---

73. Schelling was particularly struck by this embrace of disparate madnesses—the one genuine but momentarily concealed beneath an apparently sane facade, the other a literary facade concealing underlying sanity. Two chapters later, when Don Quijote self-consciously rejects Orlando's madness and feigns the desperate alienation of Amadís, the game becomes even more complex.

marked in the initial essay that when the novel works for us
and in us, as it is supposed to, it is because it presents its
fictional world in the same temporal fashion with which we
experience our own. It was this apparently spurious miracle—this making stories "true" and not just verisimilar—offered by the printed page that Cervantes realized he had
consecrated and authenticated. Whatever suspense the ridiculous adventure itself may awaken quickly disappears when
the lion turns into a giant cat, yawns, washes its face, and
turns its backside toward its challenger. What remains and
what is true are the two knights and their two ways of life in
intimate relation with ours. The human "frame" has become
the meaning of the whole—and in a fashion far more subtle
than in chapter 20 of Part I.

This particular transition from adventure to experience is
accompanied by the marked deceleration that has increasingly become the hallmark of the genre. I refer not only to
the *nouveau roman*, which overdoes it, but to Fabrice immobile
in the Farnèse tower, to Mrs. Dalloway strolling through St.
James's park, to Carlos Maia waiting patiently for patients,[74]
and to a thousand and one other favorite "passages," in the
literal sense of the word. What is remarkable about the *Quijote*, however, is that we can see the change in the process of
taking place. Cervantes had begun by inventing in "lying
fables" and in the greedy assimilation of their accelerated
time by their newly addicted public, and now he realized
how he had transformed habitual surrender to the tempta-
tions of fiction not only in order to savor and preserve its
flavor but also in order to slow it down and to verify it in our
lives; not to stun our consciousness on the roller coaster of
adventure or to coddle it in the never-never land of unre-
quited pastoral passion but rather to tap it in its own tempo.
The contrast in velocity between the aftermath of the Adventure of the Windmills and of the Adventure of the Lions is a

74. In Eça de Queiroz's fascinating amalgamation of adventure and experience entitled *Os Maias*, a book that offers endless delight to "Cervantine
creatures."

gauge of the transition from verisimilitude to truth—truth more true than that which each of us contributes because of its ability to survive history, as Balzac was to proclaim for what he called "le vrai" in his *Avant-propos*.

Immortality aside, however, it is precisely because Cervantes was conscious of the deceleration (or at least the contrived impression of deceleration) of his narrative that he warns us against descriptive stasis. With what clarity the writer of Part II foresaw the future perils of a genre he could not know he had invented!

"If it hadn't been for this
basin-helmet, he would have had a hard time"

Cervantes's agreement with Stendhal that first of all "le roman doit raconter" returns us, in conclusion, to the Romantic interpretation of the *Quijote*, for which Schelling's *Philosophie der Kunst* (1802) is the *locus classicus*. As we have just seen, for Cervantes the "true" has as little to do with the "real" or the realistic as it has to do with the "ideal" or the idealistic. Rather, he has discovered in the act of writing fiction the single certainty that underlies both the undependable external appearances (a windmill, a gentleman in a green overcoat, his house) of the post-Tridentine, or Baroque, world and the rampant *ingeniosidad* that was its literary expression. And, strangely enough, that primordial novelistic truth—conscious experience in its temporal course—is no different from that offered by the nineteenth-century authors whom Cervantes would have scrutinized caustically because of their self-proclaimed historicism, realism, and naturalism. Indeed, one suspects that he (or his Morisco translator) might have appreciated more those of his descendants who in the early twentieth century further "internalized" and thereby "derealized" the genre: James, Virginia Woolf, Proust, Joyce, Azorín.

It is on these terms that we may answer those who insist on asking such obvious but justifiable questions as, What about the windmills? Are they not real? How else to explain

Cervantes's marvelous gift for oral characterization? In contrast to Quevedo's superlatively grotesque Dómine Cabra, do not the individual galley slaves resemble Sevillian jailbirds Cervantes might have known rather than picaresque caricatures? Is not the Velázquez-like realism of the goatherds around their campfire a means of accentuating the morbid artificiality of Grisóstomo's pastoral passion? The truth is that Cervantes invented from or in everything he knew, both the books he had read and the life he had lived. His experience of Spain and, above all, of Spaniards is a *topikon* that served him as a springboard for his adventurous imagination. The truth of the lions does not depend on their nonliterary origin or behavior but on their contribution to the novel's ongoing communion of consciousness. They are no more or less real than Marcela, Grisóstomo, or Maritornes. Not the windmills, but the *baciyelmo* is the proper emblem of the whole.

It was, of course, only to be expected that nineteenth-century readers of the *Quijote* out of their own deep submersion in novelistic experience should have gone on inventing it. And the result was that Cervantes's virtual, narrative Spain, "where it never rains" (as Flaubert noted with surprise), was replaced by an imaginary and picturesque romantic Spain à la Gustave Doré. But Cervantes, who was writing neither a fictional biography (unlike Guzmán, Don Quijote is born in his fifties) nor a disguised autobiography, chooses not to describe the tranquil and semicultured[75] dwelling of Don Diego de Miranda for the same reason he wishes not to remember the name (and the grotesquely ignorant milieu) of Argamasilla. Instead, as we have seen, he was concerned first with matching the minds and dispositions of his readers, and then, once that intimacy was achieved, with inventing them and inventing in them. He would draw from each of them in each reading (whether in 1605 or 2005) the infinite variety of Stendhalian sounds that in silent chorus constitute its ulti-

75. As exemplified by his preference for the "books of honest entertainment" among the "six dozen" in his library, as well as by his dislike of poetry as such, Don Diego is not a "reader."

mate truth. If I may be permitted a final metaphor (borrowed from Américo Castro), his book would succeed more than any of its kind in its irresistibly seductive search across future history for "dancing partners."[76]

The *Quijote's carnet de bal* reached encyclopedic proportions in the nineteenth century when the novel came into its own and when each man's experience (even that of Mr. Bailey, the grocer) was revered as a meaningful "cell" of history.[77] But in its own age it was a unique and magnificent exception. How remarkable that, in a world so obsessed with temporal erosion that its two primordial poetic *isms* were dedicated either to the evasion of time or to grim delight in its grotesque acceleration,[78] this single novel should have staked its claim to truth on the evanescent duration of human experience. A valid argument can be made that the *Quijote* is a Baroque (or Manneristic) work insofar as it is rooted in critical scrutiny of the Spain in which Cervantes lived, as well as of the books into which he escaped. In its own way it portrays a world as cruel, as illusory, and as deceptive as those of Calderón or Quevedo. The difference, and the reason the *Quijote* can work in us in a way their writings cannot, is that Cervantes invented a way to transform our laughter at his crazy and foolish clowns into a rejuvenating and liberating participation in their errant and erratic existences. Their "truth" is our "truth," and vice versa!

76. This phrase is taken from the titular essay of *An Idea of History*, p. 296.
77. See Wilhelm Dilthey, *Gesämmelte Schriften*, ed. B. Groethuysen (Leipzig: Teubner, 1923–36), 7: 246.
78. The reference is to the two opposed but complementary literary "sects" called *culteranismo* (typified by Góngora) and *conceptismo* (typified by Quevedo). The former transformed or evaded the temporal world in elaborate metaphorical play and Latinate syntax and vocabulary, while the latter emphasized evanescence (*le néant* of human existence) in vicious verbal caricature. See Andrée Collard, *Nueva poesía: Conceptismo, Culteranismo en la crítica española* (Madrid: Castalia, 1967), pp. 73–76, and my own "The Ideology of the Baroque in Spain," Symposium 1 (1946), pp. 82–107.

4

Discovery

*"My sole object has been to arouse men's
contempt for all fabulous and absurd stories . . ."*

Among other conclusions, our discussion of Cervantes as an
inventor demonstrates that his ambivalent assessment of his
own talents cannot be separated from his generally acerbic
estimation of the literature of his time. What now remains to
be done is to change course and to examine the positive contribution of overt literary criticism to the creation of the *Quijote,* a book made from books and about books. Why did Cervantes entitle it simply *El ingenioso hidalgo don Quijote de la
Mancha* and not *The History of . . .* or *The Adventures of . . . ,*
as J. M. Cohen begins the title of his translation? The answer
already suggested is that its hero *is* a book just as we saw
Cardenio to be his own story. Or conversely, the book is a
person named Don Quijote, whom many of the inhabitants
of Part II have already "read"! In other words, we shall now
be concerned with comprehending the *Quijote's* symbiosis of
literature and life, not just in the simplistically comic First
Sally, but with all the deadly serious implications discovered
critically during the course of the Second.

As we have seen, when Cervantes speaks about his reasons for writing the *Quijote,* he is uncharacteristically unambiguous. And not just in the Prologue to Part I. At the end of
Part II he is equally outspoken: "My sole object has been to
arouse men's contempt for all fabulous and absurd stories of
knight-errantry" (I.74). Is this just an elementary form of
moral camouflage designed to deceive the narrow minds
of self-righteously censorious readers? Possibly, or in part.
However, no less an authority than Vicente Llorens recom-

mends that we take these statements seriously as a point of critical departure.[1] The *Quijote* began and begins as a satire of the *Amadís* and its progeny, just as *Joseph Andrews* began and begins as a satire of *Pamela* written "in the manner of Cervantes." Without taking that initial intention into account, we cannot hope to delve more deeply into what Augusto Centeno termed its "intent"[2]—the underlying thematic complexity beneath the satirical thesis.

But why did Cervantes begin in this way? As is well known (at least among Hispanists), by the year 1600 the romance of chivalry was about as moribund as the western is today, and it seems absurd to have spent so much time and effort in order to "arouse men's contempt" for it. It is as if Saul Bellow were to pick Zane Grey as his literary target. This is a classic question for students of Cervantes, and in order to answer it, let us replace the interrogative *why* with *what*. What was Cervantes trying to communicate to his readers with his persistent assertion of such a simplistic excuse for writing? An initial answer might be that that was his way of calling attention to the unprecedented interpenetration and interdependence of criticism and creation in his art of composition. As we have seen, this novel, perhaps more than any other before or since, was conceived as a systematic, calculated, carefully woven fabric, of which the woof was creative invention and the warp was critical meditation. In it fiction—somewhat as in the art of Picasso after 1914—is created in the act of destroying fiction. Understood in this way, the paradox of erecting such an enormous *máquina* (as Cervantes would have called it) for such a futile task is no longer paradoxical. Rather, these unambiguous assertions communicate forcefully the unprecedented importance of literary criticism and critical theory in the making of the *Quijote*.

Cervantine bibliography is replete with cogent and well-

1. Vicente Llorens, "La intención del *Quijote*," in *Literatura, historia, política* (Madrid: Revista de Occidente, 1967), pp. 205–27.
2. Augusto Centeno, *The Intent of the Artist* (Princeton, N.J.: Princeton University Press, 1941), Introduction.

informed studies of the novelist as a critic.[3] However, those that I have read attempt to abstract (and then to reformulate) a coherent critical doctrine from the treatises of Cervantes's neo-Aristotelian mentors, from the pertinent chapters of Part I of the *Quijote*, from the *Viaje del Parnaso*, from the *Persiles*, and from the prologues to his works. Here, on the contrary, relying on our previous discussion of the novel as representing a process of growth and realization, we shall proceed differently. Instead of trying to reconstruct Cervantes's definite poetics—the fossilized skeleton of his rhetorical "philosophy"—we shall try to trace the gradual development of his critical engagement with his own work and with those of his colleagues during the composition of the Second Sally. As he began to exploit untried sources for invention, Cervantes became increasingly aware of a more pernicious and pervasive form of identification of literature and life than that represented by Alonso Quijano's comic delusion. In so doing, as we shall see, he discovered critically the innate potentialities of his own accomplishment.

Obviously, we, too, must schematize and foreshorten (otherwise we would be repeating the strange experiment of Pierre Menard alluded to earlier), but we shall try to do so in a way that is not tangential to our experience as readers and to Cervantes's experience as a writer. Taking as our point of departure the language of his overt criticism, we shall begin by examining its puzzling and repeated use of Inquisitional comparisons and jargon. This is first apparent in the Scrutiny of the Books, undertaken by the Priest and the Barber, in Part I, chapter 6. Then, at the very end of the Second Sally, we are surprised to find the same conceits repeated in a greatly modified, almost antithetical, fashion. Between these two moments of explicit critical commentary, the invention of Part I is further elaborated in Sierra Morena (chapters 23–25), so that instead of proceeding directly from the Scrutiny to the

---

3. The basic studies have already been cited: in Spanish, Castro's *El pensamiento de Cervantes;* in English, Riley's *Cervantes's Theory of the Novel* and Forcione's *Cervantes, Aristotle, and the "Persiles."*

dialogue of the Priest and the Canon, we shall pause once again in that pre-Romantic hideaway in order to take the pulse of the literary lives—the literature-infused lives—that encounter each other there. It was in telling us about what went on in those protective fastnesses that Cervantes discovered (and hoped to lead his readers to discover) what was profoundly wrong with the literature and culture of his time.

"We must condemn it to the flames without any mercy . . ."

The battered Don Quijote of the First Sally is now sound asleep, and the Priest and the Barber have invaded his library in order to purge it of the guilty books. As they begin to speak, translators, whether in the seventeenth century or in the twentieth, begin to run into grave difficulties:

> The first volume that Master Nicholas handed the Priest was *The Four Books of Amadís de Gaula.* "This is very curious," said the Priest, "for as I have heard tell, this was the first book of chivalry printed in Spain, and all the others took their origin and beginning from it. So it seems to me that, as the first preacher of so pernicious a sect, we must condemn it to the flames without considering mitigating circumstances [*sin excusa*]."
>
> (I.6)

The Cohen translation, among other lapses, fails entirely when it converts the Priest's initial comment, "Parece cosa de misterio esta," into "This is very curious." What the Priest is commenting on is not the mere curiosity of the book but rather its mysterious generative power, the fact that it was the "origin and beginning" of a "género." And since it is a "cosa de misterio," it awakens ecclesiastical suspicion, almost as if it were a witch or an enchanter. The *Amadís* had, in fact, such a strange capacity to propagate itself in continuations and imitations that the Priest compares it to a "dogmatizador" (dogmatist or doctrine giver, not "first preacher") of a new heretical sect. His awareness of its literary "mystery" justifies the Priest's acceptance of the Niece's earlier demand for an auto-da-fé at 451 degrees Fahrenheit. He speaks like an Inquisitor and judges with the implacability of an Inquisitor. Cervantes, as usual, has expressed himself ironically, but the concealed message is necessarily elusive to readers unfamiliar with his century and culture.

The obvious *explications de texte* are clearly erroneous. One might be that the whole chapter is a spoof of the Holy Office and its procedures, comparable to Fielding's burlesque of the professional behavior of English justices of the peace. Yet even in an age accustomed to its presence (in 1605 the Inquisition was almost 130 years old), familiarity could not conceivably have bred so much contempt. The prestige of the Inquisition was too immense, its power too overwhelming, its threat too grim, and its feelings too easily hurt to allow for persiflage.[4] Cervantes, like Fernando de Rojas before him, did indeed relieve his feelings with covert verbal thrusts at the dreaded institution (as we shall see, there are at least two in the passage just cited), but this is hardly the same as poking overt fun at its vocabulary and methods. The puzzling thing (for those of us who have worked with Inquisition documents) about this sustained metaphor for literary criticism is that it appears to express a dangerously inappropriate humor.

A second possibility—that Cervantes was using the Priest as a surrogate in order to attack the cruelty and intolerance of that sanctified FBI cum Supreme Court—is for the same reason even more unlikely. Furthermore, although the Priest does say later that he would burn his own father at the stake

---

4. In H. C. Lea's exhaustive four-volume *History of the Inquisition in Spain* (New York: Macmillan, 1906–07) we find a variety of cases of "disrespect for the Inquisition," many of which concern petty matters of protocol and precedence. The Inquisitors were particularly concerned with their seating at public functions: location, pillows, canopies, carpets (1: 358). Invidious remarks reported to them about the institution and its personnel were investigated and punished with fines, various forms of public humiliation (including whipping), and exile. Even the personal servants of the Inquisitors enjoyed the same protection. For example, after a verbal quarrel with such an individual about the quality of his meat, a Murcian butcher was banished (1: 369–70). One simply did not tease or criticize the Inquisition in any way it could understand!

if he found him dressed as a knight-errant in the company of the absurd characters of the *Amadís de Grecia*, we know him as a well-meaning individual genuinely concerned for his errant parishioner. Finally, we must take into account the fact that his judgements—including the hyperbolical remark about his father—clearly represent, however ironically, Cervantes's own opinions. In the Scrutiny both the Priest and the Barber proceed hastily and ruthlessly (they end by condemning an indefinite number of books they have not read or examined), but their individual critical verdicts are those of their author. We cannot, as a result, automatically absolve Cervantes of responsibility for the literary Inquisition.

If neither teasing nor overt satire can account for the language of the Scrutiny, must we then interpret it literally and include Cervantes in the disreputable company of Savonarola, Hitler, and the rest of history's fanatical book burners? Before reaching such a drastic conclusion, we should remember that the Priest's description of the *Amadís* as a "dogmatizador de una secta" echoes the rhetoric of the then current polemic against the elaborately metaphorical *culterano* poetry of Góngora and his followers. The old-fashioned, patriotic versifier Cristóbal de Castillejo had earlier demanded nothing less than the resurrection of the monstrous Lucero, the most irresponsible and bloodthirsty of all past Inquisitors, in order that the new "secta de poetas" (comparable in his view to that of Luther) might be extirpated. Just as in the viciously aggressive style of Quevedo, who also denounced the "false sect of vain and empty poets,"[5] such remarks allow us to overhear the oral violence of literary life in that so-called Golden Century.

Unlike Cervantes, these word warriors sound as if they mean it. They would be happy to see not just the poems but also the poets go up in smoke! In view of this, we may ten-

5. See chapter 3, note 22. Castillejo was concerned to extirpate the use of eleven-syllable Italianate verse forms, but the tradition of referring to literary schools as heretical sects continued through the *culteranismo* polemic right down to that concerning the introduction of naturalism into the peninsula. A deep structure?

tatively propose that, at least in part, the Scrutiny refers to a prevalent variety of criticism that in its ferocity could not distinguish—or chose not to distinguish—between aesthetic and dogmatic evaluation. Rather than the Inquisition, Cervantes's primary target could well have been those of his colleagues who advocated inquisitorial methods in a realm for which they were wholly unsuited.

This interpretation is confirmed by the Barber's reply to the Priest's accusation and summary conviction of the *Amadís*: " 'No, sir,' said the Barber, 'for I have heard that it is the best of all books of this kind [*género*] ever written. So, since it is unique in its art, it ought to be pardoned' " (I.6). The Barber, in accord with his modish profession, is interested in styles and innovations. Acting as the defense attorney in the miniature trial, he manages to get his client acquitted for the time being: " 'True enough,' " replies the Priest, agreeing reluctantly to a stay of execution. For the Priest the *Amadís* is an open wound of moral infection and should be cauterized, but for the Barber it is the model for a genre (or subgenre) and deserves to be pardoned. Its mysterious generative capacity marks it as "the best of its kind," "unique in its art."

By the same criteria, one might admire Góngora and Lope as innovators and at the same time condemn the excesses of their followers. But whether or not Cervantes's own readers might have agreed with the Barber, it is clear that the borrowed conceit of inquisitorial judgement is a parable designed to illustrate the proper and improper concerns of criticism. Others—a Fray Pedro Malón de Chaide, a Mateo Alemán, an Avellaneda, or even a Luis Vives—might attack romances of chivalry as sinful or scandalous, but Cervantes in chapter 6 was concerned with their questionable merit as works of literature.

However, as we remarked earlier, the Inquisition does not emerge entirely unscathed. For example, we are told explicitly that neither the Priest nor the Barber really know what they are talking about. They surely had read the *Amadís* (all literate Spaniards had done so), but, like the Inquisitors they imitate, they both judge on the basis of hearsay: "según he oído decir." And when the accused is saved from the flames, the sentence is not revoked but only suspended: "se le otorga la vida por ahora" (literally, "life is granted to him for the time being"). Not only is the phraseology properly official but also the state of mortal uncertainty in which the book-person must go on living resembles that of the flesh-and-blood victims of the Holy Office. Once denounced, always on file, was the practice of those pious bureaucrats for whom full absolution, although occasionally granted, nevertheless seemed to be a defeat for the system.

If this seems perhaps too ingenious an "explication," Cervantes's contemporary readers (and ironical collaborators) surely caught on when he comments on the critical opinions of the manifestly illiterate Housekeeper and Niece. As we remember, it was the latter who originally proposed the "auto público," and when the Priest and the Barber set about separating the sheep from the goats (as good Inquisitors should), she objects strongly. Speaking with the voice of the people, she demands that because they are books, they should all be burned without discrimination. This portion of the dialogue begins when the Housekeeper, as superstitious as her master is mad, asks the Priest to exorcise the library of the enchanters who still might be haunting it:

> The Priest laughed at the Housekeeper's simplicity, and bade the Barber hand him the books one by one, so he could see what they were about; for he might find some of them that did not deserve punishment by fire.
> "No," said the Niece, "there is no reason to pardon any of them, for they have all of them caused the trouble. Better throw them out of the window into the courtyard, and make a pile of them, and set them on fire; or else take them out into the backyard and have the bonfire there where the smoke won't be a nuisance."
> The Housekeeper agreed, so anxious were they both for the massacre of those innocents; but the Priest would not consent without at least reading the titles first.
>
> (I.6)

In this context it is appropriate that this same Housekeeper should be chosen for the role of *brazo seglar* (the so-called secular arm of the state), which punished condemned heretics because it was not thought fitting for the Church to shed blood. As for the savage Niece, it is equally appropriate that she should designate the "backyard" (*corral*) for the bonfire (a reference to the custom of locating the *quemaderos* outside of town because of air pollution) and that later she should insist that the few volumes spared from the flames wear *sambenitos* (the traditional garments of public shame worn by penitents) as jackets (II.6). These sly details, along with the narrator's description of the collection as "innocents" pursued relentlessly by popular ignorance and prejudice, indicate, to say the least, that Cervantes was not in favor of book or person burning. Rather, he would have agreed with Montaigne that "c'est mettre ses conjectures à bien haut prix que d'en faire cuire un homme tout vif."[6]

Thus, while using the Scrutiny as a familiar and humorous means of communicating his opinions about literature and its criticism, Cervantes nonetheless deplored the scrutinizers and their illiterate supporters. It is also quite probable that in addition to satirizing the violent rhetoric of the *culteranismo* polemic, he intended to allude tacitly to the general examination of public and private libraries undertaken by the Holy Office in 1558 and continued, according to H. C. Lea, until the suppression of the Inquisition (see note 4). "All heretical, suspicious, and scandalous books," including those printed abroad and not on the Index, were to be sequestered, examined, and in some cases "publically burnt."[7] As Francis Thompson, the author of *The Hound of Heaven*, warned us, the double edge of Cervantine irony cuts both ways, and it is not surprising that he should have combined aesthetic judge-

6. Montaigne, *Essais*, ed. A. Thibaudet (Paris: La Pléiade, 1950), p. 1149. "After all it is rating one's conjectures at a very high price, to roast a man alive on the strength of them" (*Essays of Montaigne*, trans. E. J. Trechmann [Oxford: Oxford University Press, 1953], 1: 505).
7. Lea, *History of the Inquisition*, 3: 446, 448, and 575.

ment of contemporary books with a veiled satire of those who would abolish ("they have all of them caused the trouble") or limit freedom to read.

The remarks on Cervantes's own *La Galatea* (to which we referred in the previous essay) demonstrate the cunning of his ambivalence. Again translation is unsatisfactory, but, as we remember, the Priest describes the author as an old friend "better versed in misfortunes than in versification" and then condemns the book to secluded *enmienda*—solitary confinement and self-imposed penitence, or self-correction, imposed by the Holy Office for minor or unproven offenses. *La Galatea*, he goes on to say, "has something of skilled invention," but unfortunately "it proposes something and comes to no conclusion." However, it might be saved by rethinking and re-working—which, as we saw, is precisely what Cervantes partially accomplished in the Marcela and Grisóstomo episode. But what concerns us now is the way the Inquisitional comparison is remodeled. Solitary confinement, instead of being a punishment, is an image for the agonizing but ultimately beneficial solitude of the creator's *entendimiento*. *Reclusión* and *enmienda*, exploited aesthetically, are the indispensable prerequisites, if one is to save oneself as an artist. Instead of arrogantly condemning fiction as such and as a whole, one must learn to distinguish the good from the bad and then through a process of painful self-mortification learn how to create the good.

Aesthetic repentance and creative self-contemplation, in conclusion, constitute the "moral" of Cervantes's art and are everywhere apparent in his works. All that we talked about in the preceding essay—the need of the *ingenio* for the guidance of invention, the importance of surpassing facile generic standardization, the mediating function of the pastoral—merge in the confessional manifesto of chapters 47–50 at the end of Part I. There Cervantes tells us as clearly as he can what he has learned both from current theory—the virtue of verisimilitude and the delight of harmony and proportion—and from creative practice. On his own he had realized (in fecund opposition to theoretical strictures) that at their best, narration and reading are processes of liberation and spiritual therapy. Nevertheless, alongside these much discussed aesthetic conclusions there are a number of passages not yet examined that indicate a profound change in critical engagement. As we shall see, a sociological preoccupation—a preoccupation with the deleterious effects of literature on society— has been added.

As a result of this change, Cervantes's earlier use of inquisitorial imagery is reshaped in a fashion that at first glance seems to contradict that of the Scrutiny. The Canon remarks, for example, that the romances of chivalry, like unassimilated population groups, "deserve to be banished from a Christian commonwealth as a useless tribe" (I.47). They are indeed heretical in that their authors are "inventors of new sects" that corrupt innocent minds. The point is not to determine whether Cervantes in his heart of hearts approved or disapproved of the expulsion of the Jews and Moriscos (the good Morisco, Ricote, partially justifies his own fate) but rather to observe how Cervantes now seems to espouse the critical ferocity he had seemed to chastise at the beginning. Similarly, when the Priest attacks the "new art"[8] of the national theater as offering only mirrors of insanity, examples of folly, and images of lasciviousness, he goes on with all apparent seriousness to propose censorship by "a wise and intelligent person" (I.47). What has happened to the initial auto-da-fé parody of arbitrary criticism? And why did Cervantes change his tactics? In order to answer these questions, we must return to the stories told by Cardenio and Dorotea in Sierra Morena and consider them as further elaborations of the inventive process.

"In order to imitate . . . brave Sir Roland"

The liberation of the galley slaves in chapter 22 constitutes the narrative watershed of Part I for several reasons. In the

---

8. The reference, of course, is to the title of Lope's apologetically defiant and ironically humble *Arte nuevo de hacer comedias en este tiempo* (1609).

first place, up until that point, aside from a tangential glance at the pastoral follies of Marcela and Grisóstomo, Cervantes and his readers have mainly attended to a single and manifestly extravagant case of symbiosis of literature and life. But afterward, as we shall see, two other cases offer themselves for inspection at center stage. In the second place, as in chapter 4 when Don Quijote's belief in his own invincibility was shattered by the merchants' adolescent muleteer, he is obliged again to superimpose a new fictional identity on that invented in Argamasilla. The obsolete knight now is confronted not with a single antagonist nor with a group of *malandrines* (scoundrels)—picaros, herdsmen, galley slaves, traveling players, or contentious villagers—but with organized society itself in the form of the Santa Hermandad, or Holy Brotherhood, as the state police of the time was called. As Hegel remarked in the section of his *Aestetik* entitled "Das Ende der romantische Kunstform," the aspirations of the heroes of both romance and novel would be untenable (are untenable!) in a nation blessed or cursed with really efficient law enforcement—apparently meaning that they are fundamentally antisocial. It is curious, therefore, that elsewhere he points to this episode as particularly significant. In any case, Sancho warns his master that the liberation of the galley slaves will not be overlooked, and Don Quijote reluctantly heeds his recommendation that they retreat into the wilderness of nearby Sierra Morena. However, since flight in any form is contrary to his code, he is perplexed, and a few chapters later we find him trying to justify himself by recalling from his past reading a suitable role model.

Who shall he be now? On the one hand, there is "brave Sir Roland," who, "when he discovered in a fountain the signs that Angelica the Beautiful had committed a villainy with Medoro," ran about the countryside where he "went mad, tore up trees, muddied the waters of clear running springs, slew shepherds, set fire to huts, tore down houses, dragged mares along after him, and did a hundred thousand other outrageous deeds [*insolencias*] worthy of eternal renown and written record" (I.25). But Sancho demurs: "What evidence is

there that my Lady Dulcinea del Toboso has been trifling with
Moor or Christian?" Don Quijote's answer—"That is precisely my point, . . . and therein resides the exquisiteness of
my plan, for . . . if I do this much in cold blood, how would
I behave in the heat of passion?"—is far more comic in Spanish than in English.[9] Nevertheless, Sancho's objection (like
everything else in this intricate compendium of memories)
remains in Don Quijote's mind. In the next chapter we hear
him meditating: "I will venture to swear that my Dulcinea del
Toboso has never seen a Moor as he really is dressed in his
native garb and that today she is as intact as the mother who
bore her."[10] Imitation of Orlando's fury would therefore be a
form of chivalresque slander, a consideration that leads him
to choose a more suitable alternative—Amadís, who after
being rejected by Oriana also retreated into the wilderness.
There, "without losing his senses and without committing
mad extravagances, he won no less fame as a lover." There-

9. "Si en seco hago esto, ¿que haría en mojado?" The expression *en seco*
corresponds roughly to our army's "dry run," and the humor consists in the
knight's coining of an unexpected variation: *en mojado*, or "wet run" (under
fire?).

10. Apparently the phrase was a vulgar and nonsensical oral Spanish
commonplace, which Cervantes here relates (in the context of Dulcinea's
possible Arabian lover) to Ariosto's remark concerning Angelica in *Orlando
Furioso* (I, 55): "E che'l fior virginal così havea salvo / come se lo portò del
materno alvo." ("And how she was, in fact / As when she left her mother's
womb, intact" [Ariosto, *Orlando Furioso*, translated by Barbara Reynolds, p.
130; all translations of *Orlando Furioso* in this chapter are from this version].)
The Cervantine version has confused overlogical translators, who have reverted to Ariosto's commonsensical commonplace; for example, Samuel Put-
nam's "She is today what she was when her mother bore her." As far as the
phrase "dressed in his native garb" is concerned, it is well known that El
Toboso was at the time a village of Moriscos, meaning more or less accultur-
ated descendants of the Moors. Thus, Aldonza Lorenzo, although of Moorish descent, has never seen a genuine (or literary) Muhammadan dressed as
such, like Medoro or Cervantes's own Algerian captors. The hidden point is
that the more or less well situated Jewish converts returned the disdain of
their Old Christian peasant neighbors by pointing out that since they were
totally unaware of their own lineage, they were probably "tainted" with Morisco blood. In this sentence Cervantes teases the whole business, which, as
we have said, he found utterly ridiculous. The glorious lineages of El Toboso
are to the grandee Mendozas and Guevaras of Castile what Don Quijote is
to Amadís of Gaul.

fore, Don Quijote concludes: "Now to business! Oh memory bring to mind the doings of Amadís, and teach me how to begin imitating them."

Aside from its comic juxtaposition of the two lovelorn fictional heroes Orlando and Amadís—the one grotesque (no matter what Voltaire thought!) and the other exemplary— Don Quijote's discourse reveals what his author-enchanter has been up to surreptitiously all along. As we remember, in chapter 23 the knight and the squire enter Sierra Morena by night, and at dawn they discover, in addition to the theft of the donkey, a valise the padlock of which was so ruptured ("roto") that its contents could easily be inspected. The ensuing inventory includes gold coins, fine clothing, and a notebook containing a poem about love and death addressed to Fili (a pastoral pseudonym) along with the rough draft of a desperate letter apparently intended for the same lady. The wordplay here is once again infernal for conscientious translators. Sancho, like other Castilian illiterates of the time, substitutes *h* for all *f*'s with the result that he hears *Fili* as *hilo* and interprets it to mean the "thread" of the still unknown story suggested by the mysterious valise.[11] When, at the end of the same chapter, the participle used for the padlock (*roto*, from *romper*, meaning "to break" or "to sever") is used in Cardenio's mock-chivalric epithet "El Roto de la Mala Figura" (The Ragged—or Amputated—One of the Shameful Countenance), the careful rereader realizes that Cervantes has been engaged in subtle verbal allusion to, and continuation of, the

11. As is well known, Castilian underwent a whole series of phonetic changes in the fifteenth century, one of the most conspicuous of which was the conversion of *f* to *h*, which was at first aspirated and later became unaspirated. *Falcón*, for example, became *halcón*, and Don Quijote imitates the language of his belovedly antiquated texts by pronouncing *hermosura* as "fermosura." The oral speech of the mass of the population was the source of the change, with the result that Sancho simply cannot hear the *f* of the pastoral name *Fili*. Cervantes adored the interplay of the written with the oral just as he did that of commonplaces (whether popular or courtly) with the outlandish variations and extensions he and his characters could come up with spontaneously.

narrative play with interruption and sequence we discussed in chapter 2, "Birth."

After the finding of the valise, two more discoveries follow immediately and augment the suspense both of the reader and of the discoverers. First a hirsute individual clad in velvet tatters is seen on high "leaping from crag to crag with marvelous agility" (I.23), and then the body of a mule that had apparently been driven to death is encountered.[12] Neither Don Quijote nor Sancho know what to make of these mysteries, but our suspicion that this wild man may be a calculated reincarnation of Orlando (who, according to Don Quijote, "dragged mares after him") is confirmed by a passing shepherd. He and his companions—he informs the curious knight and squire—have been attacked by this mad desperado during the accesses of "furia" that alternate with intervals of courteous and rational behavior.[13] He might even have "killed" one of them with his fists and teeth, if they hadn't subdued him. It only remains for Don Quijote to recall in chapter 25 that Ariosto's Italianate Roland "slew shepherds" for us to be certain wherein Cervantes has now ventured to "invent."

The shepherd has just finished his account when "el Roto" himself suddenly appears on the immediate scene. He and Don Quijote, as we remember, exchange embraces and gaze into each other's eyes in wonder at their divergent varieties of eccentricity. However, in arranging the meeting with such care, Cervantes had something more in mind than to provoke laughter at comparative madness. As we have said, his narrative course has veered sharply, and he is now concerned—

12. According to the critics, Cervantes invented both in Ariosto's epic and in a lyrical (meaning artistic rather than popular and oral) ballad of Juan del Encina, "Por unos puertos arriba," in which a similarly clad figure appears on high dressed in mourning beside his dead horse. Cervantes's inventiveness, as usual, is plural.

13. The goatherd uses the rather high-flown word *furia* (instead of *locura*), and later Cervantes terms Cardenio's temporary alienation a "furioso accidente," in order to suggest to readers this more unfamiliar ingredient of his intertextual play.

with the help of Ariosto—with guiding his presumably spell-bound readers toward certain discoveries about their national literature that he has already made and that he wants them to make on their own. He is concerned with employing suspense positively (as opposed to its mockery in the fractured single combat with the Basque) by means of both mystery and a subtly orchestrated sequence of generic variations.

The careful development and the final oratorical confrontation of the Marcela and Grisóstomo episode have not been forgotten. Once again, a lyric poem and a shepherd's tale prepare us for not just one but two dramatic encounters: first, the courtly embrace, and afterward, the abrupt physical combat of the two extravagantly costumed actors. The narrative die has been cast. Nothing is now excluded except for the outrageous but sophisticated inverisimilitude that Ariosto adored. Nevertheless, the elaborate comic mystification of *Orlando Furioso* will be a means of engaging us during the whole of the Sierra Morena sojourn with unlikely encounters, with every kind of disguise, and with incessant role-playing by all the actors except Sancho and the shepherds. They—and we—make up the amused and bemused audience of a wilderness masque, an improvised and self-conscious comedia that ends, as we shall see, with a climactic denouement at the centripetal inn. When Shakespeare selected this portion of the Skelton translation (1610) for his lost Cardenio play, he understood perfectly what his contemporary had up his sleeve.[14]

But for this purpose why invent in *Orlando Furioso*? How could a seemingly endless comic epic in verse contribute to the change from sequential to dramatically structured narration? To begin with, it enabled the quasitheatrical confronta-

---

14. Guillén de Castro (who was the author of the source for Corneille's *Le Cid*) also used this episode as the plot for his *Don Quijote de la Mancha* "comedia." Therein he presents Cardenio as being of peasant origin, includes references to Ariosto, and, like Shakespeare, resolves the conflict through the intervention of the noble father. For an idea of the content of Shakespeare's Cardenio play, see Lewis Theobald's "revised" version, *Double Falsehood* (London: Lowndes, 1767).

tion of the two madmen. Obviously, the allusions to Ariosto
we have just detected were not as immediately familiar to the
general public as were chivalresque, picaresque, and pastoral
topika. But once they realized what was up, those preterit
common readers were just as entertained as we are by the
meeting, the dialogue, and the conflict of the supposedly
flesh-and-blood actors Cardenio and Don Quijote, each representing in his own way—the one desperately and the other
playfully—Orlando and Amadís, two antithetical archetypes
of fictional heroism at moments of extreme erotic distress.

In addition, Ariosto provided his devotee, Cervantes, with
a model for a new kind of narrative sophistication. As we
remember, the latter had imitated—at second hand—the
characteristic thread cutting of the former when he interrupted the single combat with the Basque. And now the
Spaniard, in direct rapport with his favorite poem, could
go on to weave skeins that suddenly appear out of the blue
(the still anonymous ragged acrobat seen leaping like a goat),
that are just as suddenly interrupted (Cardenio mute and
"furioso"), that reappear when least expected (the story re-
commenced with "almost the same words"), and that inter-
twine with others (that of Dorotea). Ariosto, to the amusement of the cynical "knights of the court" to whom he read
his poem aloud, was a superb manipulator of the comedy
and theatricality that are inherent in chivalry as a self-
conscious social show. A consummate puppetmaster, he
taught Cervantes how to vary episodic sequence with plotted
sequence. Dialogue and memory aside, prior to chapter 22
the *Quijote's* narrative form had been essentially that of
Amadís; in Sierra Morena it is that of *Orlando Furioso*.

In Ariosto's poem the drawn-out suspense—an essential
ingredient of Stendhal's "happiness"—seemingly could have
lasted for a thousand and one cantos. But for Cervantes, at
once a theorist of the drama and in his own opinion an un-
fairly neglected playwright, plots were by definition Aristotelian. They had to have a beginning, a middle, and an end,
as indeed they do, first in Sierra Morena and afterward at the
inn—just as Sancho surmised proverbially, when he heard

the name Fili in the poem, that *hilo* (strand) might lead to the *ovillo* (the whole ball of yarn or the heart of the matter).[15] And when Cervantes, using the same topical image, describes his new narrative tack as a "rastrillado, torcido y aspado hilo," he does not mean tangled up, as unprepared readers might assume, but rather "cleansed, twisted, and reeled-up" (I.28).[16] Like Sancho in chapter 20, Cardenio and Dorotea can only spin their yarns (with or without interruption) in a straight line. Cervantes, however, thanks to Ariosto, can convert their lives and stories into a "reeled-up" dramatic plot and thereby save them at the end of "Act III" from the apparently inevitable results of their follies—which is what traditional comedy on stage, as contrasted to Don Quijote's tragicomic or comitragic novel, is all about.

But this is by no means all there is to it. The presence of *Orlando Furioso* in Sierra Morena acts as a catalyst that reveals aspects of Spanish life of far more concern to Cervantes than the comic confrontation of two madmen (each of whom lives his own mad story in his own mad fashion) or than the increment of narrative sophistication. Although Cardenio's wretched and antiheroic account of loss of nerve in a small-town Andalusian ambiance may seem antithetical to the only too justifiable fury of Orlando, a fantasy hero in a fantasy demesne, they do have one thing in common. Both are "knights" who, having reason to believe their ladies have betrayed them, fail to live up to the exigencies of their knighthood. In concocting this essay in comparative chivalry, Cervantes is as subtle as ever. Orlando's furious alienation, maliciously arranged by that super-stepfather Ariosto, needs

15. "Por el hilo se saca el ovillo" (I.23). Cervantes's constant play with the notion of the narrative thread led him inevitably to this proverb as an image for plot.

16. In this collection of verbs having to do with the preparation of yarn (for weaving a story), *cardar* is conspicuously absent. However, Beth Tremallo, who is equally competent in both Spanish and Italian literatures and who suggested the relevance of Ariosto's verbal play with weaving and thread cutting to the narrativity of the *Quijote*, pointed out to me that it is audible in Cardenio's name. To card the wool is the first step in the process, and he is the initiator of the new story sequence.

no further comment here, but the *caso* (a socioliterary case history) of Cardenio is far more complex. Told in the first person instead of the third, it reflects Cervantes's awareness of a curious congruence in the Italian poem, which the poet had suggested but did not emphasize—that of the severed narrative threads with the severed identity of Orlando.[17] We have seen the results. Cardenio is his story, and when it is interrupted, he interrupts himself. Ariosto's gleeful narrative malice is Cardenio's unbearable burden.

On the face of it, it would appear that this change in point of view (from third-person "epic" insouciance in the historical present to anguished *ich-Erzählung* in the autobiographical past) should impede or render impossible the transition from lyric lament and oral tale of woe to the theatrical denouement that here concerns us. However, that appearance is misleading insofar as it ignores two pertinent factors: the ambivalence of the designation *caballero* (at once gentleman and knight) in the Spain of the time, and the reflection of that ambivalence in the drama of honor that prevailed on the stage. As far as the first is concerned, Cardenio is a gentleman "of noble lineage and wealth," a native of one of the

17. When the shepherd shows Orlando the bracelet the latter had bestowed on Angelica as a token of his adoration (and she in turn had given to the former in gratitude for having saved Medoro's life), that piece of evidence is "la secure / che'l capo a un colpo gli levò dal collo" (XXIII, 121) ("the axe which at one final blow / His head then severed from Orlando's neck" [p. 723]). Seven octaves later he concludes: "Non son, non son io quel che paio in viso: / quel ch'era Orlando, è morto ed è sottera" ("I am not he, I am not he I seem / He who Orlando was is dead and gone" [p. 725]). From then on Orlando will not have the "lucid intervals" that Don Quijote, also desperately in love, shares with Cardenio (XXIV, 3), but, curiously enough, after emerging from his madness, Orlando does share with the latter a phantom recollection of his previous mad behavior. In Cervantes's version "the bout which he had with Don Quijote came to his memory as if out of dreams" (I.29), whereas Ariosto's hero, having swallowed the magic potion, awakes as if from a "noioso e grave sonno" (XXXIX, 58). Flaubert, who began his literary experience by listening to the *Quijote* read aloud, exaggerated the connection when he remarked, "Cervantes plus grave et plus pur refit l'oeuvre de l'Arioste" (cited in Jean Bruneau, *Les débuts litteraires de Gustave Flaubert: 1831–1845* [Paris: Armand Colin, 1962], p. 161). But he does indicate his awareness of the intricate ties, of which a few have concerned us here.

most "illustrious" birthplaces in all Andalusia. Because of his membership in this social class, he is honor-bound to play the role of chivalric knight when called on to do so, a role for which he knows all the proper rhetoric and vocabulary. He promises Dorotea later on:

> I swear to you as a Christian caballero that I will not forsake you until I see you don Fernando's wife; and if my arguments cannot bring him to acknowledge his duty to you, I shall invoke the right which my rank as a caballero confers on me and with just cause challenge him on account of the injury [*en razón de la sinrazón*] which he has done to you—without remembering the wrongs he has done to me which I shall leave Heaven to avenge while I take yours in my charge here on Earth.
>
> (I.29)

When first heard, this speech sounds worthy of Don Quijote himself.[18] We are not surprised to learn in the course of his story that both Cardenio and his lady, Luscinda, are (like Dorotea) avid readers of romances of chivalry, or that, like Alonso Quijano and the Innkeeper, he believes their characters to be historically real. The role of caballero is ready-made and not questioned, but, as his story reveals, he cannot perform it. Not only does he hesitate to interrupt the wedding, but even in the defiant speech we have just heard he proposes to begin with pleading. We have been well prepared for the theatrical climax at the inn, during which he first hides in Don Quijote's room and then behind his offender's back in order to avoid recognition. However, to explain Cardenio's behavior in psychological terms—alienation as the result of inhibition—as is often done, amounts to reading him in the same way he read the *Amadís* or to guessing the number of Lady Macbeth's offspring. Like everybody else in the *Quijote*, Cardenio is born and lives verbally—if not from

---

18. In addition, there is an echo of the second paragraph of the book, which no Spanish reader can fail to notice. Alonso Quijano is there described as being particularly titillated by such chivalresque conceits as "La razón de la sinrazón que a mi razón se hace . . . "

books, then as a failed incarnation of the most painfully problematical words of the national theater: *caballero* and *honor.*
His is an abject and Hispanicized replica of Orlando's heroic
undoing.

At this point English readers of Cervantes may well have
reservations. Obviously, Cardenio's *furia* is antithetical to
Don Quijote's idée fixe. Instead of being a simultaneous
"cuerdo loco" (II.17),[19] he is alternately mad or sane and so
does not conceal beneath a chosen role a sentient self, the
"profession" of which (according to Mark van Doren) is acting.[20] From what he tells us about himself and his background (small-town middle-class nobility), there is no reason
to suppose that he has ever heard of Ariosto's epic, let alone
that he has read it and been incited as a result. His "furia" is
entirely his and stems from his excruciating awareness that
he has been, and still is, "a coward and a fool" (I.27). However, as we have suggested and as perceptive readers of the
first edition surely realized, Cervantes has not abandoned literary satire. The big game he now intends to hunt is no
longer the romances of chivalry (already deliquescent as a
genre, as we noted) and certainly not *Orlando Furioso* (which

19. This crucial descriptive paradox was designed expressly by Cervantes
to avoid what Castro termed the "programming" of his character, meaning
any kind of fixed, stereotyped, generic or causal explanations of Alonso Quijano's unique *life* as Don Quijote. Here, as elsewhere, his intent is to leave
everything up in the air (the author, the characterizations, the narrative
world, the possible reactions of readers) except the immediate truth of experience emergent from adventure. The expression has been rendered in
many ways by translators in many languages; for example, "a mixture of
good sense and extravagance," "a sensible madman," "tantôt pour un
homme fou, tantôt pour un homme sensé," "einen gescheiten Kopf, der ein
Narr sei." As we can see, the temptation is to convert a living paradox into
syntactical sense.

20. The readers I seek are surely familiar with Mark van Doren's admirable study, *Don Quijote's Profession* (New York: Columbia University Press,
1968), and if they have followed the general tenor of this one (reiterated in
the penultimate sentence of the preceding note), they will understand the
reasons for my partial disagreement with Professor van Doren. Don Quijote
often puts on an act, but he is not a professional, and he slips from posturing
and oratory into profound authenticity as imperceptibly, continuously, and
unsurveyably as do his adventures into experience.

he adored) but instead the overwhelmingly popular "new comedy" of Lope de Vega and his followers. Precisely because the *Amadís* and its progeny extolled the same irrationally heroic exaltation as the comedia with a comparable lack of verisimilitude, the former provided Cervantes with a perfect straw genre for the purpose of "arousing men's contempt" for the latter.

Cardenio, socially speaking, is a caballero, but in accord with his century he does not wear armor, mount a charger, or joust with skeptics in defense of the perfection of his lady's eyebrows.[21] Rather, on foot with cape and sword he courts her—arranging trysts, smuggling in missives and poems, contending with treacherous rivals. In short, the role he plays—and fails to play at the moment of truth—is that of

21. Tournaments (such as the one in Zaragoza in which Don Quijote planned to compete) continued to be held in the seventeenth century, but after the middle of the sixteenth the participating *caballeros de la corte* (whom Cervantes as an old soldier despised) became increasingly aware of their artificiality and historical obsolescence. As a result, in contrast to the fierce prearranged battles of the thirteenth and fourteenth centuries, tournaments took on a marked burlesque character. Comedy, at once sophisticated and gross, became the dominant note of the mottos, pseudonyms, outfits, stentorian announcements, and general pomp and circumstance of the festivity. It was precisely this attitude toward the institution of chivalry—a refusal to abandon it combined with the kind of mockery employed by Quevedo in his portrait of the Cid—that Cervantes exploits when he has Don Quijote present himself with deadly seriousness as a "caballero andante." With this in mind, we may better understand the ambivalent reactions to the comic hero—acceptance and ridicule—both by the readers of the time and by those whom he encounters along the road. In any case, the *Quijote* did not laugh Spain's chivalry away, as Lord Byron believed; courtly society was taking care of that task on its own. What it did do was to transform that very laughter into salvation of all that had been admirable and noble in chivalry's mad institutionalization of heroism. It was this that Nabokov and Unamuno, each of whom in his own way revered the knight and disdained his author, failed to understand.

Two more tangential observations may be in order. First, as Don Quijote observed to the Knight of the Green Overcoat, the really dangerous—but stupid—antagonists of the seventeenth-century caballeros were not their human rivals but bulls. Second, if it had not been for that really execrable admirer of Lope who hid behind the name of Avellaneda, what a marvellous mockery of such decadent mockery would have been in store for us! What an opportunity (only partially realized in the joust with Tosilos) for Don Quijote to exhibit his "true" valor!

those typical *galanes* who, during the performance of count-less comedias, were concerned with surpassing each other in valor, in amorous conquest, in intrigue, in conceits (in both the moral and poetic senses of the term), and in maintenance of honor. These were the new "knights," as stereotyped as their chivalric predecessors and, in Cervantes's opinion, fic-tionally far more deleterious. Why? Not only because be-neath the masque of honor their behavior was often ignoble but also because the stage on which they strutted and fretted was perceived by its audience as an exemplary mirror of so-cial behavior. Cardenio, in other words, before retreating in shame into Sierra Morena, has lived as if he were a hero of a comedia, and then he is forced to realize he is neither brave nor shrewd. As a result, he loses both his lady and his honor and is reduced to a nonentity. He is literally a broken man "who is not who he is," in the parlance of the time.[22]

Thus, Cervantes is deeply concerned with the latest and, for him, peculiarly sinister literary rage—the comedia; not only because of the aesthetic objections that were expressed surreptitiously in the Scrutiny but, more important, because of the theater's toxic effects on Spanish society and on the individual's self-image as a member thereof. Cardenio's is an extreme case—a well-calculated parable of inability to cope with the *Literarisierung des Lebens* imposed by the increasingly self-conscious theatricality of interpersonal relations.[23] In this

22. See Leo Spitzer's article, "Soy quien soy," *Nueva Revista de Filología Hispánica* 2 (1947), p. 275. Self-affirmation is endemically Hispanic, and to open up one's interior self (see Octavio Paz's explication of *rajarse*, in *El laberinto de la soledad*) is what Jalisco should avoid above all according to the mariachis. The point is that Cardenio's is a case of self-negation. What Amér-ico Castro has referred to as the "imperative dimension" of Spaniards (pos-sessed in exemplary fashion by Don Quijote) has been fractured beyond re-pair.

23. At a recent (autumn 1985) gathering at Ohio State University dedi-cated to discussion of Shakespeare's history plays, this aspect of seventeenth-century European consciousness was mentioned by many of the assembled scholars, often in connection with Essex's use of *Richard II* as political propaganda. As a student of Romance languages, I found it curious that they uniformly ascribed it to the Renaissance. Although I no longer find the generalizations of *Geistesgeschichte* as illuminating as I did years ago, this seems mistaken. I would suggest that my colleagues in English literature take

connection we should remember Lope's dictum that "cases of honor" (in which a character loses and regains his or hers) provided the kind of plot that most "forcefully moved" the national public.[24] Such suspense, neatly resolved at the end by the playwright's *ingenio*, relieved individual theatergoers of the tensions of problematical existence in an honor-obsessed society that demanded more of its members than fragile human nature can usually provide. This is precisely why Cervantes arranged Cardenio's happy ending in a fashion so contrived as to be caricaturesque. If society has turned you into a puppet, Ariosto may save you by revealing the strings that connect you with that collective puppeteer.

"A voice reached his ears which suspended his senses . . ."

The only possible ending of Cardenio's story (as such a story and not as narrative preparation for an unbelievable theatrical denouement) is that which he himself predicts just prior to the interruption by an unknown "voice": no ending at all, but "only sorrow and suffering without surcease even in death" (I.27). He knows no more about himself and his situation than he has told us until the voice begins to speak and completes his awareness (and ours) of what an abject creature he is. Dorotea's account of victimization at the hands of the same ignoble grandee has generally been interpreted as an exercise in parallel narration, an echo-play of rhetoric and situations.[25] Yet it ends in a significantly different way: "I implore Heaven to take pity on me and grant me favor and in-

the time to read Richard Alewyn's *Das grosse Welttheater* (Hamburg: Rowohlt Verlag, 1959) or the French translation of it by Danièle Bohler, entitled *L'Univers du Baroque* (Geneva: Gonthier, 1964).

24. For a discussion of the importance of this phrase from Lope's *Arte nuevo* to the mass reception of the comedia, see the initial chapter of Américo Castro's *De la edad conflictiva*, already cited.

25. Cardenio begins his tale by saying that his native town is one of the best in "esta Andalucía," and Dorotea, who has not heard him, begins: "En esta Andalucía . . ." Later on, when they speak of Don Fernando, both stress the terms *grande* and *grandeza*, and both compare him to a topical list of famous traitors. However, whereas Ariosto's Merlin only mentions classical examples in speaking of Ezzellino da Romano (III, 33), Cardenio adds names

genuity so that I may either escape from my misfortunes or
else abandon my life among these solitudes, leaving no memory of an unhappy being who, by no fault of hers, has fur-
nished matter for talk and scandal at home and abroad"
(I.38). In other words, unlike Cardenio, she is not desperate,
and she continues to hope that her characteristic ingenuity
may yet win through; unlike Cardenio, who is utterly frank,
she rationalizes her past folly and considers herself an innocent victim; and finally, unlike Cardenio, she is socially conscious and hence concerned above all with her reputation—
that is, not with her actions but with the scandal arising from
her actions.

Taking these points in order, let me begin by saying that
those professional and amateur readers who find in Dorotea
the most admirable and attractive woman in the entire *Quijote*—indeed the only admirable and attractive woman
therein—are entranced not just by her beauty but also by her
resolution and acumen. Precisely! Because she is every inch
a heroine (in contrast with Cardenio), they should go on to
ask themselves how she could have possibly arrived at the
wretched state in which we first encounter her. The topic of
maidens exposed in the wilderness had first been broached
in the discourse on the Golden Age, which prepares us both
for Marcela's behavior and for that of her pursuers. In that
"happy" time, Don Quijote asserts, "Maidens and modesty
wandered at will, alone and unattended, without fearing bra-
zen importunities or lascivious assaults, and, if they were undone, it was of their own will and pleasure" (I.11).[26] Dorotea,

---

from the ballad tradition, as well as Judas and the Count Julian, who supposedly was responsible for the Moorish invasion; Dorotea, less educated,
can only remember the two ballad miscreants. This is exactly the point. Cervantes uses these parallelisms as a way of bringing out the profound differ-
ences between the stories and their tellers.

26. Ariosto seems more skeptical than Don Quijote:

> Delle lor donne e delle lor donzelle
> si fidâr molto a quella antica etade.
> Senz'altra scorta andar lasciano quelle
> Per piani e monti e per strane contrade;
> ed al ritorno l'han per buone e belle,
> nè mai tra lor suspizïone accade.

in other words, who has already been undone of her own will (and hopefully pleasure) and who fears nothing more in the world than village gossip, is as naively Quixotesque as the speaker of the words just quoted. It is as if entirely unwittingly she has just emerged from her own private version of the Golden Age into the Iron Age.

Dorotea's description of her previous life provides the nec-

Fiordiligi narrò quivi al suo amante,
che fatto stolto era il signor d'Anglante.

(XXXI, 61)

In olden days they seemed to place great trust
In women whether middle-aged or young;
Permitted to indulge their wander-lust,
They travelled unaccompanied along
Strange roads, up hill, down dale, from coast to coast,
But those at home suspected nothing wrong.
Fair Fiordiligi started to relate
What she had witnessed of Orlando's state.

(*Orlando Furioso*, p. 238.)

These remarks refer to Fiordiligi, who, wandering on a quest similar to that of Dorotea, shows up exactly at the moment when Orlando's madness is discovered (XXIV, 56). However, although her honor is still intact, Angelica in exile (before meeting Medoro) is as worried as Dorotea about her reputation:

Ma che me possi nuocere non veggio,
più di quel che sin qui nociuto m'hai.
Per te cacciata son del real seggio,
dove più ritornar non spero mai:
ho perduto l'onor, ch'è stato peggio;
chè, sebben con effetto io non peccai,
io do però materia ch'ognun dica,
ch'essendo vagabonda, io sia impudica.

(VIII, 41)

I do not see what ill can more be done,
So greatly have you wronged me before now.
By you I'm exiled from my royal throne,
And no return to it will you allow;
And, what is worse, my honour's lost and gone,
For though I have not sinned, and this I vow,
Because I wander homeless, men make haste
To slander me and say I am unchaste.

(*Orlando Furioso*, p. 273.)

essary explanation. The only daughter of a wealthy peasant family, she has never known rural poverty but rather has been nourished abundantly at "the broad fertile bosom of Mother Earth" (I.28); she has returned parental adoration with complacent and efficient assumption of administrative responsibilities ("as I was mistress of their hearts, I was also mistress of their possessions . . . with a diligence on my part and a satisfaction on theirs which I cannot well describe"); and her leisure time has been spent, not in the manner of Aldonza Lorenzo (flinging crowbars with the village lads), but in such genteel occupations as sewing, embroidering, playing the harp, and reading devotional books. Here she seems purposefully to omit what we later learn from her dialogue—her even greater devotion to romances of chivalry!

Most crucial, however, is the fact that, like other young women in her milieu, Dorotea has been brought up in a state of virtual and virtuous isolation:

> It is thus the case that, passing my time with these occupations, and living in a state of retirement which only could be compared to that of a convent, I was never observed (as I believed) by anybody but the servants, because on the days I went to Mass it was so early in the morning and I was so closely accompanied by my mother and maidservants and I was so thickly veiled and circumspect that my own eyes could scarcely see the ground I trod on.
>
> (I.28)

As a result of such an upbringing (for which, of course, she is not personally responsible) she is as rashly self-confident and as abysmally ignorant of the outside world (the Iron Age with its cynical, violent, and concupiscent male inhabitants) as Alonso Quijano in his library. Like his makeshift armor, her flowing hair (which she should have cut) and her dress and jewels (poorly hidden in a pillowcase) are the costume for the role of heroine, which she still hopes to play triumphantly. Alonso Quijano has himself "armed" as a caballero in an ignoble time; she falls into those of the first ignoble heir to that rank (an unscrupulous *galan* who professes to be bound by the chivalresque obligations of secret matrimony.[27]) who catches a glimpse of her. And afterward, instead of being disillusioned and realizing the truth of her preliminary hypocritical remarks on the domestic and social undesirability of such a match,[28] this Damsel of the Resplendent Countenance sallies forth determined to retrieve her honor and win matrimonial fame.

Dorotea's penchant for rationalization and self-justification in its own way is even more imprudent than the courage that distinguishes her from Cardenio. Apparent throughout, it is at its most specious in the reproduction of her inner thoughts just prior to her surrender: my suitor may well be sincere; others before me have followed this path to high estate; it will be better to be married than raped; screaming would reveal to my parents that he is inexplicably in my room. Anything but have him ejected forthwith or admit to herself the strength of her carnal attraction! The same almost inhuman control of consciousness characterizes the tone of her narrative (delivered "without any hesitation, with so much ease, and in so sweet a voice that her auditors were no less charmed by her intelligence than by her beauty") as well as its style, which, as we said, sounds as if she enjoyed listening to herself. Among other indulgent artifices there are paired synonyms ("pleadings and prejudices," "promises and oaths," "sought and prized"), preceding adjectives (which have the same effect in Spanish as "house beautiful" in English), untranslatable plays on words,[29] and above all

27. This literary "institution"—which Cervantes, needless to say, found both absurd and risky—was fundamental to amorous relationships in the romances. Dorotea is as deluded as Don Quijote in her belief in chivalric conventions. See Justina Ruiz de Conde, *El amor y el matrimonio secreto en los libros de caballerías* (Madrid: Aguilar, 1948).

28. "I told him to think it over . . . because the initial pleasure of such unequal matches does not last very long." She is far more sincere when she says, "I esteem myself as a subject and a peasant as much as you do as a lord caballero," and, above all, when she admits her satisfaction "at seeing herself so loved and esteemed by such an illustrious caballero." *Estimar*, like *crédito*, *respeto*, *desigualdad*, and *humilde*, all repeated, are characteristic of her socially self-centered lexicon.

29. For example, when her shepherd master made an attempt on her

that ever-present Golden Age puzzle for modern readers
called zeugma, a form of "allusion and elusiveness,"[30] of
which a classic example occurs at the very moment of her
seduction. Exactly like Don Quijote's romance when he sets
out over the plain of Montiel ("Scarce had the rubicund
Apollo spread o'er the face of the broad and spacious earth
. . ." [I.2]), her story for her is a work of literary art that re-
sists interruption and possesses its own autonomous reality.
After a pause she continues in this fashion: "What happens
in my story . . ."

Unlike poor Cardenio, who is his story and as a result is
periodically insane, Dorotea fabricates (or at least arranges)
her story imaginatively, admires it as she repeats it aloud,
and proceeds to try to live it. As a genuine "loca-cuerda," she
provides herself with a series of interacting roles that constitute the fabric of her self-understanding and therefore of her
existence. She is successively the apple of her parents' eyes,
the wise and respected mistress of their estate and house-
hold, the secluded maiden surprised and gratified by the po-
tency of a beauty she pretends she had not realized was hers
(and which she continues modestly to deprecate), and the

---

virtue, she could not find another convenient cliff "de donde despeñar y
despenar al amo." *Despeñar,* from *peña* (cliff), means throwing him over it as
she had done to her servant, while *despenar,* from *pena* (grief), means—as
they say in the blues—to satisfy his mind. The artificiality of the telling is
intentionally contrasted to the grim naturalism of what is told.

30. "Alusión y elusión" is Dámaso Alonso's fortunate expression for Góngora's style, but it also applies to Golden Age rhetoric in general with its
fondness for zeugma, roughly describable as a grammatical short circuit
based on the ambivalence of an antecedent. The following example is repre-
sentative: "con volverse a salir del aposento mi doncella, yo dejé de serlo"
("when my maid left the bedroom once more, I ceased to be one"). *Doncella*
means both "lady's maid" and "maiden." Dorotea "alludes" to what happened but at the same time renders the joy and the sin "elusive" by short-
circuiting them stylistically, absorbing their living experience into linguistic
play. Unlike Cervantes, she is not writing a novel, though her subject, as we
shall see, in later centuries would be quintessentially novelistic. I should add
that the poets of the time also used the classical form of zeugma, a single
predicate for several subjects. Karl Vossler, the great German Romanist, was
the first to explore the meaning of, and call our attention to the importance
of, the Golden Age variety. See his *Introducción a la literatura española del Siglo
de Oro* (Mexico City: Séneca, 1941), pp. 50–55.

innocent victim of unexpected and undeserved faithlessness who bravely sets out in perilous quest of just reparation. One does not have to remember certain women one has known all one's life—women as admirable in their way as Alonso Quijano is in his—in order to appreciate Cervantes's profound portrait of female Quixotism in contrast with the male variety. Neither shares Cardenio's authentic alienation; both suffer the harsh consequences of folly and self-delusion. But while Don Quijote returns in dejected defeat to mortal resignation in Argamasilla, Dorotea (admittedly with the indispensable Ariosto-like intervention of her author) will predictably settle into a long run in the role of aristocratic matriarch of an adoring family. And her seducer, Don Fernando (all literary creatures aspire to biological and biographical life in spite of our critical "fallacies"!), will have reaped the opposite of his just deserts.

If Dorotea's self-indulgent audition of her own story and her incurable propensity for role-playing lead first to seemingly inevitable perdition in Sierra Morena and later to contrived wedded salvation, her acute consciousness of herself as a social being is for Cervantes less excusable. Let us begin with her parents, whose easily imagined consternation and grief at the disappearance of "the support of their old age" has no place in her self-centered confession. Although wealthy and upwardly mobile ("coming by degrees" she remarks complacently, "to be treated as hidalgos and even as caballeros" [I.28]), they nevertheless belong by birth to the third estate.[31] That is, they are traditional tillers of the soil

31. Upward mobility or change of status to that of hidalgo was achieved by *conversos* and rich peasants alike by arranging for what was called a *probanza de hidalguía*, a legal deposition in which neighbors and friends (often bribed) testified to the ancestral status of the family. This social farce was widespread; the standard questionnaire was composed in a specialized language Cervantes frequently enjoyed teasing. For example, when the Priest tells Sancho that Dorotea is the heiress of the kingdom of Micomicón in Guinea "por linea recta de varon" ("directly descended from the masculine line"), this stock *probanza* formula, which has absolutely nothing to do with royal lineage, is an implicit critique of all the false dignities and titles that abounded in Spain as well as the general social absurdity of the time. Then Sancho continues the game by remarking that Micomicona is a suitable name

(*villanos,* or villeins) and, as she does not fail to point out, for that very reason (like Sancho) Old Christians proud of the "untainted blood" that distinguished them from those hidalgos and caballeros whose ancestors had intermarried with wealthy descendants of Jews or Moors or were maliciously suspected of having done so. As a result, the very humility of her lineage endowed Dorotea with that "peasant honor" that was peculiar to that culture and that in its opposition to the proud and overbearing honor of the nobility had become a prominent theme of the drama. It is precisely this unprecedented variety of honor that Don Fernando besmirches, an action that in certain well-beloved comedias would have resulted (inverisimilitude aside!) in his poetically justifiable murder or execution.

Cervantes, however, purposefully eschewed the kind of plot we find in Lope's *Fuenteovejuna* or Calderón's *Mayor of Zalamea*. Rather, as a part of his ongoing offensive against what he considered to be the destructive national myths of Old Christianity, cleanliness of blood, and codified honor itself, he probes more deeply into Dorotea's acute social self-awareness. As the result of the politics of the Catholic Monarchs (and with the theatrical collusion of Lope), the caste to which she belongs, the axiologically rebellious and often proudly illiterate descendants of erstwhile villeins, had con-

---

for a princess from Micomicón, not because *mico* means "monkey," but because in Spain, too, many surnames and lineages are taken from place names. As Sancho and everybody else knew, Jews at the moment of baptism often took as their own the name of the town where the sacrament was administered. Thus, Dorotea's assertion of clean blood and peasant honor and her adoption of a ridiculous "aristocratic" name derived from a kingdom of blacks (a race to which she herself, skin aside, is presumed to belong) are presented in comic contrast. Just beneath the narrative surface the *Quijote* is replete with contemporary social *alusiones* and *elusiones* that probably should be ignored by foreign readers. Moreover, if they are not, anachronistic interpretations can result. For example, in a course given at the University of California at San Diego, a very gifted black student objected to the "racism" of this episode. It took an office hour to get him to understand Cervantes's malicious burlesque of Spanish discrimination and presumptuousness. And when he did, he—quite pardonably—continued to object to the use of Africa for such a purpose.

verted the disdain suffered by its forebears into an assertive superiority, which for Cervantes (and other intellectuals and professionals who shared his stigma) was, to say the least, questionable. In Dorotea's case, however, such claims to social preeminence were insufficient in themselves; instead, they incited her into believing that she was entitled to the real thing: aristocracy with all the trimmings. When Sancho claims that his Old Christianity qualifies him for his future governorship, and Don Quijote replies, "It's quite enough and maybe even a bit too much," Cervantes's intention is comic. But here, without his staged intervention, the results of such presumption would have been tragic.

Is the author of the *Quijote*, then, intent on defending a stratified social order against presumptuous Becky Sharps? Does he in any way admire Don Fernando or justify his behavior? Not at all! Rather, he is intent on continuing his exploration of illusion and its consequences—but now as a social, rather than an individual, aberration. For example, absolving herself as usual from responsibility, Dorotea wonders whether her parents' "misfortune" in not possessing an "illustrious" family tree may not be the cause of her own misfortune. Don Fernando, she believes, would have kept his word and married her if only . . . Still an inhabitant of her fairy-tale Golden Age, she cannot comprehend the Iron Age treachery she was never taught to expect. As she sees it, it is not her own ambitious gullibility that is to blame but the accident of her birth.

Here comparison with Becky Sharp and other protagonists of nineteenth-century novels is valid. Cervantes with uncanny prescience has discovered that those who live in between one social category and another must manufacture their own identities.[32] It was a startling discovery, not because such lives were exceptional at the time, but because

32. In the picaresque novel the protagonists often conceal their shameful or lowly origins with a series of disguised false identities—which is not the same thing as Dorotea's serious effort to create for herself a new one that will be authentic.

seventeenth-century Spaniards preferred to celebrate the blessed petrifaction of their culture and their community. Lope de Vega's theatrical heroes are those who best perform their assigned roles in the face of adversity, and his villains (not villeins!) those who fail to do so. As the ultimate anti-novelist, Lope would not have understood Cervantes's problematical approach to self and society, nor would he have acknowledged his responsibility for having exacerbated the problem.

Dorotea's discontent with her social heritage is most censurable (which is not to say that she is a Lopesque villain) in her relationship with the "servant of her father's," to whom she confides her secret and whom she asks to accompany her in her sally as a squire. As she admits, "Though he remonstrated with me for my boldness and condemned my resolve, when he saw how intent I was, he offered to accompany me, as he said, to the end of the world" (I.28). A man of decent instincts and of peasant origin, he might—wealth aside—have been a suitable partner for her. Yet when our Cinderella learns of the inevitable rumor that she has run away with him, what cuts her to the heart is to realize the stain on her reputation: "Losing my good name because of my flight was bad enough, but even worse was to be thought to be involved with a fellow so far beneath me and so unworthy of my favors." But what follows is worst of all: "My good servant, until that moment faithful and trusty, finding me all alone in this desert and *incited* by his own perversity rather than by my beauty, tried to take advantage of the occasion" (italics mine, for obvious reasons!). Beginning with "words of love," which were harshly rejected, he ends by resorting to force. However, Dorotea "with the help of Heaven" manages to throw him over a convenient cliff and leaves him there without caring whether he is "alive or dead." Had this homicidal, rather than suicidal, precursor of Emma Bovary heard Don Quijote's oration on the Golden Age in its entirety, she would have known what might happen and perhaps would have been able to handle the situation less savagely. At the very least, she might have been less self-righteous.

In presenting Dorotea as an Old Christian who lives her seduction as a case of honor, Cervantes waited until the denouement at the inn before revealing the theatrical—or antitheatrical—significance of her plight; not so when it came to her transparent masculine disguise. As we have seen, she is an inveterate role-player, and this was a role that was immediately recognizable both to the readers and to the other characters. The mass audience of the Golden Age theater was particularly fond of the legshows provided by harebrained heroines who donned tights and buskins and set out with conventionally assured success to recapture the hero of their choice.[33] It was exactly this show that the Priest, the Barber, and Cardenio enjoy when, like the Elders and Susanna, they spy her washing herself at the fountain with "her gaiters . . . rolled halfway up her legs which seemed truly to be as white as alabaster" (I.28).

Once begun, the show must go on. After Dorotea's story has been spun to the end, the Priest explains the peculiar rescue mission he and the Barber have undertaken—whereupon, without being asked, Dorotea volunteers for the starring role of damsel in distress. She has read "many books of chivalry and knows by heart the style [they] use when they ask a boon of a knight-errant." Without further ado, she dons the fancy feminine costume saved for the scene she had been planning upon encountering Don Fernando. She is ready to perform, and she scores her first hit with Sancho, who is all the more impressed when the Priest announces the program: "Just to say it out of the blue, brother Sancho, this fair lady is no less than the heiress . . . of the great Kingdom of Mico-

33. Carmen Bravo Villasante in *La mujer vestida de hombre en el teatro español* (Madrid: Revista de Occidente, 1955), gives some twenty-five examples from Lope prior to 1603 (the date of his own first published catalogue of plays). Her book is particularly interesting for us in that she demonstrates the origins of such transvestism in the Italian novella and epic, above all in Ariosto, a relationship Cervantes clearly intuited. His originality consisted in combining that variety of willful heroine with a second theatrical prototype, that of the Old Christian maiden concerned with her peasant honor.

micón who has come to ask your master as a boon to redress the tort and injustice a wicked giant has done to her" (I.29).

In commenting on this episode, many critics have noticed the irony of an ostensibly real damsel in distress—Dorotea—whose honor is restored as the result of her impersonation of an ostensibly fictional counterpart—the Princess Micomicona. Don Quijote, without realizing it, has actually been instrumental in the defeat of an evil giant, the perverse grandee Don Fernando. Yet however comic and suggestive this paradoxical coincidence may be, it seems to me to ignore the deeper malice of Cervantes's critical intent. Quite clearly, for him both literary roles—that borrowed tacitly from the theater and that imitated verbally from the romances of chivalry—are equally artificial and absurd. There is, however, a crucial difference between Don Quijote as an actor and Dorotea as an actress. If the former could survive his three sallies (insofar as his mad humor awakened at least as much amused sympathy as careless brutality), Dorotea's story demonstrates the inevitable dangers awaiting attractive young ladies (and there are records of such cases[34]) who might be tempted to enact in life what they had seen working out so well on the stage.

Even worse is the fact that Dorotea—except at the end when she triumphs—is not very talented. Her impersonation of a shepherd boy is as unconvincing as Huck's impersonation of Sarah Williams; as the Princess, she forgets her new name, confuses her itinerary, and has to depend on the Priest, who takes the role of prompter.[35] Although Cervantes (like Fielding in the eighteenth century) is here concerned with reproving the sloppy acting of the traveling companies of his time, that is not his real target. Rather, what he wants to do is to lead his reader to contemplate on his own the inner

---

34. Bravo Villasante, *La mujer vestida*, pp. 183–203.

35. In this case the reference to the theater is literal and specific. Dorotea forgets her new name, and the Priest reminds her with an "apuntamiento," or prompting. She replies, "from now on I don't think it will be necessary to *apuntarme*" (I.30).

similarity of two equally reprehensible genres, the one grotesque and ridiculously obsolete, the other at the height of its popularity, a purveyor of unlivable and stereotyped images of self for the whole of the nation.[36] There on stage the audience could pick and choose among identities: aggressively honorable peasant, fearless gallant, irresistible seducer, heavy father, or adorable heroine willing to risk all for love. It was serious nonsense, for, as Don Quijote himself observes to the Bachelor later on, "the most discreet character in comedias is the fool" (II.3).

The perceptive reader has been warned, and others will have to wait for the four-way encounter at the inn with its disguises and gestures, its confrontations and anagnorises, its cunningly timed entrances and exits, its mysteries and revelations, its tears and orations, and its two undeserved happy endings to perceive how a plot that began with two words, *roto* and *Fili*, gradually evolved from verse to voice, story, and theater—or rather, to a semiburlesque exaggeration of theatrical exaggeration. It was precisely this kind of superbly controlled comic narration that Henry Fielding referred to as "the manner of Cervantes," and since his version of it will be familiar to my presumed readers, I shall spare them further analysis.[37]

If I have dwelt on the affairs of Cardenio and Dorotea, it is simply because those who read (or teach) the *Quijote* in English are often so puzzled or put off by these so-called interpolations that they shunt them aside. The *Viking Portable Cervantes* omits them; Nabokov superciliously refers to them as "the dregs of Italianate fiction"; and Virginia Woolf in her diary (August 5, 1923) terms them "dull." The author himself

36. See Marcos Moríñigo, "El teatro como sustituto de la novela en el Siglo de Oro," *Revista Universitaria de Buenos Aires* 11 (1957), pp. 41–61.
37. One of the reasons I undertook to rewrite these essays for readers whose Spanish is either nonexistent or rudimentary is the failure of many students of Fielding to "receive" the *Quijote* with Fielding's uncanny accuracy and insight. I have also contributed an article entitled "On Henry Fielding's Reception of *Don Quijote*" to *Medieval and Renaissance Studies in Honor of R. B. Tate* (Oxford: Dolphin Books, 1986). It is intended for anyone who may be curious about a Hispanist's view of the relationship.

even sounds a bit apologetic at the beginning of Part II, when he remarks that the most "jovial" among his readers only ask that he allow Don Quijote to go on "charging" and Sancho to go on "talking" for their complete satisfaction. That is precisely the point at issue: joviality is fine, but it is not a sufficient qualification for reading a text of this magnitude. One must apply one's *entendimiento* to the whole in all its parts, not just because what happens and what is said in Sierra Morena is as fascinating a technical accomplishment as the generic play that preceded it (a well "cleansed, twisted, and reeled-up" yarn complementary to the "subtle design" of the "cloth woven from various and beautiful skeins") but also because in the process of inventing in *Orlando Furioso* and in the comedia, Cervantes discovered the full potentiality of the new kind of narrative—the novel to be—that here concerns us.

"To the discredit of the truth and the detriment of history . . ."

Once the inner resemblance of the two genres has been recognized by Cervantes's readers, they are led to realize that all his objections to the romances of chivalry can be extended to the comedia. In chapter 33 the Priest and the Barber return to their inquisitorial role and conduct a miniscrutiny of four books that have been left at the inn by a "traveler"—presumably a sly reference to Cervantes himself, since he also left the manuscript of *El curioso impertinente*. The episode is beloved because of the Innkeeper's description of how romances were read aloud: "When it is harvest time, the reapers flock here on holidays, and there's always one who knows how to read and he takes up one of these books. We gather around him thirty or more and we sit there listening to him with such pleasure that it takes away our grey hairs." It is an image that, as we saw, corresponds in popular terms to the Canon's heretical "new mode of life." Then, those present who have listened avidly to these sessions describe their personal varieties of incitation: the Innkeeper loves the blows and, like another Alonso Quijano, feels the urge to join in the fray; Maritornes is thrilled by the scenes of physical love-making, which, she says, "taste like honey"; and the daughter emotes upon hearing the lovelorn rhetoric of caballeros who are out of favor with their ladies.

The fondness of nineteenth- and twentieth-century readers for this particular chapter has a certain dose of anachronism. Cervantes did not intend to sketch a folkloric *scène de campagne* but rather to point out that the above reactions were stimulated only by the two absurd romances of chivalry selected for burning and not by the two other chronicles of authentic Spanish heroism—that of the so-called Great Captain and that of the latter-day peninsular Hercules, Diego García de Paredes.[38] The Innkeeper naturally objects: if half his circulating library has to be burned, let them choose the latter pair and not the former, beneath the grotesquely fictional surface of which he submerges himself as joyously as Ortega does beneath that of the *Chartreuse,* which is exactly why the amateur Inquisitors have decided to condemn them!

Spain's genuinely heroic "old life," Cervantes implies, is being literally buried not only by junk sentimentality and violence but also, far worse, by an avalanche of pseudohistory and pseudoheroism accepted as true by the masses of illiterate innkeepers, reapers, and their like. Alonso Quijano is an isolated case of folly: the audience at the inn (identical to those that filled both fixed and ambulatory theaters[39]) is the

38. "El gran capitán" was, of course, Gonzalo Fernández de Córdoba, King Ferdinand's heroic and victorious general in Italy, while Diego García de Paredes, "the Spanish Bayard," fought in the same ranks and was famed for his legendary physical strength. It is interesting that Cervantes, unlike Lope, picks out sixteenth-century heroes rather than those of the early Reconquest, whose fame had already been blurred by apocryphal chronicles and ballads.

39. In order to understand Cervantes's alarm, one must take into account the almost incredible proliferation of theatrical activity after Lope perfected his three-act formula with its incessantly changing versification. Lope's endless fecundity corresponded perfectly to the insatiable appetite for plays of those he called with good reason "my Spaniards." His own plays are uneven in quality, ranging from masterpieces such as *El Caballero de Olmedo* to pot-boilers, but in the hundred or so I have read I have not found a single one lacking moments of sheer poetic delight. His example, however, as Cer-

nation itself. When the Priest tries to explain to the Innkeeper the difference between history and fiction, he replies (like Don Quijote, who later uses the same argument) that his romances cannot lie because they are vouched for "by the license of the Lords of the Royal Council." The proposition of official censorship of the theater is obviously waiting in the wings. If two romances of chivalry could so mislead these simple souls, the same responsible Lords had better begin supervising the mass folly of the comedia.

Overt criticism of the national theater only appears in chapter 48 after the lesson on fictional verisimilitude and harmonious narrative structure, and in it we perceive immediately the increment of social preoccupation that modifies the aesthetic criteria of the initial Scrutiny. Cervantes, of course, does not employ twentieth-century terminology—role models and the like—but when citing Cicero he observes that drama should be a "mirror of human life, model of manners, and image of the truth," he is clearly worried about the health of the nation's collective consciousness. When he goes on to say that the kind of plays that are put on in 1605 are instead "mirrors of insanity, examples of folly, and images of lascivi-

---

vantes points out in *El viaje del Parnaso*, inspired numerous followers to emulate the fecundity, but in most cases without the quality. Along with the immense number of playwrights and plays, there was a corresponding increment in performances of all kinds. Unlike France and England with their limited number of institutionalized theaters and traveling companies, in Spain, aside from the two theaters and the officially recognized troupes in Madrid, there were countless bands of nomadic actors—ranging from those thirteen or fourteen strong that toured the larger towns to lone beggars in remote hamlets able to recite a single comedia from memory in exchange for a handout. Both the peninsula and the American viceroyalties were literally inundated with a theater that celebrated values that Cervantes found questionable and that unashamedly falsified the heroic past. The soul of the nation had been literally captured by what we now would call mass culture—commercialized and standardized mass culture as against prior oral and spontaneous folk culture. This theater was made possible, of course, by the existence of the ballad tradition, and many of the stories and characters as well as fragments of that tradition were utilized in comedias; but it was mass production, mass consumption, and mass performance that made Spanish theater an unprecedented socioliterary phenomenon.

ousness," we begin to comprehend the lesson of Sierra Morena. Once they have come to the end of their insane, foolish, and lascivious stories, Cardenio and Dorotea are ready to be transported from that labyrinth to the impromptu stage of the inn, where they find the happy ending they do not deserve. A population that only knows itself as reflecting the shadow lives of the comedia will perforce be exiled from its past and lost in its present. Enslaved to a commercial product ("mercadería vendible"), it will ignore both its own "history" and the authenticity or "truth" of its human existence. Hence the urgent need of appointing "an intelligent and discreet person in the capital to examine all plays before being put on . . . and whose approval, seal, and signature would be required in each case." Cervantes himself?

Cervantes's precepts for drama reflect the standard neo-Aristotelian doctrine of the time (the three unities and the rest) and need not be summarized here. But the implications of communal alienation and axiological degeneration in the Priest's discourse were singularly prescient. One only has to look at the state of Spanish literature at the end of the seventeenth century in order to realize how clearly Cervantes foresaw the shape of things to come. Much as we may admire the great plays of Lope, Tirso, and Calderón, what we would now term the mass culture out of which they sprang was to become a cultural wilderness, in which unleashed *ingenio* would entirely supplant insight, and accelerated and compartmentalized adventures (an express freight train!) would lose all semblance of recognizable experience. Cervantes may not have believed that his proposition of censorship was practicable, but when he has the Canon justify the flames ("Such punishment they certainly deserve for being liars and imposters and as the founders of new sects and a new mode of life" [I.49]), he implies that instead of being "innocent," as in chapter 6, such literature (romances of chivalry and, by extension, the comedia) is far more dangerous to the traditional values of a Christian commonwealth than minor religious deviations. He then proves his case by returning to the theme of Spain's authentically heroic past, its collective identity embodied in individual heroes, which is in danger of being lost forever:

> Lusitania had a Viriatus, Rome a Caesar, Carthage a Hannibal, Greece an Alexander, Castile a Count Fernán González, Valencia a Cid, Andalusia a Gonzalo Fernández, Extremadura a Diego García de Paredes, Jerez a Garcí Pérez de Vargas, Toledo a Garcilaso, Seville a don Manuel de León, and reading about their valiant deeds can entertain, teach, delight and inspire the most elevated of *ingenios*.
>
> (I.49)

If we have to have an Inquisition—the question seems to be—why not invent one that would be intelligent and discreet and that would attend to what was really polluting ("staining," in the parlance of the time) the soul of the nation?

Cervantes's "modest proposal" of censorship is once again a case of "duplicity within duplicity, a sword turning all ways," but it does correspond to what he had discovered in the course of writing Part I: that, like decent theater (how much he would have admired Molière!), fiction—reformed as he had reformed it—instead of just inundating the public with fantasy, could confront it with sanity and truth. In the First Sally he had taken the narrative pulse of an individual aberration, and by the end of the Second Sally he had arrived at a profound diagnosis of his Quixotic society. In drawing on each reader's experience for the validation of his fiction, he had—or at least hoped he had—led him or her to realize its collective dimension and to assess the degeneration of its collective worth.

Ironically and without the slightest trace of bombast, Cervantes had discovered in himself a historian and a prophet, a Homer and an Isaiah, who could teach his fellows how to free themselves from collective determinism. For the proto-novelist Cervantes, being who he was and living in the time he lived, that determinism was literary (the endemic "Literarisierung des Lebens" he found at once deplorable and wildly amusing), but the lesson was not lost on the nineteenth century. We may not go to Heaven, and we cannot aspire to the spiritual heights and depths of Don Quijote, Huck Finn, Emma Bovary, Fabrice del Dongo, Raskolnikov, Captain Ahab, Parson Adams, or Prince Myshkin, but having lived their lives novelistically, we are freed from having to be Cardenio or Dorotea—or their descendants: a money-mad Dombey, a power-mad Vautrin, or a Madame Verdurin mad for a variety of social gratification that was itself a strange aberration.

In conclusion, since we have taken pains to analyze the composition of the Sierra Morena narratives (the author's own and those of the two protagonists) as a characteristically Cervantine fusion of genres (an "epic, lyric, tragic, comic" cocktail, according to the Priest [I.48]), let us reflect on what was discovered therein in terms of generic theory. For Cervantes the fundamental aberration of the comedia as formulated by Lope was not just facile fecundity and absurd plots but, more important, the fact that both audience and authors took its literary vision of life as seriously as Alonso Quijano took that of the *Amadís.* Far more than either the English or the French theaters, it provided seventeenth-century Spaniards with the same instrument that the novel was to provide nineteenth-century Europeans: a mirror of mores, a reflection of the relations and accepted roles of servants and masters, fathers and grown-up children,[40] gallants and damsels, kings and subjects, nobles and commoners, peasants and landlords, and husbands and wives.

Unlike those of the future novel, however, the mores of the comedia[41] were not the typical "manners" or "affectations" of a given time portrayed critically, humorously, and, at times, affectionately by an ironical outsider. Rather, as we

40. Since the comedia was alternately celebrative and conflictive, there was no place in it for Shakespearean pathos or for the intimate tenderness of the mother-child relationship. With a few exceptions—Jesus as a child of macho matriarchs—neither is to be found in the typical cast.

41. Although elaborate scenery was current by the time of Calderón later in the seventeenth century, Lope specialized in what were termed purely oral *comedias de ingenio,* in which standardized "scenes" were recognized only from the dialogue.

have stressed, they reflect the exigencies of honor—that is to say, of a code inherited from the centuries of the Reconquest, exaggerated fictionally in the romances of chivalry, exacerbated socially by unrelenting caste tensions, and celebrated unanimously by playwrights, characters, and the public. In so saying, we must take care not to confuse honor with religious faith or loyalty to king and country. The latter were unquestioned and unquestionable values, whereas honor functioned dramatically both as fateful anguish for those who had to conform to its dictates (must I kill my wife, my son, my liege lord, or my fiancée's father?) and, at the end of the play (in a fashion antithetical to the tragedy of Othello), as an "ingenious" form of resolution, a recipe for comforting conformance. Thus, as we have seen, in his two intertwined meditations on the comedia Cervantes took care to explore more profoundly the dishonored anguish (or lack of it) of the protagonists and to emphasize the artificiality of the climax.

The contrast of Spain's seventeenth-century theater and the nineteenth-century European novel as mirrors of society is elementary. We believe in the inhabitants and the milieu of the Maison Vauquer—"Mais, ils sont vrais!"—because Balzac's use of caricature in their portrayal converts them into heightened and thereby all the more recognizable vessels of personal experience. Instead of being admirable or reprehensible enactors of standard roles (determined by a consecrated social code of behavior) in a conventional setting (anteroom, public square, bedroom, court, or battlefield), in their particular speech and in their milieus they provide clues—unexpected but immediately comprehensible signs—to their privacy. It was precisely the absence of that kind of individuation that seemed so false and misleading to Cervantes. What, he asks, might actually be the actions and reactions (the possible experience) of a second- or third-tier caballero whose fiancée is coveted by an all-powerful grandee or of a peasant maid determined to reclaim her honor by sallying forth in a wide and *obdachlos* world in search of her seducer?

Obviously, these two interpolated tales and performances are not novelistic in the nineteenth-century sense; they are at best social fables for Cervantes's time. The *isms* indispensable for depiction of the full complexity of private existence in a historical milieu had not yet been invented—which, of course, is why everything had to take place in Sierra Morena and on the improvised stage of the inn and not in the urban world of "this Andalusia" remembered fragmentarily by Cardenio and Dorotea. Nevertheless, the counterposed indications of just "how it felt to exist in the happening" (the "twinning" perfected by Fielding), the awareness of the intricacies of social stratification (as against simply "I am a caballero" or "I am an Old Christian"), and the skeptical contemplation of the convention of honor (by an author who was nonetheless a patriot and an Erasmian Catholic) taken together indicate that Cervantes had drawn an intuitive chart of the future course of the novel, or that at least he had erected a sign post pointing in the right direction.

Thus, emergent from his generic criticism of the comedia, the critic was granted a brief vision of a strange and unprecedented genre of which his own *Quijote* was to be the precursor. Even more, without the experimental isolation and the absence of social contamination made possible by the human laboratories of Sierra Morena and the inn, the protonovelistic episodes that take place in the manor house of Don Diego de Miranda, in the Duke's palace, in Barataria, and in Barcelona would all have been impossible. If the romances of chivalry had provided Cervantes with a model for printed narration, the comedia, by portraying contemporary Spain in terms of honor—at once traditional and fictional—provide his ironic mirror with a society for ironic reflection. The anachronism that was the life of Don Quijote could now be observed on the national stage. The chivalresque, picaresque, and pastoral *topika* of the beginning remain no less serviceable, but they have been infiltrated by others derived from the theater's *Literarisierung* of social mores. Like Columbus, without knowing exactly what it was, Cervantes had set foot on a new continent later to be called the novel.

Appendix

If Don Quijote and Sancho experienced their wide-open succession of chivalric adventures, and Cardenio and Dorotea experienced their artificially plotted theatrical happening, the novelistic protagonists who followed them came to experience society as a challenging giant. But whether vanquished (as is Zola's Gervaise Lantier) or spiritually triumphant (as is Galdós's Fortunata Izquierdo), the interplay of adventure and experience in their lives took on an apparently infinite number of new aspects, possibilities, and variations. As a final listing of first names, let us meditate on the gamut that runs from Joseph, Tom, and Clarissa through Wilhelm, Becky, Julien, Emma, and Huck to Marcel and Stephen. However, in the mid-twentieth century the perils imposed from without (the literally unspeakable horrors that were becoming manifest) and self-disintegration from within (Strindberg's "creatures of rags and tatters") rendered untenable the always precarious collaboration, or deeply moving embrace, of adventure and experience. It is true that Cervantes still lives in such novels as *Brave New World, The Leopard,* and *Henderson the Rain King* (as good reading as one could desire!), but in each case we are taken out of our history and society: into the future, the past, or farther back into savagery.

As illustrations of what I think happened to the genre, I offer two extensive extracts in French, followed by English translations, from the two best-known novelistic harbingers during my generation's early maturity. The first is from Camus's *La peste,* in which the sealing off of the stricken town (Simmel's hermetic adventure as ultimate ghastliness) constricts and eventually murders the possibility of personal experience. The second, from Sartre's *La nausée,* reveals the nauseating deliquescence of that experience once the carapace of adventure is removed and the helpless human crustacean is exposed (*obdachlos*) for ever and ever.[1]

. . .

1. Albert Camus, *La peste* (Paris: Gallimard, 1947), pp. 181–83; Jean-Paul Sartre, *La nausée* (Paris: Gallimard, 1985), pp. 57–61. All italics are mine.

Nos concitoyens, ceux du moins qui avaient le plus souffert de cette séparation, s'habituaient-ils à la situation? Il ne serait pas tout à fait juste de l'affirmer. Il serait plus exact de dire qu'au moral comme au physique, ils souffraient de décharnement. Au début de la peste ils se souvenaient très bien de l'être qu'ils avaient perdu et ils le regrettaient. Mais s'ils se souvenaient nettement du visage aimé, de son rire, de tel jour dont ils reconnaissaient *après coup* qu'il avait été heureux, ils imaginaient difficilement ce que l'autre pouvait faire à l'heure même où ils l'évoquaient et dans des lieux désormais si lointains. En somme, à ce moment-là, ils avaient de la mémoire, mais une imagination insuffisante. Au deuxième stade de la peste, *ils perdirent aussi la mémoire.* Non qu'ils eussent oublié ce visage, mais, ce qui revient au même, il avait perdu sa chair, *ils ne l'apercevaient plus à l'intérieur* d'eux-mêmes. Et alors qu'ils avaient tendance à se plaindre, les premières semaines, de n'avoir plus affaire qu'à des ombres dans les choses de leur amour, ils s'aperçurent par la suite que ces ombres pouvaient encore *devenir plus décharnées, en perdant jusqu'aux infimes couleurs que leur gardait le souvenir.* Tout au bout de ce long temps de séparation, ils n'imaginaient plus cette intimité qui avait été la leur, ni comment avait pu vivre près d'eux un être sur lequel, à tout moment, ils pouvaient poser la main.

De ce point de vue, ils étaient entrés dans l'ordre même de la peste d'autant plus efficace qu'il était plus médiocre. Personne, chez nous, n'avait plus de grands sentiments. *Mais tout le monde éprouvait des sentiments monotones.* «Il est temps que cela finisse», disaient nos concitoyens, parce qu'en période de fléau il est normal de souhaiter la fin des souffrances collectives, et parce qu'en fait, ils souhaitaient que cela finisse. Mais tout cela se disait sans la flamme ou l'aigre sentiment du début, et seulement avec les quelques raisons qui nous restaient encore claires, et qui étaient pauvres. Au grand élan *farouche* des premières semaines avait succédé un abattement qu'on aurait eu tort de prendre pour de la résignation, mais qui n'en était pas moins une sorte de consentement provisoire.

Nos concitoyens s'étaient mis au pas, ils s'étaient adaptés, comme on dit, parce qu'il n'y avait pas moyen de faire autrement. Ils avaient encore, naturellement, l'attitude du malheur et de la souffrance, mais ils n'en ressentaient plus la pointe. Du reste, le docteur Rieux, par exemple, considérait, que justement, c'était cela le malheur, et que l'habitude du désespoir est pire que le désespoir lui-même. Auparavant, les séparés n'étaient pas réellement malheureux, il y avait dans leur souffrance une illumination, qui venait de s'éteindre. A présent, on les voyait au coin des rues, dans les cafés ou chez leurs amis, placides et distraits, et l'œil si ennuyé que, grâce à eux, toute la ville ressemblait à une salle d'attente. Pour ceux qui avaient un métier, ils le faisaient à l'allure même de la peste, méticuleusement et sans éclat. Tout le monde était modeste. Pour la première fois, les séparés n'avaient pas de répugnance à parler de l'absent, à prendre le langage de tous, à examiner leur séparation sous le même angle que les statistiques de l'épidémie. Alors que, jusquelà, ils avaient *soustrait* farouchement leur souffrance au malheur collectif, ils acceptaient maintenant la confusion. *Sans mémoire et sans espoir, ils s'installaient dans le présent.* A la vérité, tout leur devenait présent. Il faut bien le dire, *la peste avait enlevé à tous le pouvoir de l'amour et même de l'amitié. Car l'amour demande un peu d'avenir, et il n'y avait plus pour nous que des instants.*[2]

Was it that our fellow citizens, even those who had felt the parting from their loved ones most keenly, were getting used to doing without them? To assume this would fall somewhat short of the truth. It would be more correct to say that they were wasting away emotionally as well as physically. At the beginning of the plague they had a vivid recollection of the absent ones and bitterly felt their loss. But though they could clearly recall the face, the smile and voice of the beloved, and this or that occasion when (as they now saw *in retrospect*) they had been supremely happy, they had trouble in picturing what he or she might be doing at the moment when they conjured up these memories, in a setting so hopelessly remote. In short, at these moments memory played its part, but their imagination failed them. During the second phase of the plague *their memory failed them, too.* Not that they had forgotten the face itself, but—what came to the same thing—it had lost fleshly substance and *they no longer saw it in memory's mirror.*

Thus, while during the first weeks they were apt to complain that only shadows remained to them of what their love had been and meant, they now came to learn that even shadows can *waste away, losing the faint hues of life that memory may give.* And by the end of their long sundering they had also lost the power of imagining the intimacy that once was theirs or understanding what it can be to live with someone whose life is wrapped up in yours.

---

2. Pestilence is, of course, a metaphor for the historical disease of a "time" that squeezes the last residues of meaningful experience out of the hermeticism of adventure. Unlike the "sueño" of Calderón's Segismundo, our collective "long sommeil" is empty and so suppresses "les jugements de valeur" (pp. 184–85). As a result, and as we no longer need to be told, "il vient toujours une heure dans l'histoire où celui qui ose dire que deux et deux font quatre est puni de mort" (p. 135). ("There is always a time in history when the one who dares to say that two and two make four is condemned to death" [my translation].)

In this respect they had adapted themselves to the very condition of the plague, all the more potent for its mediocrity. None of us was capable any longer of an exalted emotion; *all had trite, monotonous feelings.* "It's high time it stopped," people would say, because in time of calamity the obvious thing is to desire its end, and in fact they wanted it to end. But when making such remarks, we felt none of the passionate yearning or fierce resentment of the early phase; we merely voiced one of the few clear ideas that lingered in the twilight of our minds. The *furious* revolt of the first weeks had given place to a vast despondency, not to be taken for resignation, though it was none the less a sort of passive and provisional acquiescence.

Our fellow citizens had fallen into line, adapted themselves, as people say, to the situation, because there was no way of doing otherwise. Naturally they retained the attitudes of sadness and suffering, but they had ceased to feel their sting. Indeed, to some, Dr. Rieux among them, this precisely was the most disheartening thing: that the habit of despair is worse than despair itself. Hitherto those who were parted had not been utterly unhappy; there was always a gleam of hope in the night of their distress; but that gleam had now died out. You could see them at street corners, in cafés or friends' houses, listless, indifferent, and looking so bored that, because of them, the whole town seemed like a railway waiting-room. Those who had jobs went about them at the exact tempo of the plague, with dreary perseverance. Everyone was modest. For the first time exiles from those they loved had no reluctance to talk freely about them, using the same words as everybody else, and regarding their deprivation from the same angle as that from which they viewed the latest statistics of the epidemic. This change was striking since until now they had jealously *withheld* their personal grief from the common stock of suffering; now they accepted its inclusion. *Without memories, without hope, they lived for the moment only.* Indeed, the here and now had come to mean everything to them. For there is no denying that *the plague had gradually killed off in all of us the faculty not of love only but even of friendship. Naturally enough, since love asks something of the future, and nothing was left us but a series of present moments.*[3]

.   .   .

Antoine Roquentin's foil and principal interlocutor, l'Autodidacte, is now speaking:

3. Albert Camus, *The Plague*, trans. Stuart Gilbert (New York: Modern Library, 1948), pp. 163–65.

. . .

—Quand j'aurai fini mon instruction (je compte encore six ans pour cela), je me joindrai, si cela m'est permis, aux étudiants et aux professeurs qui font une croisière annuelle dans le Proche-Orient. Je voudrais préciser certaines connaissances, dit-il avec onction, et j'aimerais aussi qu'il m'arrivât de l'inattendu, du nouveau, des aventures pour tout dire.

Il a baissé la voix et pris l'air coquin.

—Quelle espèce d'aventures? lui dis-je étonné.

—Mais toutes les espèces, monsieur. On se trompe de train. On descend dans une ville inconnue. On perd son portefeuille, on est arrêté par erreur, on passe la nuit en prison. Monsieur, j'ai cru qu'on pouvait définir l'aventure: un événement qui sort de l'ordinaire, sans être forcément extraordinaire. On parle de la magie des aventures. Cette expression vous semble-t-elle juste? Je voudrais vous poser une question, monsieur.

—Qu'est-ce que c'est?

Il rougit et sourit.

—C'est peut-être indiscret . . .

—Dites toujours.

Il se penche vers moi et demande, les yeux mi-clos:

—Vous avez eu beaucoup d'aventures, monsieur?

Je réponds *machinalement:*

—Quelques-unes, en me rejetant en arrière, pour éviter son souffle empesté. Oui, j'ai dit cela machinalement, sans y penser. D'ordinaire, en effet, je suis plutôt fier d'avoir eu tant d'aventures. Mais aujourd'hui, à peine ai-je prononcé ces mots, que je suis pris d'une grande indignation contre moi-même: *il me semble que je mens, que de ma vie je n'ai eu la moindre aventure, ou plutôt je ne sais même plus ce que ce mot veut dire.* En même temps pèse sur mes épaules ce même découragement qui me prit à Hanoi, il y a près de quatre ans, quand Mercier me pressait de me joindre à lui et que je fixais sans répondre une statuette khmère. Et l'IDÉE est là, cette grosse masse blanche qui m'avait tant dégoûté alors: je ne l'avais pas revue depuis quatre ans.

—Pourrai-je vous demander . . . , dit l'Autodidacte.

Parbleu! De lui en raconter une, de ces fameuses aventures. Mais je ne veux plus dire un mot sur ce sujet.

—Là, dis-je, penché par-dessus ses épaules étroites et mettant le doigt sur une photo, là, c'est Santillane, le plus joli village d'Espagne.

—Le Santillane de Gil Blas? Je ne croyais pas qu'il existât. Ah! monsieur, comme votre conversation est profitable. On voit bien que vous avez voyagé.

J'ai mis l'Autodidacte à la porte, après avoir bourré ses poches de cartes postales, de gravures et de photos. Il est parti enchanté et j'ai éteint la lumière. A présent, je suis seul. Pas tout à fait seul. Il y a encore cette idée, devant moi, qui attend. Elle s'est mise en boule, elle reste là comme un gros chat; elle n'explique rien, elle ne bouge pas et se contente de dire non. Non, je n'ai pas eu d'aventures.

Je bourre ma pipe, je l'allume, je m'étends sur mon lit en mettant un manteau sur mes jambes. *Ce qui m'étonne, c'est de me sentir si triste et si las. Même si c'était vrai que je n'ai jamais eu d'aventures, qu'est-ce que ça pourrait bien me faire?* D'abord, il me semble que c'est une pure question de mots. Cette affaire de Meknès, par exemple, à laquelle je pensais tout à l'heure: un Marocain sauta sur moi et voulut me frapper d'un grand canif. Mais je lui lançai un coup de poing qui l'atteignit au-dessous de la tempe . . . Alors il se mit à crier en arabe, et un tas de pouilleux apparurent qui nous poursuivirent jusqu'au souk Attarin. Eh bien, on peut appeler ça du nom qu'on voudra, mais, de tout façon, c'est un événement qui *M'est arrivé* [Sartre's italics].

Il fait tout à fait noir et je ne sais plus très bien si ma pipe est allumée. Un tramway passe: éclair rouge au plafond. Puis c'est une lourde voiture qui fait trembler la maison. Il doit être six heures.

Je n'ai pas eu d'aventures. Il m'est arrivé des histoires, des événements, des incidents, tout ce qu'on voudra. Mais pas des aventures. Ce n'est pas une question de mots; je commence à comprendre. Il y a quelque chose à quoi je tenais plus qu'à tout le reste—sans m'en rendre bien compte. Ce n'était pas l'amour, Dieu non, ni la gloire, ni la richesse. C'était . . . Enfin je m'étais imaginé qu'à de certains moments ma vie pouvait prendre une qualité rare et précieuse. Il n'était pas besoin de circonstances extraordinaires: je demandais tout juste un peu de rigueur. Ma vie présente n'a rien de très brillant: mais de temps en temps, par exemple quand on jouait de la musique dans les cafés, je revenais en arrière et je me disais: autrefois, à Londres, à Meknès, à Tokio j'ai connu des moments admirables, j'ai eu des aventures. C'est ça qu'on m'enlève, à présent. Je viens d'apprendre, brusquement, sans raison apparente, que je me suis menti pendant dix ans. Les aventures sont dans les livres. Et naturellement, tout ce qu'on raconte dans les livres peut arriver pour de vrai, mais pas de la même manière. C'est à cette manière d'arriver que je tenais si fort.

Il aurait fallu d'abord que les commencements fussent de vrais commencements Hélas! Je vois si bien maintenant ce que j'ai voulu. De vrais commencements apparaissant comme une sonnerie de trompette, comme les premières notes d'un air de jazz, brusquement, coupant court à l'ennui, raffermissant la durée; de ces soirs entre les soirs dont on dit ensuite: «Je me promenais, c'était un soir

de mai.» On se promène, la lune vient de se lever, on est oisif, vacant, un peu vide. Et puis d'un coup, on pense: «Quelque chose est
arrivé.» N'importe quoi: un léger craquement dans l'ombre, une silhouette légère qui traverse la rue. Mais ce mince événement n'est
pas pareil aux autres: tout de suite on voit qu'il est à l'avant d'une
grande forme dont le dessin se perd dans la brume et l'on se dit
aussi: «Quelque chose commence.»

Quelque chose commence pour finir: l'aventure ne se laisse pas
mettre de rallonge; elle n'a de sense que par sa mort. Vers cette
mort, qui sera peut-être aussi la mienne. Je suis entraîné sans retour.
Chaque instant ne paraît que pour amener ceux qui suivent. A
chaque instant je tiens de tout mon cœur: je sais qu'il est unique;
irremplaçable—et pourtant je ne ferais pas un geste pour l'empêcher
de s'anéantir. Cette dernière minute que je passe—à Berlin, à
Londres—dans les bras de cette femme, recontrée l'avant-veille—
minute que j'aime passionnément, femme que je suis près d'aimer—
elle va prendre fin, je le sais. Tout à l'heure je partirai pour un autre
pays. Je ne retrouverai ni cette femme ni jamais cette nuit. Je me
penche sur chaque seconde, j'essaie de l'épuiser; rien ne passe que
je ne saisisse, que je ne fixe pour jamais en moi, rien, ni la tendresse
fugitive de ces beaux yeux, ni les bruits de la rue, ni la clarté fausse
du petit jour: et cependant la minute s'écoule et je ne la retiens pas,
j'aime qu'elle passe.

Et puis tout d'un coup quelque chose casse net. L'aventure est
finie, le temps reprend sa mollese quotidienne. Je me retourne; der-
rière moi, cette belle forme mélodique s'enfonce tout entière dans le
passé. Elle diminue, en déclinant elle se contracte, à présent la fin
ne fait plus qu'un avec le commencement. En suivant des yeux ce
point d'or, je pense que j'accepterais—même si j'avais failli mourir,
perdu une fortune, un ami—de revivre tout, dans les mêmes circonstances, de bout à bout. Mais une aventure ne se recommence ni
ne se prolonge.

Oui, c'est ce que je voulais—hélas! c'est ce que je veux encore.
J'ai tant de bonheur quand une Négresse chante: quels sommets
n'atteindrais-je point si ma *propre vie* [Sartre's italics] faisait la ma-
tière de la mélodie. *L'Idée est toujours là, l'innommable.* Elle attend,
paisiblement. A présent, elle a l'air de dire:

«Oui? C'est *cela* [Sartre's italics] que tu voulais? Eh bien, précisé-
ment c'est ce que tu n'as jamais eu (rappelle-toi: tu te dupais avec
des mots, tu nommais aventure du clinquant de voyage, amours de
filles, rixes, verroteries) et c'est ce que tu n'auras jamais—ni personne autre que toi.»

Mais pourquoi? POURQUOI?[4]

---

4. The true conclusion of the "novel" occurs during Antoine's encounter

"When I've finished my instruction (I allow six more years for that) I shall join, if I am permitted, the group of students and professors who take an annual cruise to the Near East. I should like to make some new acquaintances," he says unctuously. "To speak frankly, I would also like something unexpected to happen to me, something new, adventures."

He has lowered his voice and his face has taken on a roguish look.

-----

with Anny after years of separation: "C'est ça, c'est bien ça. Il n'y a pas d'aventures—il n'y a pas des moments parfaits . . . nous avons perdus les mêmes illusions" (p. 210). ("That's it, that's really it, there are no adventures, there are no perfect moments . . . we have lost the same illusions [my translation].) Here is a clue to the nature of the unspeakable "idée" (aside from the possible sly reference to Hegel); it is whatever makes adventure illusory: remorseless time, malevolent divinity, "le néant," nauseating flux, or whatever. The reference to Hanoi and the "statuette khmère" is, one suspects, to that most flamboyant of novelist-adventurers, André Malraux. Finally, it should be noted that in addition to denying adventure to our lives, Sartre also disputes the validity of that other mainstay of the novel—*Erfahrung,* or cumulative experience.

> Comme je voudrais lui dire qu'on le trompe, qu'il fait le jeu des importants. Des professionnels de l'expérience? Ils ont trainé leur vie dans l'engourdissement et le demisommeil, ils se sont mariés précipitamment, par impatience, et ils ont fait des enfants au hasard. Ils ont rencontré les autres hommes dans les cafés, aux mariages, aux enterrements. De temps en temps, pris dans un remous, ils se sont débattus sans comprendre ce qui leur arrivait. Tout ce qui s'est passé autour d'eux a commencé et s'est achevé hors de leur vue; de longues formes obscures, des événements qui venaient de loin les ont frôlés rapidement et, quand ils ont voulu regarder, tout était fini déjà. Et puis, vers les quarante ans, ils baptisent leurs petites obstinations et quelques proverbes du nom d'expérience, ils commencent à faire les distributeurs automatiques: deux sous dans la fente de gauche et voilà des anecdotes enveloppées de papier d'argent; deux sous dans la fente de droite et l'on reçoit de précieux conseils qui collent aux dents comme des caramels mous.
>
> (pp. 100–101)

How I would like to tell him he's being deceived, that he is the butt of the important. Experienced professionals? They have dragged out their life in stupor and semi-sleep, they have married hastily, out of impatience, they have made children at random. They have met other men in cafés, at weddings and funerals. Sometimes caught in the tide, they have struggled against it without understanding what was happening to them. All that has happened around them has eluded them;

"What sort of adventures?" I ask him, astonished. "All sorts, Monsieur. Getting on the wrong train. Stopping in an unknown city. Losing your briefcase, being arrested by mistake, spending the night in prison. Monsieur, I believed the word adventure could be defined: an event out of the ordinary without being necessarily extraordinary. People speak of the magic of adventures. Does this expression seem correct to you? I would like to ask you a question, Monsieur."

---

long obscure shapes, events from afar, brushed by them rapidly, and when they turned to look all had vanished. And then, around forty, they christen their small obstinacies and a few proverbs with the name of experience, they begin to simulate slot machines, put a coin in the left hand slot and you get tales wrapped in silver paper, put a coin in the slot on the right and you get precious bits of advice that stick to your teeth like caramel.

(*Nausea*, p. 68)

It is curious to observe the contrast between this fundamentally antinovelistic manifesto and Wilhelm Dilthey's celebration of autobiography as the basis of the nineteenth century's novelistic comprehension of history:

Die Selbstbiographie ist die höchste und am meisten instruktive Form, in welcher uns das Verstehen des Lebens entgegentritt. Hier ist ein Lebenslauf das Äussere sinnlich Erscheinende von welchen aus das Verstehen zu dem vorandringt, was diesen Lebenslauf innerhalb eines bestimmten Milieu hervorgebracht hat. Und zwar ist der, welcher diesen Lebenslauf versteht, identisch mit dem, der ihn hervorgebracht hat. Hieraus ergibt sich eine besondere Intimität des Verstehens. Derselbe Mensch, der den Zusammenhang in der Geschichte seines Lebens sucht, hat in all dem, was er als Werte seines Lebens gefühlt, als Zwecke desselben realisiert, als Lebensplan entworfen hat, was er rückblickend als seine Entwicklung, vorwärtsblickend als die Gestaltung seines Lebens und dessen höchstes Gut erfasst hat—in alledem hat er schon einen Zusammenhang seines Lebens unter verschiedenen Gesichtspunkten gebildet, der nun jetzt ausgesprochen werden soll. Er hat in der Erinnerung die Momente seines Lebens, die er als bedeutsam erfuhr, herausgehoben und akzentuiert und die anderen in Vergessenheit versinken lassen. Die Täuschungen des Momentes über dessen Bedeutung hat dann die Zukunft ihm berichtigt. So sind die nächsten Aufgaben für die Auffassung und Darstellung geschichtlichen Zusammenhangs hier schon durch das Leben selber halb gelöst.

(Wilhelm Dilthey, *Gesämmelte Schriften*, 3: 199–200)

Autobiography is the highest and most instructive form in which we face an understanding of life. Here is a vital itinerary whose perceivable external appearance emerges from an understanding of what con-

"What is it?"

He blushes and smiles.

"Possibly it is indiscreet!"

"Ask me anyway."

He leans towards me, his eyes half-closed, and asks:

"Have you had many adventures, Monsieur?"

"A few," I answer *mechanically,* throwing myself back to avoid his tainted breath. Yes. I said that mechanically, without thinking. In fact, I am generally proud of having had so many adventures. But today, I had barely pronounced the words than I was seized with contrition; *it seems as though I am lying, that I have never had the slightest adventure in my life, or rather, that I don't even know what the word means any more.* At the same time, I am weighed down by the same discouragement I had in Hanoi—four years ago when Mercier pressed me to join him and I stared at a Khmer statuette without answering. And the IDEA is there, this great white mass which so disgusted me then: I hadn't seen it for four years.

"Could I ask you . . ." the Self-Taught Man begins . . .

By Jove! To tell him one of those famous tales. But I won't say another word on the subject.

"There," I say, bending down over his narrow shoulders, putting my finger on a photograph, "there, that's Santillana, the prettiest town in Spain."

"The Santillana of Gil Blas? I didn't believe it existed. Ah, Mon-

---

ditions, within a certain milieu, have produced this itinerary. And he who understands it is indeed identical with the one who has produced it. Hence there arises a special intimacy in the process of understanding. The same human being who seeks some coherence in the history of his life, who has, in all that he felt were the values of his life, or accomplished as its purposes, or designed as a project for life, or embraced either as development, looking backwards, or, toward the future, as shaping of his life and its highest good—in all this he has already formed a coherent structure for his life from different viewpoints, which now need to be expressed. He has brought out and emphasized in his memory those moments of his life that he experienced as being significant, and allowed the others to sink into oblivion. The deceptions of the moment as to such significance, the future has proceeded to correct. In this manner the imminent tasks, concerning the conception and representation of a historical coherence, have been half resolved through life itself.

(Cited in Patricia Drechsel Tobin, *Time and the Novel* [Princeton, N.J.: Princeton University Press, 1978], p. 22, from Wilhelm Dilthey, *Pattern and Meaning of History,* trans. H. P. Rickman [New York: Harper, 1962], pp. 85–86)

sieur, how profitable your conversation is. One can tell you've travelled."

I put out the Self-Taught Man after filling his pockets with post cards, prints and photos. He left enchanted and I switched off the light. I am alone now. Not quite alone. Hovering in front of me is still this idea. It has rolled itself into a ball, it stays there like a large cat; it explains nothing, it does not move, and contents itself with saying no. No, I haven't had any adventures.

I fill my pipe, light it and stretch out on the bed, throwing a coat over my legs. *What astonishes me is to feel so sad and exhausted. Even if it were true—that I never had any adventures—what difference would that make to me?* First, it seems to be a pure question of words. This business at Meknes, for example, I was thinking about a little while ago; a Moroccan jumped on me and wanted to stab me with an enormous knife. But I hit him just below the temple . . . then he began shouting in Arabic and a swarm of lousy beggars came up and chased us all the way to Souk Attarin. Well, you can call that by any name you like, in any case, it was an event which *happened to ME* [Sartre's italics].

It is completely dark and I can't tell whether my pipe is lit. A trolley passes: red light on the ceiling. Then a heavy truck which makes the house tremble. It must be six o'clock.

I have never had adventures. Things have happened to me, events, incidents, anything you like. But no adventures. It isn't a question of words; I am beginning to understand. There is something to which I clung more than all the rest—without completely realizing it. It wasn't love. Heaven forbid, not glory, not money. It was . . . I had imagined that at certain times my life could take on a rare and precious quality. There was no need for extraordinary circumstances: all I asked for was a little precision. There is nothing brilliant about my life now: but from time to time, for example, when they play music in the cafés, I look back and tell myself: in old days, in London, Meknes, Tokyo, I have known great moments, I have had adventures. Now I am deprived of this. I have suddenly learned, without any apparent reason, that I have been lying to myself for ten years. Adventures are in books. And naturally, everything they tell about in books can happen in real life, but not in the same way. It is to this way of happening that I clung so tightly.

The beginnings would have had to be real beginnings. Alas! Now I see so clearly what I wanted. Real beginnings are like a fanfare of trumpets, like the first notes of a jazz tune, cutting short tedium, making for continuity: then you say about these evenings within evenings: "I was out for a walk, it was an evening in May." You walk, the moon has just risen, you feel lazy, vacant, a little empty. And then suddenly you think: "Something has happened." No matter what: a slight rustling in the shadow, a thin silhouette crossing the street. But this paltry event is not like the others: suddenly you see that it is the beginning of a great shape whose outlines are lost in mist and you tell yourself, "Something is beginning."

Something is beginning in order to end: adventure does not let itself be drawn out; it only makes sense when dead. I am drawn, irrevocably, towards this death which is perhaps mine as well. Each instant appears only as part of a sequence. I cling to each instant with all my heart: I know that it is unique, irreplaceable—and yet I would not raise a finger to stop it from being annihilated. This last moment I am spending—in Berlin, in London—in the arms of a woman casually met two days ago—moment I love passionately, woman I may adore—all is going to end, I know it. Soon I shall leave for another country. I shall never rediscover either this woman or this night. I grasp at each second, trying to suck it dry: nothing happens which I do not seize, which I do not fix forever in myself, nothing, neither the fugitive tenderness of those lovely eyes, nor the noises of the street, nor the false dawn of early morning: and even so the minute passes and I do not hold it back, I like to see it pass.

All of a sudden something breaks off sharply. The adventure is over, time resumes its daily routine. I turn; behind me, this beautiful melodious form sinks entirely into the past. It grows smaller, contracts as it declines, and now the end makes one with the beginning. Following this gold spot with my eyes I think I would accept—even if I had to risk death, lose a fortune, a friend—to live it all over again, in the same circumstances, from end to end. But an adventure never returns nor is prolonged.

Yes, it's what I wanted—what I still want. I am so happy when a negress sings: what summits would I not reach if *my own life* [Sartre's italics] made the subject of the melody.

The idea is still there, unnameable. It waits, peacefully. Now it seems to say:

"Yes? Is *that* [Sartre's italics] what you wanted? Well, that's exactly what you've never had (remember you fooled yourself with words, you called the glitter of travel, the love of women, quarrels, and trinkets adventure) and this is what you'll never have—and no one other than yourself."

But Why? WHY?[5]

. . .

5. Jean-Paul Sartre, *Nausea*, trans. Lloyd Alexander (New York: New Directions, 1964), pp. 51–55.

To conclude, I should like to stress that the above passages were not selected in order either to predict or to lament the "death of the novel," but rather to illustrate its birth and its flourishing years in terms of its mid-life crisis. If that final demise does take place, it will not be because of the inner contradictions of the genre or its irrelevance to a society as mad as that of Cervantes, but rather, as suggested, because of massive illiteracy. As their entire history demonstrates, the organisms called novels are comparable to those viruses that survive by means of a phenomenal capacity for mutation. Thus, rather than being moribund, novels posterior to the pre– and post–World War II existential self-negation of *La nausée* and *La peste* have displayed an exhilarating—if somewhat feverish—vitality. *Catch 22* is by now a classic along with *Catcher in the Rye*. However, because of the nature of my foregoing theses, I am particularly interested in those that substitute the experience of an ongoing collectivity submitted to the adventure of history for the individual experience of the biographical model. I refer specifically to such novelists as Robert Penn Warren, Marguerite Yourcenar, and Günter Grass. Spanish literature offers all kinds of examples, including Goytisolo's *Conde don Julián*, Fuentes's *Terra nostra*, and García Márquez's novelistic romance of chivalry and antichivalry, *Cien años de soledad*. In all these cases, instead of abandoning what Patricia Drechsel Tobin (in her brilliant *Time and the Novel*) terms the "genealogical imperative" of the genre,[6] it is reexplored in new directions as limitless and startling as Don Quijote's venture "over the ancient and memorable plain of Montiel."

6. Tobin, *Time and the Novel*, p. 15.

Index

Addiction, 7

Adventure: experience and, 23–30, 185–86; illusory, 192n4; typology of settings for, 95–96. *See also names of specific episodes, works*

Adventure of the Fulling Mills, 130, 137, 138

Adventure of the Lions, 132, 134, 137

Adventures of Huckleberry Finn (Twain), 19–21, 26–29, 32–33, 35–36, 41, 47

Aestetik (Hegel), 152

Aestetik des reinen Gefühls (Cohen), 31, 33

A la recherche du temps perdu (Proust), 25

Alemán, Mateo, 87–88, 92, 98

Algiers, Cervantes's captivity in, 58

Alienation, 188; Cardenio and, 160, 170; Cervantes's, 105–6; communal, 180; Third Sally and, 75–76

Amadís de Gaula (Rodríguez de Montalvo), 3, 4, 8, 46, 87, 89, 104, 120, 144, 146

Ambrosio, 98

El amigo Manso (Galdós), 124

Angelica, 166n26

Annotations, 14

Anselmo, and narrative thread, 51–52

Antiadventures, 87

Antiheroism, 34

Ariosto, Ludovico, 50, 99, 155–64 passim

Aristotelian *topika*, 78, 94, 139

Authors: annotations by, 14; game of communication with, 9; intervention by, 13, 52; listening to self, 47. *See also names of specific authors*

Autobiography, Dilthey on, 193–94n4

Azaña, Manuel, 74–75

Bakhtin, Mikhail, xiv, 7, 39–40, 57

Ballad tradition, 121n56, 179n39

Balzac, Honoré de, 62–63, 138, 183

Bend Sinister (Nabokov), 14, 43

Bergson, Henri, 21

The Brothers Karamazov (Dostoevsky), 14

Camus, Albert, 186

Canon and Priest dialogue, 125–27, 144

Captive's Tale, 99n38, 129

Cárcel de Amor (Diego de San Pedro), 57

Cardenio, 59, 154, 158, 197; alienation of, 170; background of, 50, 159–61; *caso* of, 159; as Orlando, 156–57; stories of, 57

Caricatures, temporalized, 36–37

Casos de amor, 96

Castillejo, Cristóbal de, 146

Castro, Américo, vii, xvii, 16, 18, 21, 34, 127, 134

La Celestina, 88, 98, 121

Centeno, Augusto, xvi, 142

Cervantes Saavedra, Miguel de, 5; alienation of, 105–6; on *Amadís*, 4; as bookworm, 72; on comedia, 163, 177–84; as critic, 89, 108–9, 118, 132, 142–51; death of, 58; drama precepts of, 180; future consciousness and, 75–76; hero-